⟨*Global Showdown*⟩

(*Global Showdown*)

How the New Activists
Are Fighting Global
Corporate Rule

Maude Barlow and Tony Clarke

Published in 2001 by Stoddart Publishing Co. Limited
895 Don Mills Road, 400-2 Park Centre, Toronto, Canada M3C 1W3
180 Varick Street, 9th Floor, New York, New York 10014

Distributed by:
General Distribution Services Ltd.
325 Humber College Blvd., Toronto, Ontario M9W 7C3
Tel. (416) 213-1919   Fax (416) 213-1917
Email cservice@genpub.com

05 04 03 02 01 1 2 3 4 5

Canadian Cataloguing in Publication Data

Barlow, Maude
Global showdown : how the new activists are fighting global corporate rule

Includes bibliographical references and index.
ISBN 0-7737-3264-0

1. World Trade Organization. 2. International business enterprises.
3. International trade – Political aspects. 4. International trade – Social aspects.
5. Economic policy – Citizen participation. I. Clarke, Tony. II. Title.

HF1385.B37 2001   382'.92   C00-932829-7

Quotations from the following sources have been reprinted with permission:
Globalization from Below: The Power of Solidarity, by J. Brecher, T. Costello, and B.
Smith, © 2000 (used by permission of South End Press); "Globalisation: Creed of
Greed," by Chalmers Johnson, in *Australian Financial Review*, November 18, 1998
(used by permission of the author); "The Year of Living Dangerously," by Peter
Newman, in *Maclean's*, © 1995 (used by permission of the author); *Wrestling with the
Elephant: The Inside Story of the Canada–U.S. Trade Wars*, by Gordon Ritchie,
© 1997 (used by permission of Macfarlane Walter & Ross); *Citizen's Guide to the World
Trade Organization*, by Steven Shrybman, © 1999 (used by permission of the
Canadian Centre for Policy Alternatives); "Report to the Council of Canadians, June
2000," by Steven Shrybman, © 2000 (used by permission of the author); *GATS: How
the World Trade Organization's New "Services" Negotiations Threaten Democracy*, by Scott
Sinclair, © 2000 (used by permission of the Canadian Centre for Policy Alternatives);
"The WTO and War: Making the Connection" from *The WTO and the Global War
System*, a forum held at Seattle, WA, November 1999, © 1999 (used by permission of
the author). Every reasonable effort has been made to contact the holders of copy-
right for materials quoted in the book. The authors and publisher will gladly receive
information that will enable them to rectify any inadvertent errors or omissions in
subsequent editions.

Jacket design: Bill Douglas @ The Bang
Text design: Tannice Goddard

THE CANADA COUNCIL | LE CONSEIL DES ARTS
FOR THE ARTS | DU CANADA
SINCE 1957 | DEPUIS 1957

*We acknowledge for their financial support of our
publishing program the Canada Council, the Ontario Arts
Council, and the Government of Canada through the
Book Publishing Industry Development Program (BPIDP).*

Printed and bound in Canada

To the movement's youth activists,
who inspire us

Contents

Acknowledgements

We are deeply grateful to the hundreds of colleagues, activists, and friends in Canada and around the world whose research, analysis, and organizing have inspired this movement and this book. Many of your names appear in the text; many do not. There are simply too many to acknowledge in person — a sign that the power and the size of our movement are growing. We are privileged to have worked with you for over a decade.

We wish to thank our editors, Kathryn J. Dean and Marnie Kramarich, and the whole terrific team at Stoddart. Special thanks as well to Sarah Dopp for research assistance and Patricia Perdue for her administrative support and unending optimism. As well, the whole team at the Council of Canadians continues to be a joy. Finally, we are very grateful to our families for their support of this project and the overall goals of our work.

MB and TC

Introduction

*T*he fall of the Berlin Wall in 1989 was supposed to have marked "the end of history." Capitalism had conquered communism. Ideology was dead. Ahead lay universal prosperity delivered to an affluent, savvy world of consumers on a global conveyor belt of goods and services. Economic freedom and consumer choice would replace the political decisions required in the old system; people would be kept busy being knowledgeable customers in a world of dazzling material abundance.

Ten years later, on a glorious sunny November day in Seattle, many thousands of protesters shut down the most powerful institution on earth. The World Trade Organization, easily the most obvious manifestation of post–Berlin Wall triumphalism, had come to the West Coast city to launch the "Millennium Round" — the next phase in creating a seamless global economy with universal rules set by big business for its own advancement. That it came as a total surprise to the likes of Bill Gates of Microsoft and Phil Condit of Boeing — the co-hosts of the event — exposes just how isolated from reality their wealth had left them.

How is it that they had not noticed the appalling inequities their system had created in the world: the millions without work, the billions without the necessities of life, the ecological destruction reaching into even the most remote corners of the planet? How was it possible to hold a show like the Millennium Round in a city, a country, and a world beset by the injustice and inequality of Washington Consensus–style unregulated free market capitalism and not expect the revolution that took place?

This book is the story of that revolution. It documents the rise of the most compelling civil society movement of modern history and lays out a blueprint for its future.

All over the world, the role of governments has dramatically changed in the last twenty years. Deregulation, funding cutbacks, privatization, and free trade have left governments with little to do but give more power to global economic institutions like the WTO and the World Bank and provide the security forces needed to protect the system against its detractors.

In the 1980s, Structural Adjustment Plans imposed by the International Monetary Fund forced Third World governments to abandon their traditional role of providing social security for their citizens; a decade later, free trade agreements did the same in the Industrialized Nations of the North. The enormous ensuing power vacuum was quickly filled by giant corporations that had used technology and trade agreements to escape nation-state boundaries; they soon became transnational power blocks more formidable than the governments they replaced.

Workers, social justice advocates, and environmentalists, largely abandoned by their governments, fought back, at first using traditional methods of lobbying the very politicians they opposed. Thousands of citizens' organizations and progressive research institutes came together to voice their concerns about social injustice. And bit by bit, civil society groups began to replace the work previously done by governments in providing social services, feeding the poor, monitoring health and safety standards, and becoming advocates for the environment in an era of environmental deregulation. Unknown even to itself, a powerful "third sector" of civil society was being created, largely unnoticed by the new global royalty of government and corporate elites for whom all appeared to be going as planned.

Lester Salamon, director of the Center for Civil Society at Johns Hopkins University, has undertaken a massive study of the nonprofit sector in forty-two countries around the world. He's revealed some remarkable data since the completion of the first of three phases of the project. The world, he reports, is experiencing a rise in the nonprofit sector unprecedented in modern history. So fast is this sector growing in size and importance that it will appear in retrospect as significant an historical development as the creation of the nation-state in the last part of the nineteenth century.

The third-sector growth rate is dazzling, he says. According to early reports prepared as part of Salamon's study, in nine large countries, the nonprofit sector is growing at four times the rate of the economy. In fact, says Salamon, with annual global expenditures of well over one trillion dollars, if all the third-sector groups were amalgamated in one country, they would form the eighth-largest economy in the world. Nongovernmental organizations also employ more people than the private sector by a margin of six to one — hardly surprising when we examine the massive layoff records of the world's biggest transnationals.

But very little is known about this "veritable associational revolution." Salamon bemoans the "gross" lack of basic information about the third sector and how it operates. "The non-profit sector remains the 'lost continent' on the social landscape of modern society, invisible to most policymakers, business leaders, and the press, and even to many people within the sector itself."

One powerful, political arm of the nonprofit sector, however, became angered that governments appeared to be ignoring their citizens. In attempts to advance their national corporate interests, governments were promoting economic globalization through the World Bank, the North American Free Trade Agreement (NAFTA), the Asia-Pacific Economic Cooperation forum (APEC), the International Monetary Fund, and the World Trade Organization. Governments did set up "dialogues" with civil society, in some cases even holding public hearings like Canada's public consultations on the WTO on the eve of Seattle. Over and over again, however, groups would offer the benefit of their expertise in these consultations, only to find that their advice had been entirely omitted when their governments issued final policy positions.

Governments, and global institutions like the WTO, began to suffer from a "crisis of legitimacy," to use the term coined by the great social movement strategist Antonio Gramsci nearly three-quarters of a century ago. Gramsci pointed out that political power and control cannot be sustained in the long run without popular support — the endorsement that can be derived only from civil society. The legitimacy crisis occurs when political institutions are stripped of their moral and cultural prestige and reduced to their basic "economic-corporate" existence, a condition that reveals more clearly the real cause of oppression.

For a growing number of people, particularly young people, governments around the world, including our own in Canada, were no longer carrying out the mandate they had been elected to fulfill. They were becoming captive to global corporate forces that increasingly dictate all policy — economic, social, and environmental. Citizens watched with dismay as transnational corporations took control of the world's food supply, genetically engineering it with their governments' consent. They watched as politicians and bureaucrats gave giant pharmaceutical companies carte blanche to set drug prices while millions went without basic health care. They saw their politicians turn a blind eye to sweatshop conditions around the world and around the corner, all in the name of competition and profits.

They watched as governments smoothed the way for the commodification of the commons — areas like seeds and genes, culture and heritage, health and education, even air and water — access to which was once considered to be a fundamental right. Citizens questioned the very existence of democracy in such a system.

Unprecedented numbers of young people stopped voting. For them, politicians, political parties, and elections became irrelevant. Citizens' groups, particularly those with young members, began to feel that the politics of consultation and cooperation with governments were nothing more than co-optation and diversion. They began to advocate a more effective form of civil society politics.

The tactics were direct and confrontational — nonviolent civil disobedience. The communications tool was the Internet, which gave enormous power to the grassroots and created what some are calling "globalization from below." The goal was to build an independent international citizens' movement with the power to directly confront not only transnational corporate rule, but also the global institutions that serve it.

The first victory was the defeat of a global investment treaty called the Multilateral Agreement on Investments (MAI) — an advance that sent shock waves through the halls of power around the world. By the time WTO officials admitted defeat in Seattle a year later, the world was put on notice that a new force had emerged on the international scene — one that would change the nature of politics forever.

This is a story in progress. No populist movement emerges full blown, knowing what it wants and how to get it. The values, goals, policies, and strategy of this movement are still to be worked out, not from some authority on high, but on a day-to-day basis, by groups around the world with a diversity of passions and beliefs. But one thing is clear: civil society politics are the politics of the twenty-first century. It is time to take them seriously.

1

Seattle Showdown

How the Battle of Seattle has become the symbol of resistance to corporate globalization

*I*t was a war zone. As dusk approached, the sulphurous air was thick with clouds of smoke, tear gas, and pepper spray. A military curfew was in effect. Thousands of heavily armed police, looking for all the world like extras on a Star Wars set, roamed the rainy streets around the Washington State Convention and Trade Center, randomly beating and pepper-spraying anyone who was still outside. Roving groups of young people, some in anarchist black, played cat and mouse with police; others, chained to one another, held sit-ins at police barricades, taking the full brunt of the officers' brutality up close and personal. A few city buses, driven by public-sector workers disobeying the curfew, drove through the deserted downtown corridor, rescuing injured protesters. Dozens of army helicopters circled overhead, their searchlights casting concentric pools of light on the silhouetted warriors below. The date was November 30, 1999; the event was the 134-member-country Ministerial Meeting of the World Trade Organization, which came to be known as the Millennium Summit.

It was to have been an historic event. As the last major gathering of the millennium for this august body, it was scheduled to launch a whole new round of world trade negotiations, the logical outcome of the successful Uruguay Round of the GATT (General Agreement on Tariffs and Trade), which had resulted in the creation of the WTO itself in 1995. The stakes were extremely high. Globalization and unregulated free trade were in trouble with the public, particularly in the United States. Three times Congress had denied President Bill Clinton "fast track" authority — the legislation required for the U.S. government to endorse free trade agreements without changes — leaving the president without a mandate to expand trade liberalization automatically throughout the world. The show in Seattle would put all that right; both Clinton and Al Gore, by now openly running for the highest political office in the U.S., would make triumphant appearances at strategic points throughout the week. American capitalism and U.S. corporate interests around the world would be secured in a global show of political and economic harmony.

MILLENNIUM DREAMS

The agenda for the "Millennium Round" was extremely ambitious. The United States, joined by the Cairns Group of eighteen food-exporting countries, had vowed when they'd formed in 1986 to systematically reduce or remove most remaining trade barriers and subsidy programs in agriculture. They also sought to establish rules forcing all member-countries to import genetically modified foods, even if there were questions about the safety of these products among their citizens. Meanwhile, the U.S., the European Union, and Canada were vigorously promoting a new round of negotiations that would strengthen corporate intellectual property rights and open up the global service sector — including education, health care, culture, and water — to the full force of WTO discipline.

In addition, through "procurement" and "competition" negotiations, governments were to agree to tender more contracts on the open global market and weaken legislation preventing global corporate concentration. This last move was meant to open up government procurement and competition policy in order to give transnational corporations more access to domestic contracts at the expense of local providers. Tariff barriers and so-called "non-tariff barriers" (including environmental regulations on forest products) were to be reduced, and there was even pressure to start negotiations on a free trade agreement in manufactured chemicals.

Seattle was chosen as the site for the WTO Summit for a very simple reason. For the first time, the event was to be fully funded by the private sector. It was necessary to find a city where corporate sponsors would raise the $10 million needed, and Seattle's Bill Gates of Microsoft and Phil Condit of The Boeing Company came forward to volunteer their considerable talents. As co-hosts of the Seattle Host Organization, Gates and Condit successfully approached companies like AT&T, Hewlett-Packard, Bank of America, and General Motors for generous contributions in return for promised access — proportional to the size of their donations — to American and foreign government officials attending the Summit. Also offered were optional before-and-after-WTO skiing excursions and outings to the best golf courses in the area.

DEMOCRACY ON THE STREETS

What almost no one in authority foretold was the massive number of protesters who would also descend on Seattle, delighted that the less accessible alternative, Honolulu, had not been chosen. Plans for a counter-action were difficult to miss; for months before, the Internet had been filled with the call to come to Seattle. Antiglobalization movements, which had been building in strength for several years, had targeted the WTO and Seattle for the kinds of protest that would put their agenda and anticorporatist message on the public radar screen all over the world. Authorities in Seattle, Washington, and Geneva, where the WTO is housed, ignored or belittled the activists' plans — an attitude they would come to regret. So did much of the mainstream media. Thomas L. Friedman of the *New York Times* called the demonstrators "a Noah's ark of flat-earth advocates, protectionist trade unionists and yuppies looking for their 1960s fix." In fact, had organizers and media representatives chosen to take the movement seriously, they would have recognized its growing stature among civil society groups around the world.

For many months, and in some cases, years, before Seattle, a powerful coalition of international civil society groups in numerous countries had struggled to produce a common analysis and arrive at a common position on the WTO. While not blaming the WTO for all the world's woes, civil society groups had been steadily coming to the conclusion that the WTO was now a dangerous player, whose promotion of corporate-led globalization was writing off millions of people and whole regions of the earth and whose mandate of growth at all costs was destroying the natural world.

Unlike any other global institution, the WTO has both the legislative and the judicial authority to challenge laws, policies, and programs of countries that do not conform to WTO rules and to strike them down if they are seen to be too "trade restrictive." Cases are decided — in secret — by a panel of three trade bureaucrats, and once a WTO ruling is made, worldwide conformity is required. A country is obliged to harmonize its laws or face the prospect of perpetual trade sanctions or fines.

The WTO, which has no minimum standards to protect the environment, labour rights, social programs, or cultural diversity, has already been used to eliminate a number of key nation-state environmental, food safety, and human rights laws. The rate of natural resource extraction has greatly accelerated in the last five years of WTO action, as has the gap between rich and poor in every country and between countries. The WTO has, in fact, become the most powerful tool available to transnational corporations who have worked hand in hand with the trade bureaucrats in Geneva and Washington to establish what is a system of unofficial but real global corporate governance.

Many of the most influential labour, environmental, human rights, cultural diversity, Indigenous, farmer, consumer, and social justice organizations in the world have now developed sophisticated critiques of economic globalization and the WTO. They came together and formed a loose "common front" to exert their influence on the Seattle proceedings, producing a unified demand for the meeting, best summed up by the slogan "No New Round — Turnaround." The message was adopted by over 1,600 organizations internationally. Their members came to Seattle from all over the world, determined to prevent the launching of a new round of WTO negotiations, and joined forces with the powerful U.S. coalition of civil society groups, who were ready for a major confrontation with their own government.

There were several streams of protesters. Public Citizen's Global Trade Watch, which had spent months preparing, with the help of local coalitions, operated the nerve centre for the week's activities and ran a very effective alternative media centre. The U.S. labour central, the American Federation of

Labor–Congress of Industrial Organizations (AFL-CIO), joined by Greenpeace, Friends of the Earth, and others, organized the official march, attended by almost sixty thousand protesters. The more grassroots activities were organized by People's Global Action, which rallied national support in the U.S.; the Direct Action Network, the main organizer of the downtown protests; and the Ruckus Society, which sponsored a week-long camp in the Cascade Mountains, run by the Rainforest Action Network, to train activists in the skills of nonviolent civil disobedience.

The weekend before the WTO Ministerial Meeting began, the San Francisco–based International Forum on Globalization (IFG) held a "teach-in" at Seattle's Benaroya Hall. Over sixty experts on economic globalization and the WTO presented information, analysis, and strategy advice to a highly motivated, supercharged audience of 2,500, and almost as many were turned away at the door. This set the stage for civil society workshops, panels, and seminars held all over the city throughout the entire week.

An air of tension hung over the city as dawn broke on Monday, November 29th. A planned consultation between WTO officials and nongovernmental organizations (NGOs) had to be postponed because of a bomb threat. Hundreds of delegates, locked out of the Convention Center, mingled with an assortment of protesters (some dressed as sea turtles and butterflies and others as genetically mutant corn) as hundreds of "robo-cops" paraded up and down the streets, rhythmically beating their truncheons against their shin pads in a menacing show of force. By early afternoon, the Convention Center was cleared and the NGO "symposium" commenced.

Chairs Michael Moore, director general of the WTO, and Charlene Barshefsky, U.S. trade representative and chair of the WTO Millennium Summit, took the gloves off. They told the audience (which included corporate lobby groups — considered by the WTO to be NGOs) that they should be grateful to be present at this first such dialogue in the fifty-one-year history of the GATT and that the WTO was the best thing ever for the environment and for human and labour rights. Moore even invoked the name of Martin Luther King, Jr., saying that King would have been a WTO booster. Many in the room were appalled at the controlled nature of the so-called dialogue and left to join the protesters on the street.

The next morning, before dawn, thousands of youth protesters converged on the Paramount Theater near the Washington State Convention and Trade

Center, where the official opening ceremonies were to take place, and ringed it with a human chain almost impossible to break through. Highly disciplined "flying groups" of protesters placed themselves at strategic spots downtown, preventing delegates from travelling to the ceremony or their meetings. Using a variety of tactics, the groups held key intersections of the downtown and surrounded the Convention Center and the adjacent five-star hotels, effectively blocking delegates from moving around at all.

Pierre Pettigrew, Canada's Minister for International Trade, and Sergio Marchi, Canada's Ambassador to the WTO, only managed to enter the Convention Center through a second-floor window, having been unceremoniously lifted there in a flower box! Charlene Barshefsky, who was to deliver the keynote address at the official opening, was stuck in her hotel room. The official opening ceremonies were cancelled, and for the first time in the city's history, the mayor of Seattle called in the National Guard.

The sun broke through the clouds later that morning as tens of thousands of peaceful marchers, including over two thousand Canadians, left their rally at a nearby stadium and headed downtown in a massive, colourful, music-filled march. While many turned around at the end of the demonstration and headed back to waiting buses, many others joined the direct action on the streets, running right into armoured cars, horses, and security squads in full riot gear.

Without warning, police started firing tear and nerve gas and rubber bullets, indiscriminately pepper-spraying and randomly attacking protesters with truncheons. Special forces from the FBI, the United States Secret Service, and the Pentagon's top-secret Delta Force were soon joined by highly trained National Guard forces. Anyone walking, sitting, or even going to or from work was fair game for the random and excessive force that followed. At several locations, the combined "security" forces simply unleashed barrages of tear gas, and fumes soon filled the entire downtown core with acrid smoke. One by one, police grabbed the heads of seated protesters from the rear and sprayed pepper directly into their eyes. Then, in some cases, officers used their thumbs to grind the chemical in. People writhed in agony on the sidewalks or went unconscious from the fumes and the pain. Blood and broken teeth could be seen on the streets. Produce at Seattle's famous waterfront market was ruined after being sprayed; local residents were beaten up; and police even invaded Seattle's trendy Capitol Hill suburb, chasing phantom protesters and lobbing tear-gas canisters onto verandahs.

SEATTLE FIREPOWER

Seattle police were armed with the following: U.S. military-standard M40A1 double-canister gas masks; uncalibrated, semi-automatic, high-velocity Autocockers loaded with solid plastic shot; Monadnock disposable plastic cuffs; Nomex slash-resistant gloves; Commando boots; Centurion tactical leg guards; combat harnesses; DK5-H pivot-and-lock riot face shields; black Monadnock P24 polycarbonate riot batons with Trumbull stop side handles; No. 2 continuous discharge CS (orthochlorobenzylidene-malononitrile) chemical grenades; M651 CN (chloroacetophenone) pyrotechnic grenades; T16 Flameless OC Expulsion Grenades; DTCA rubber bullet grenades ("Stingers"); M-203 (40 mm) grenade launchers; First Defense MK-46 oleoresin capsicum (OC) aerosol tanks with hose and wands; .60-caliber rubber ball impact munitions; lightweight tactical Kevlar composite ballistic helmets; combat butt packs; .30-cal. 30-round magazine pouches; and Kevlar body armor. None of the police had visible badges or forms of identification.

Paul Hawken, "Journal of the Uninvited," *Whole Earth*, Spring 2000

Most protesters were armed with nothing but a bandana soaked in vinegar, to protect their eyes and noses from pepper spray and tear gas, and jackets with hoods to fend off the elements. It is true that several dozen black-clad anarchists roamed the downtown core, smashing selected windows of businesses whose human rights and environmental records have been called into question by many activists: Starbucks, The Gap, Nike, and McDonald's (symbols, says Vancouver APEC protester Rob West, that "look like Disney, taste like Coke, and smell like shit"). To the distress of local residents and peaceful demonstrators, the police did not arrest these people, but they used the media's property-damage images to justify their brutal crackdown against the peaceful majority. Illegal detentions ensued; over six hundred young people were held in harsh conditions, and many were denied food and water until the WTO Summit was over and the delegates returned home. Criminal proceedings against the vast majority of those arrested were dropped in the weeks following the fiasco.

One professor from Seattle University, a protester himself, remarked that the police behaviour had done what he hadn't been able to do in his class-rooms — it had radicalized his white, middle-class students, who had never been political in their lives.

DEMOCRACY INSIDE THE WTO

Inside the Convention Center, WTO officials did their best to ignore the outbreak of democracy on the streets. What they didn't count on was the outbreak of democracy inside the Center itself. Delegates from Nonindustrialized Countries, who almost universally believe that the WTO has not delivered on promised benefits to the South, were furious at the high-handed treatment they were receiving from the powerful countries of the North. Many, particularly in Asia and Africa, were opposed to the agenda of the powerful QUAD countries — the United States, Europe, Canada, and Japan. They wanted to deal first with the issue of power imbalances between South and North — a discussion that had been promised at the conclusion of the Uruguay Round. But they soon found their concerns dismissed by the Northern countries.

After much wrangling and foot dragging on the part of the U.S., the Third World delegates were finally assured, for the first time, an equal role in the Summit deliberations. But Charlene Barshefsky was blunt in her warning. WTO officials were attempting to take a democratic approach, she declared, by "allowing" Nonindustrialized Nations to participate. But if the process didn't work to her satisfaction, she told the international press and all WTO delegates, she would exercise her authority and unilaterally impose her agenda on the meeting.

One had only to observe the differences between the official country delegations walking the halls of the Washington State Convention and Trade Center to understand the power imbalance between rich and poor countries. The U.S., Europe, Canada, and Japan all had hundreds of delegates attended by trade lawyers, spin doctors, and government officials and supported by state-of-the-art technology. Many Nonindustrialized Countries had only two or three delegates, with no aides, no spin doctors, and not even any cellphones.

Overarching the entire proceedings was the arrogance of the United States, which bungled the whole event, underestimating the size of the protests, mishandling the Third World nations, and generally acting as a bully. Many felt it inappropriate that Charlene Barshefsky did not act as a neutral chair, and her inflexibility provoked an unprecedented amount of public criticism from all sides.

Tension quickly built. Taking the promise of inclusion seriously, Third World delegates started demanding a democratic process inside the meetings, which resulted in paralysis. When, on December 1st, President Clinton publicly called for labour standards in the WTO, representatives of Nonindustrialized Nations were upset; they felt that the statement was cheap political posturing carried out in preparation for the upcoming American national election and that, if Northern countries really cared about the Third World, they would work to build true equalization mechanisms into trade relations. Third World delegates credited the street protests with giving them the resolve to fight to be heard at the talks, even if it meant scuttling the negotiations. Said Papua New Guinea Trade Secretary Michael Maue, "The people who demonstrated basically represent the world's silent majority." But the efforts of the delegates from the South came to naught. After hearing their demands, Charlene Barshefsky, who hadn't slept more than an hour or two a night for close to a week and was in no mood for compromise, made good on her promise to exercise her authority and unilaterally imposed discipline on the meeting.

On Friday, December 3rd, sleep-deprived delegates from Industrialized Countries held "Green Room" sessions with dissenting sleep-deprived Third World delegates, where, seated in airless rooms and not given coffee or even water to drink, they were badgered one or two at a time. The Third World delegates were palpably furious. One stomped out into the hall, muttering that this was a "hell of a way to run the world."

Late that evening, Barshefsky received a call from a stern President Clinton. The meeting had become an international embarrassment. Three thousand journalists from all over the world were there to cover the liberalization of global trade and to sing the praises of the American economic miracle. Instead, they were sending home stories about protesters, endangered sea turtles, sweatshops, child poverty, the plight of Third World farmers, and demands for the democratization of the WTO. Clinton ordered his trade rep to close the mess down.

The news spread through the Convention Center and spilled out onto the streets like an electric current. Canadian Minister for International Trade

Pierre Pettigrew and other government officials were already concocting the best spin they could think of — statements like "We never had great expectations for this meeting anyway" and "The protesters had nothing to do with this." But they couldn't hide the truth of this remarkable week. The only way they could even conduct their business was with the support of excessive physical policing, and even that hadn't worked. Protest organizer Lori Wallach of the U.S. group Public Citizen summed up the mood of the crowd: "The allegedly unstoppable force of globalization just hit the immovable object called grassroots democracy. The world will never be the same again." "Summit Ends in Failure," blared the headline in the *Seattle Post-Intelligencer* the next day. It was, the newspaper noted, "an ugly conclusion to an ugly week."

The world of international trade and finance was stunned. How could this have happened? Who were these people? How did they organize something like this? Why were so many of them young? Why were their own children so sympathetic to the protesters? Would this be a one-time wonder or was it the beginning of a movement?

TOWARD A NEW MOVEMENT

In fact, the seeds of Seattle had been growing for some time. In a variety of ways, protest against economic globalization had been building toward this crescendo for years. It had begun in the early 1980s with protests in India, when peasants and farmers had mobilized against the so-called Green Revolution, whereby Industrialized Nations forced crop monoculture on Indian farmers and opened the door to corporate takeover of food production in that country. When the WTO used its muscle to allow transnational corporations to take out patents on the genetic heritage inherent in the Third World's traditional crops, groups across the South began to unite.

In North America, free trade became a controversial issue in the 1980s, first in Canada, with the opposition of the majority of Canadians to the Canada–U.S. Free Trade Agreement. The anti–free trade movement then expanded to the U.S. and Mexico with the North American Free Trade Agreement (NAFTA) and later to Latin America with the planned expansion of NAFTA to become the FTAA — the Free Trade Area of the Americas. Environmentalists across the hemisphere came together to express deep concerns about the impact of trade liberalization on natural resource protection and about clauses in the agreements that give corporations the right to seek compensation for profit lost when they are affected by environmental regulations. Labour unions formed cross-border alliances as pressure was exerted to downgrade labour standards and wages in what workers saw as a "race to the bottom." Public educators and public health care providers across the continent started sharing concerns about the planned privatization of their sectors and discussed common strategies to preserve their public functions.

In Europe, farmers and consumers formed powerful cross-border alliances to protect the purity of their food, save their agricultural communities, and fight against genetically engineered foods and the trade agreements that were advancing them. Their movement is now worldwide. Asian human rights, worker, and environmental groups found common cause in their opposition to APEC — the Asia-Pacific Economic Cooperation forum — an ongoing corporate-government process to force the liberalization of trade and investment in Asia Pacific, with no protection for people or communities.

YOUNG ASIA DINES OUT
A recent GenerAsians survey asked 5,700 young people from the Asia-Pacific region to name their favourite food and drink. Their answers:
Australia: McDonald's, Coca-Cola
China: McDonald's, Coca-Cola
Hong Kong: McDonald's, Coca-Cola
Indonesia: McDonald's, Coca-Cola
Japan: McDonald's, Coca-Cola
Malaysia: KFC, Coca-Cola
Singapore: McDonald's, Coca-Cola
Taiwan: McDonald's, Coca-Cola
Thailand: KFC, Pepsi

GenerAsians summer poll, 1999

Artists, writers, filmmakers, and musicians around the world became increasingly concerned about cultural homogenization — what Indian physicist and activist leader Vandana Shiva calls "monoculture of the mind." Combined with the destruction of the habitat of Aboriginal citizens and the loss of thousands of languages, the deadening and harmonizing effect of economic globalization, enforced through trade agreements like the WTO, has set off alarm bells in the cultural community.

International movements, many of them including church and human rights coalitions like Jubilee 2000, an international ecumenical coalition, grew up to challenge the enormous debt burden carried by the Nonindustrialized World. Using money gained from wealthy oil-exporting nations, Northern banks had lent huge sums to the nations of the South. When the debts kept mounting, the International Monetary Fund (IMF) stepped in and imposed austere economic policies on the Nonindustrialized Nations, to ensure that some of the money was recouped. The result was increased misery among the poor. The international justice organizations are concerned that millions are losing out in a global economy that disrupts traditional economies and weakens the ability of governments to assist their citizens. Left to fend for themselves in failed states against destitution, famine, and plagues, the world's growing poor are forced to migrate, to offer their labour at wages below subsistence levels, and to sacrifice their children, their natural environment, and their personal health. One powerful coalition, called "Fifty Years Is Enough," in reference to the fact that the World Bank and the IMF are now half a century old, has created a moral crisis inside the World Bank and the IMF. It has forced them to address Third World poverty, which they now admit they had a major hand in causing.

All over the world, students were becoming politicized because of the corporate invasion of their schools and universities. Transnational corporations sit on boards of governors, shaping policy and promoting privatization of the institutions. Students on many campuses have fought back against exclusive deals in which their universities have received funding from Coca-Cola and against other attempts to "name brand" their schools. Universities are increasingly being used to foster profit-making projects funded partially or in whole by corporations who are then in a position to dictate the academic direction of the research and who will own any resulting products when the project is complete. At the same time, tuition fees have skyrocketed and students are carrying enormous debt burdens, often for years into the future. A profound politicization of youth has taken root in these institutions; it is from them that the antiglobalization youth movement, deeply cynical about traditional politics, has sprung.

THE NEW SOVEREIGNS

The top two hundred global corporations are now so big that their combined sales surpass the combined economies of 182 countries, and they have almost twice the economic clout of the poorest four-fifths of humanity. Of the hundred largest economies in the world, fifty-two are now transnational corporations. Wal-Mart is bigger than 163 countries. Mitsubishi is larger than Indonesia. Ford is bigger than South Africa. The new merged Time Warner–America Online colossus has a market value greater than the economy of Australia.

On a more personal front, four hundred and forty-seven billionaires have a combined wealth greater than the income of half of humanity. The three richest people in the world have assets that exceed the combined gross domestic product of forty-eight countries. Eighty-nine countries have lower per capita incomes today than they did a decade or more ago and 200 million more people this year are living in absolute poverty (less than one dollar a day). The world's two hundred richest people have doubled their wealth in the last four years.

Institute for Policy Studies, Washington, D.C.,
and *1999 UN Human Development Index Annual Report*

Many international movements and campaigns have also focused on individual corporations in the past decade, alleging that corporations such as Nike and The Gap use sweatshop labour; that the Shell Oil Company and the mining company Rio Tinto are implicated in environmental pollution and human rights abuses; that agribusiness giants such as Monsanto Company are destroying biodiversity by aggressively producing and promoting genetically modified foods; and that water distribution giants like Suez Lyonnaise des Eaux are privatizing the world's water for profit. Antisweatshop activists combined forces with international campaigns such as Free the Children to protest the barbarous conditions inside many Nonindustrialized World workplaces. Almost every sector now has a "watchdog" group that monitors its actions, and many corporations have been forced to deal with the public relations nightmares that have been created by these campaigners.

Recently, these disparate groups and others have started to challenge more than some individual corporations alleged to be engaging in illegal or immoral acts; they are questioning the actual structural power and authority of transnational corporations and the body of rights they have acquired nationally and internationally. This powerful global anticorporate movement is carrying out a more systematic analysis of the power of corporations and is questioning their right to exist in their current manifestation.

These are the movements that came together in Seattle. It wasn't the first time they had shown their power. In North America, coalitions had staged marches and rallies against both the Canada–U.S. Free Trade Agreement and NAFTA, in Canada, the U.S., and Mexico. Protesters dogged the World Bank, the IMF, and the group of seven leading industrial countries (G7) throughout the 1990s — in Auckland, London, Kuala Lumpur, and New Delhi. Thousands turned out for a "street party/demonstration" in Birmingham, England, on May 16, 1998, for the G7 meeting; two days later, protests were staged all over the world on the fiftieth anniversary of the creation of the GATT. Over two hundred young people were arrested in Geneva during days of rioting. When APEC leaders met in the Philippines in 1996, thousands of protesters formed a vehicle convoy and clogged the highways for miles from Manila to Subic Bay, where the leaders were meeting. When APEC came to Vancouver the next year, thousands more marched in the streets, and student protesters were pepper-sprayed and intimidated by police. Forty thousand people demonstrated in Cologne, Germany, in June 1999 at the meeting of the G8 countries (the G7 plus Russia) to demand greater assistance for the world's poorest nations.

Seattle was only one in a series of antiglobalization protests that captured media attention around the world, but it was also something special — a culmination of worldwide activity on the part of citizens deeply concerned about global corporate interests that are violating the laws of nature and taking precedence over democratic freedoms.

2

Militant Roots

*How grassroots activism
set the stage for
"globalization from below"*

*The government of Japan was terrified. In July 2000 the leaders of the seven
most powerful countries on earth, along with the new Russian president, were
holding their annual G8 meeting on the island of Okinawa, home to a
controversial U.S. naval base. Fearful of another Seattle, Japan spent an
unprecedented Can$1 billion on the tightest security in the country's history.
Undeterred, with gags over their mouths to symbolize their forced silence, more
than twenty-five thousand Okinawans surrounded the U.S. Kadena Air Force
Base when President Clinton arrived, to protest the continued presence of the
U.S. military on Japanese soil.*

*   The message was clear. No amount of security can silence a movement
whose time has come.*

MAI VICTORY

The momentum that culminated in the Battle of Seattle had been building for some time. In October 1998, the countries of the Organization for Economic Co-operation and Development (OECD) abandoned their quest to ratify a global treaty on direct foreign investment — the Multilateral Agreement on Investment (MAI) — in the face of massive public resistance. Under the MAI, signatory governments would have agreed to give up their rights to set conditions on foreign investment, losing substantial sovereignty over their natural resources, cultural institutions, social security programs, and environmental regulations. Transnational corporations would even have been able to sue governments directly for "appropriation compensation" if those governments introduced or even exercised certain existing health, safety, human rights, environmental, or labour laws. The MAI was dubbed, and was truly, a global charter of rights and freedoms for transnational corporations.

It was in 1996 that Martin Khor of the Third World Network first alerted members of the International Forum on Globalization that a global investment treaty was being negotiated; it was his understanding from his contacts in Geneva that the deal was fairly close to the ratification stage. But Khor had no actual document as proof. Groups began demanding information from their governments about the MAI but were less than happy at the responses. Most governments fudged their answers or denied the existence of the treaty altogether. The document, the original of which was drafted by the International Chamber of Commerce, was finally obtained in Canada and shared with groups around the world, who collectively launched the first successful Internet campaign to defeat a global government-corporate project.

In the fall of 1997, seventy labour, environmental, and citizens' groups met with government MAI negotiators at the posh headquarters of the OECD in Paris. The groups had worked late into the night to come up with a consensus demand for a one-year moratorium on the negotiations to allow them to meet with their governments and hold public briefings back home. The OECD arrogantly refused, talking down to the activists as if they were incapable of understanding the intricacies of the deal. Angered at this treatment by representatives of their own governments, the groups dispersed to fight the MAI back in their own countries.

Throughout the next year, coalitions were formed in many countries among all the sectors that would be affected. Public meetings were held in town halls and church basements. Grassroots groups sprang up everywhere — on campuses, in seniors' communities, in health care clinics, union halls, and churches — and many of these places were declared "MAI-Free Zones." Hundreds of bumper stickers, brochures, books, pamphlets, buttons, and fact sheets were created in several lead countries, and dozens of municipal governments around the world passed resolutions against the MAI.

Country coalitions worked closely with one another across borders, sharing information and strategies. One successful approach was to create dissension within government by exposing how the MAI, being negotiated largely in secret by trade bureaucrats and kept secret even from other members of the same government, would affect ministries like culture, environment, and health. As a result of this strategy, pressure grew from within governments to exempt many areas from the MAI, and the number of reservations being demanded from the various member governments rose dramatically to over thirteen hundred, paralyzing the talks.

In a tactic called "monkey wrenching," groups informed each other of politically sensitive issues concerning their own governments' negotiating positions so that the information could be used to establish friction between the different government delegations. Although the groups perhaps didn't realize it during the heat of the battle, this was a milestone in the movement.

Until this time, groups fighting free trade and economic globalization had been nation-state-based; they had come together only as loose coalitions, to cooperate temporarily on a common project. The anti-MAI campaign, however, was fundamentally different. Because they were abandoned by their own governments, which had bought the rhetoric on investment liberalization lock, stock, and barrel, workers, environmentalists, and citizen advocacy groups had to create a movement outside their nation-state boundaries, one that was based in cyberspace and undergirded by a common set of values and beliefs.

Precedents of international cooperation did exist: the movements for women's rights, food security, and environmental stewardship had resulted in deep bonding across borders. The United Nations had also served as a place for like-minded groups to come together to fight for charters on human rights, the rights of women and children, and many other forms of justice. However, with the possible exception of the peace movement and some parts of the international environment movement, these campaigns usually worked fairly closely with their governments, lobbying, cajoling, and pressuring them to participate in their projects. But during the anti-MAI campaign, activists saw little hope in relying on their own national leaders, so they turned to each other for support.

All the groups who'd met in that Paris room were in touch with each other on a daily basis, and they disseminated information to the grassroots in their own countries. Using the creative talent of the international cultural community, which became very active in the campaign, they framed the public message long before governments did. And so, by sending the first "take" on the issue into the public arena, they set the conditions for winning.

In February 1998, the OECD held an emergency meeting to attempt to salvage the talks, which, only months before, had been nearly complete. The chairman of the OECD MAI negotiating group, Franz Engering, "relapsed into evangelism," according to a leaked Canadian government memo, to try to save the deal, and the role of the international citizens' movement was ruefully recognized by all present. In March, the European Parliament passed resolution 437–8, urging its members to reject the treaty, and the next month, another Ministerial Meeting on the proposed agreement ended in failure. A grim-faced OECD secretary general, Donald Johnston, admitted that the talks were on hold and informed a packed press conference that the delay was the fault of an effective "disinformation" campaign waged by groups around the world.

That fall, the government of France published a Cabinet report praising the work of the international anti-MAI campaign and said that the groups had put out better material and better research than had the OECD. France pulled out of the talks, followed by Canada. The MAI was dead.

The success of the campaign was based on several factors, not the least of which was trust — not easy to build between groups halfway around the world from one another. Another crucial element was the grassroots nature of the activism — thousands of small campaigns working in concert, but not directed from on high. Large groups with money produced plenty of research and information, but the material was crafted by individual groups for their own needs and local use. People and groups all over the world took personal ownership of the campaign and took personal credit for the win — as they should have.

The anti-MAI movement also used the Internet effectively to bolster its campaign. A Toronto *Globe and Mail* front-page article began with the headline "How the Internet Killed the MAI" and went on to say that "high-powered politicians" were no match for a "global band of grass-roots organizations" who had transformed international politics. The *Financial Times* compared the fear and bewilderment that had seized the governments of industrialized countries in the wake of the MAI's collapse to a scene from the movie *Butch Cassidy and the Sundance Kid*. Politicians and diplomats looked behind them at the "horde of vigilantes" in close pursuit, "whose motives and methods are only dimly understood in most capitals," and they asked despairingly, "Who *are* these guys?" The hordes, according to the paper, were "an international movement of grass-roots pressure groups" who claimed their first success in this fight and "drew blood." It quoted a veteran trade diplomat who said, "This episode is a turning point. It means we have to rethink our approach to international economic and trade negotiations."

The anti-MAI groups' use of the Internet has had an interesting ramification. As journalist Naomi Klein has written, the communications technology that facilitates antiglobalization campaigns is moulding the movement in its own image. Like the Internet, they have sparse bureaucracy, decentralized power, and minimal hierarchy. Forced consensus and laboured manifestos, she notes, are being replaced by a culture of constant, loosely structured, and sometimes compulsive information swapping. The small, moving packs of protesters in Seattle — the coalition of coalitions — were the "Internet come to life."

Perhaps the most crucial reason for the success of the MAI campaign was that separate citizens' groups began to see themselves as constituting a movement with its own power base. They came from a position of strength and the knowledge that their governments were going to listen to them not because they had good arguments, but because they had political muscle. So they entered the debate with their own demands, their own analysis, and their own vision. They didn't ask for a seat at the OECD table; they built their own table and forced their governments to deal with them as a new political force.

A MOVEMENT IS BORN

When they came to Seattle, they came as individual sectors to express their concerns about the impact of the WTO on their areas of activism — the environment, farmers' rights, food safety, worker rights, and cultural and biological diversity. But they also came as a nascent common front, and by the time the week was over, a more unified movement had been born. While the groups had diverse interests and some real differences, they had created an antiglobalization civil society movement greater than the sum of its parts. Some have charged that the movement has no coherence; but its character is distinct, both in ideology and in tactics.

First and foremost, antiglobalization activists believe that the current system of economic globalization, based on the ideology of the growth imperative, is causing such distress to our ecosystems that the planet is coming dangerously close to meltdown. Under the current system of market-driven economic globalization, no limits are placed on where capital can go to "harvest" nature. Economic globalization has forced Nonindustrialized Nations to destroy their natural ecosystems and environmental regulations in order to pay their debts.

Antiglobalization analysts are also convinced that wide-open worldwide markets promote a form of global class warfare. They refute the current counterargument from the WTO and the World Bank that the benefits of economic globalization simply have not yet reached enough people and that it is only a matter of time before they do. Opponents of the worldwide economic free-for-all say that economic globalization is based on sorting winners from losers, that there could not be "winners" on the present scale without deliberately creating losers, and that the world is unfolding not as it should but as intended by the corporate elites who are attempting to redesign it.

The members of this movement are one in their belief that transnational corporations have gained far too much power and that they now dictate government policies at all levels. Unaccountable corporate leaders, making obscene amounts of money, are setting the domestic and international rules by which people all around the world are being forced to live. Activists call this "corporate rule." They think that the WTO and its "sister" organizations, the World Bank and the International Monetary Fund, are run *by* transnational corporations *for* transnational corporations and exist to dictate to governments what they can and cannot do on behalf of their citizens. They therefore question whether real democracy still exists anywhere in the world.

The activists who opposed the MAI understand that many of the world's environmental and social crises are being provoked or aggravated by global deregulation and privatization. They know that deregulated capital flows have caused massive poverty and financial instability while benefiting wealthy hedge-fund operators, investors, and Industrialized World governments. These practices have worsened public health care conditions around the world, leaving millions without the basic medical support needed for life. In a world of commodification, everything is now for sale, and the "commons" of humanity — be they human and social rights or a safe environment — have been hijacked by corporate interests for profit.

Finally, antiglobalization activists share a profound disappointment with their governments, which, one after the other, have bought into the system and become part of the problem. They watch with anger as their political leaders lose touch with the poor in their own countries and hand over decision making to global institutions averse to the interests of the majority of the world's citizens.

This antipathy toward government is evident in the declining rate of voter participation, particularly among the young, taking place all over the world. In Europe, membership in political parties has fallen 50% in the last fifteen years; in U.S. presidential elections, fewer than half of the eligible voters cast a ballot; and in Canada, voter turnout for the November election was the lowest in the country's history. For many, partisan politics have become irrelevant. Elections have been reduced to a form of political "consumerism" in which the public gets to choose from among a class of professional politicians who appear far too alike and who govern according to a set of dictates far removed from the electorate.

For a growing number of activists, democracy within government will never be realized as long as it does not exist in society. For them, the urgent task is to address the latter first.

ONE NO, MANY YESES

The civil society movement is unified in its understanding that the global trade free-for-all will damage all nations of the world. However, activist groups within the movement are proposing many different solutions to the problem. The greatest divergence exists between those who believe nongovernmental organizations (NGOs) should be in dialogue with governments and institutions like the WTO and those who contend that such interactions will co-opt the movement, taking the wind out of its sails and transforming it into a mere "reformist" agenda. Otherwise, however, the movement's diversity has produced a wealth of processes, studies, proposals, and publications dealing with alternatives to economic globalization — proposals that range from poetic and literary imaginings of possible common futures to technical briefs on the changes that need to be made to international financial and trade rules. (See Chapter Nine.) The very diversity of these ideas is their strength, and while many are working to bring about social change within the context of existing processes and achievements (such as the 1948 United Nations' Universal Declaration of Human Rights and its accompanying covenants), there is general consensus that the vision cannot be reduced to simply an amendment of existing global institutions. More radical, systemic change is needed — from transforming our relationship to nature and other species to undertaking a profound shift in the management of wealth and power.

Antiglobalization activists believe that humans have to start living within the natural limits of the world's ecosystems once more — growing and making more products closer to home, for example. They are not opposed to trade or even (fair) trade rules but they dispute the transcendence and over-arching power of deregulated global trade and finance in every sphere of life. They believe that the "commons" have been stolen from people and nature and that they should be restored to public and democratic control. They believe in respect for cultural and biological diversity and in protecting the infinite variety of the natural world, including other species. They share the notion that one of the most potent antidotes to economic globalization is the return to community and to the reactivation of more effective local democracy; they believe that the economy exists to serve people and communities, not the other way around.

At the same time, the movement is international in its scope and spirit — community includes people around the corner and halfway around the globe. In a world where governments have abandoned the interests of their citizens, people need to act themselves to take back control from transnational corporations. And that means joining forces with international movements, as well as local ones. It also means targeting corporations and global trade and financial institutions directly, since governments are now inadequate to the task, having already made their deals with the devil. What is really at stake, and what all the campaigns address regardless of other differences, is the need for civic culture to prevail over corporate culture. As Ralph Nader says, "You can have democracy, or you can have corporate control. You cannot have both."

NEW WINESKINS

Globalization from below grew both out of previous movements and out of their breakdown. There is much to be learned from the historical heritage of centuries of struggle to restrain or replace capitalism, and we should draw on its values and practices in shaping our own. But it would be a mistake to simply treat this new movement as an extension of those that went before — or to attach it to their remnants. Globalization in all its facets presents new problems that the old movements failed to address — that is part of why they declined so radically. It also presents new opportunities that will be lost if the new wine is simply poured back into the old bottles. Besides, the historic break provides an invaluable opportunity to escape the dead hand of the past and to reground the movement to restrain global capital in the actual needs and conditions of people today. Like pioneers entering a new country, we should try to bring over the flowers and leave the weeds behind.

Jeremy Brecher, Tim Costello, and Brendan Smith,
Globalization from Below: The Power of Solidarity

A VOICE FOR THE MARGINALIZED

A striking characteristic of the new civil society movement is its insistence that its most marginalized voices shall be heard at the centre. In reaction to the top-down structures it opposes, it insists on levelling hierarchies — even those of the movements from which it has grown. Although it has spokespersons, or "spokes," who speak publicly for the movement, it eschews "stars" and formalized leaders. The new organizational form takes the shape of horizontal advocacy networks — groups and individuals linked in concentric rings, bound by common values. While building its own base, the movement chooses not to create the kinds of institutions or power structures that could directly challenge the major state and corporate institutions it opposes; rather, it works under and around these behemoths, cutting away their power base like grains of sand or rivulets of water undermining the foundations of an old building.

And the movement, as anyone watching television can see, is young. Not exclusively, of course. But the youth wing of the new global civil society movement is having an enormous impact on its values, tactics, and structure. It was not the many thousands of the official march who shut down the opening ceremonies of the WTO in Seattle or captured the media attention of the whole world, but the several thousand young people, many of them high school students, who claimed the streets in the name of democracy. Young activists, who, as Ralph Nader says, have "grown up corporate," understand the corporate culture in ways older people cannot. They have been the targets of brand identification and corporate logos since infancy, hooked on McDonald's and Coca-Cola from childhood. Unless they are among the small minority of young millionaire techno-wizards and financial speculators who have parlayed the culture into personal success, they know that to them as a generation, the opportunities of the so-called new economy are slim pickings indeed. Many have chosen to opt out of corporate culture altogether, turning off their televisions, refusing to wear brand name clothing, "culture jamming" their way to a new consciousness. In Seattle, they made it clear that the older generation of activists does not own the movement. "Elvis Is Dead" buttons graced many a T-shirt and black jacket.

The young members of the new civil society movement are more confrontational than members of more traditional NGOs. They believe that political and corporate elites have stopped listening and will be moved only by expressions of direct action against the institutions they have created. Tattooed, pierced, painted, and multiracial, they look power structures in the face and chant, "This is what democracy looks like."

For street demos, many defenders of the civil society undergo training for body, mind, and soul. The Ruckus Society in the U.S., one of the numerous teaching groups around the world, has been sponsoring camps and seminars since 1995, to help protesters learn how to carry out nonviolent civil disobedience. "Through these trainings," says one of their representatives, "we help people learn the skills they need to practice civil disobedience safely and effectively. These trainings contain cerebral elements as well as physical, including classroom-style instruction for action planning and communicating with the media and nonviolent philosophy and practice. Safety and nonviolence are integral themes of each subject taught."

Participants are organized into "affinity groups," small bands who commit to coming to shared decisions (such as whether or not to get arrested) and who look out for one another. Affinity groups sometimes break down into smaller "clusters," who will stake out a door or police barricade for a sit-in, and "flying groups," which are free to move to wherever they are needed. All these decisions are made ahead of time at "convergence centres," where affinity group representatives gather for "spokescouncil meetings" and where protesters regroup for food, medical aid, and support after a stint on the street.

FLEXIBLE FIGHTERS

In practice, [the nonhierarchical] organization [of the defenders of civil society] meant that groups could move and react with great flexibility during the [Seattle] blockade. If a call went out for more people at a certain location, an affinity group could assess the numbers holding the line where they were and choose whether or not to move. When faced with tear gas, pepper spray, rubber bullets, and horses, groups and individuals could assess their own ability to withstand the brutality. As a result, blockade lines held in the face of incredible police violence. When one group of people was finally swept away by gas and clubs, another would move in to take their place.

No centralized leader could have coordinated the scene in the midst of chaos, and none was needed — the organic, autonomous organization we had proved far more powerful and effective. No authoritarian figure could have compelled people to hold a blockade line while being tear gassed — but empowered people free to make their own decisions did choose to do just that. The affinity groups, cluster, spokescouncils, and working groups involved made decisions by consensus — a process that allows every voice to be heard and that stresses respect for minority opinions. Consensus was part of the nonviolence and jail trainings and we made a small attempt to also

offer some special training in meeting facilitation. We did not inter-
pret consensus to mean unanimity. The only mandatory agreement
was to act within the nonviolent guidelines. Beyond that, the Direct
Action Network organizers set a tone that valued autonomy and freedom over conformity, and stressed coordination rather than pressure
to conform.

The action included art, dance, celebration, song, ritual, and magic.
It was more than a protest; it was an uprising of a vision of true abundance, a celebration of life and creativity and connection that
remained joyful in the face of brutality and brought alive the creative
forces that can truly counter those of injustice and control.

E-mail from Starhawk, a San Francisco activist

A MOVEMENT GROWS

Post-Seattle, the world of international politics was put on notice: wherever
you go, wherever you meet, the antiglobalization movement will be there.
Flashed instantaneously around the world were the dates for the next actions
— written in a new code, each named after the month and day of the upcoming event: A16 — the April World Bank and IMF meetings in Washington; M1
— May Day 2000 protests around the world; M8 — a meeting of the Asian
Development Bank (ADB) in Thailand; J5 — the June gathering of the
Organization of American States in Windsor, Ontario; J12 — the June meet-
ing of the World Petroleum Congress in Calgary; J15 — an antiglobalization
rally in Bologna, Italy; J31–A14 — the Republican and Democratic national
conventions in the United States during the summer of 2000; S11 —
September's meeting of the World Economic Forum in Melbourne, Australia;
S26 — again, the IMF and the World Bank, this time in Prague in September;
A17 — the April 2001 Summit of the Free Trade Area of the Americas (FTAA)
in Quebec City.

A16

Twice a year, the World Bank and the International Monetary Fund hold
official meetings. While they have been dogged by nongovernmental organ-

izations and some protests throughout the 1990s, they knew that their meeting in Washington in mid-April 2000 would be different. As delegates began to gather in the capital's five-star hotels, thousands of protesters (including about two thousand Canadians), organized by an international coalition of 450 groups, were converging on the city's youth hostels, churches, student residences, and parks. Thanks to Seattle, their impact was felt even before they arrived.

Just a month before, Stanley Fischer, the IMF's acting managing director, had met with Friends of the Earth International, Oxfam International, and other groups, who came away from the meeting heartened that some headway was finally being made. A major furor in academic circles and in the U.S. Congress was caused when Joseph Stiglitz, the recently departed chief economist with the World Bank, and Jeffrey Sachs, a Harvard economist hardly known for progressive views, issued a stinging rebuke of the policies of the two "sister" institutions. Even James Wolfensohn, president of the World Bank, was making public statements deploring the world's growing poverty and promising to make poverty reduction a priority of the Bank. Canada's finance minister, Paul Martin, added that politicians were hearing public demands for reform of the World Bank and the IMF "loud and clear."

But these statements were not going to mute the street protests. Once again, the city took on the air of a war zone, with the area around the meetings locked down under massive security, thousands of police in riot gear patrolling the empty streets, and the steady whir of army helicopters overhead. Many of the protesters had been initiated on the streets of Seattle (or wished they had), and several young women who had been locked up in a Seattle jail for five days had used the occasion to plan for Washington: "For five days, the only thing we talked about was how to take this to the next level," said one. Added another, "You go through that, you know, and you're hooked."

The major difference between the events, however, was the massive and highly prepared security presence in Washington, D.C. The whole downtown core was under military occupation and sixty blocks around the World Bank's headquarters were sealed off; every avenue to the official meetings was barricaded with riot police, the National Guard, and metal fences. On the morning of April 16th, the day before the meetings were to begin, police raided the protesters' convergence centre, evicting the protesters, thus sending them out onto wet streets without medicine, personal belongings, or food. The next day, knowing the protesters would try to block delegates from going to their meetings, police ferried the officials into their meetings at 5:00 a.m., before the affinity groups had even arrived on the scene.

As the World Bank and the IMF held their meetings behind the barricades, between ten and fifteen thousand protesters marched, chanted, and snaked their way through police lines or lay down in front of them, chained to one another. They also attended rallies and panels and another large teach-in sponsored by the International Forum on Globalization. The amount and level of police brutality were not nearly as severe as in Seattle, because the Washington security forces were well prepared in advance. But once again, dreadful images of blood-soaked young people, indiscriminate pepper spraying and vicious clubbings were disseminated by the media around the world. Over a thousand protesters were arrested in two days of action — far more than in Seattle. They were prepared for arrest and had the phone number 202-842-4479 — the hotline for legal-aid lawyers — written somewhere on their bodies. Solidarity protests were held in several communities around the world on the same day. In Istanbul, Turkey, police viciously attacked about two hundred peaceful student demonstrators, spraying chemical gases directly into their mouths. Fifty were injured and sixty arrested.

M1

Using Seattle and Washington as their guideposts, May Day 2000 events took on the theme of fighting corporate power and globalization directly. Marches took place in Hamburg, Berlin, London, Zurich, and Bern. In Harare, Zimbabwe, three thousand workers came out to protest working conditions in that country.

Tens of thousands rallied in Moscow and Cuba, and protests in Toronto, Vancouver, Chicago, and New York called for an end to corporate-dominated globalization. Even Pope John Paul II marked the occasion by urging rich countries to forgive the debts of the Nonindustrialized World. "Globalization of finance, of the economy," he said, "should never be allowed to violate the dignity and centrality of the human person or the democracy of peoples."

M8

At the annual May meeting of the Asian Development Bank in Thailand, four thousand protesters, spurred on by the events of Seattle and Washington, caught the Thai police by surprise and stormed over barricades, interrupting the meeting with demands for an end to Bank policies that punish the poor. (The Asian Development Bank has become a target for antiglobalization groups in Asia, who believe the institution is more comfortable doing deals with corrupt governments and big business than with consulting the poor it is supposed to help.) Security forces were quick to move: the luxury hotel in which the meeting was held instantly became an armed encampment, surrounded by thousands of riot police in full gear.

The protesters, who gathered daily outside the hotel, demanded that the ADB stop funding megaprojects and put an end to loans that increase the indebtedness of poor countries in the name of financial restructuring and reform. Although they were not allowed to return to the meeting, protesters were given assurances in writing by Tadao Chino, the Bank's Japanese president, that the ADB would study their concerns and meet with them in the near future. Edwin Truman, the U.S. Treasury's assistant secretary for international affairs, told the Bank that it must find ways to understand popular opinion.

J5

The Organization of American States is a forum for multilateral dialogue and decision making for the thirty-four countries of North and South America. While originally formed to bring peace, democracy, and financial stability to Latin America, it has long been criticized for its soft treatment of dictators and human rights abusers. Recently, it has become the primary political vehicle mandated to carry out economic integration of the Americas, based on the free-market, unlimited-growth model embraced by the WTO. Its annual gathering of foreign ministers of its member countries has usually gone unnoticed apart from sporadic protests about particular human rights concerns.

Its June 2000 meeting, however, came on the heels of Seattle and Washington and included a planning forum for the upcoming meeting of the Free Trade Area of the Americas (FTAA) in Quebec City in April 2001, where the heads of state associated with the OAS were to come together to expand free trade throughout the Americas. So this meeting became a logical next target for the antiglobalization movement in the region. Canada had joined the OAS ten years earlier, and to celebrate that fact, the Canadian government successfully lobbied the OAS to hold its anniversary meeting in Windsor, Ontario.

Even though protest organizers had assured police that there would be no violence and had never predicted having more than six thousand demonstrators at the event, weeks before the meeting, the local newspaper, the *Windsor Star*, then still owned by right-wing media baron Conrad Black, so terrified the local residents with horror stories about the upcoming protests that some were holding prayer vigils to ward off the expected pandemonium. The climate of fear made it difficult for protesters to find housing.

All delegates were housed in two hotels on Windsor's waterfront, and several huge tents were erected on the beach for their meetings. A six-square-block chain-link fence was erected to seal off their compound, and large concrete blocks had been placed in front of two gated entry points by a forklift, to prevent the gates from being pushed open. Enclosed walkways leading from the hotels to the beach tents were erected. Delegates ate, slept, worked, and were entertained inside a virtual fortress. Five thousand police were assembled to protect them, including members of the Windsor Police Service, the Ontario Provincial Police, and the Royal Canadian Mounted Police, as well as undercover intelligence squad officers and uniformed mounted police from Toronto.

The barricade was ringed inside and outside with heavily armed police, and there were police on rooftops with binoculars, armed riot police patrolling the empty downtown streets, police helicopters overhead, and an unprecedented degree of police intimidation and surveillance of organizers. So tight was the security that many delegates, including Prime Minister Jean Chrétien, had to be flown into the meeting by helicopter. Across the river, four thousand police assembled to monitor a planned solidarity march in Detroit, and the city passed an ordinance making it illegal for anyone to carry gas masks or wear face coverings. Police forces on both sides of the border cooperated in preventing hundreds of demonstrators from entering Canada.

Throughout the week, local organizers and labour unions staged lively teach-ins, panels, rallies, and marches. Estimates of the number of protesters ranged from five thousand to eight thousand, a police-officer-to-activist ratio of nearly one-to-one, which led to plenty of jokes about participants finding "their" cop. As promised, the demonstrations were peaceful, but this did not prevent an inordinate amount of pepper spray from being used on anyone who came to close to the chain-link fence. The massive visible police presence frightened away many who were planning to attend. Said one, "I am sad that there's an official shutdown of the city. It's ironic that to stop a shutdown, they're initiating a shutdown."

J12

Prior media warnings preceded the June 2000 annual meeting of the Sixteenth World Petroleum Congress in Calgary, a global get-together of more than 2,200 oil-industry players. Although the Congress never attracted the kind of attention given to official global institutions like the WTO, protests were planned because of the industry's alleged association with pollution, graft, and human rights abuses. Teach-ins, a peaceful march, and some street protests were planned, but organizers made it clear from the beginning that the numbers would be modest. "I have a feeling there are going to be more police on the street than protesters," said Dan Gillean of the Calgary-based End of Oil Action Coalition.

The Conrad Black–owned *Calgary Herald* described the demonstrators as "bent on disrupting" the event and predicted the city's teens would be used as "cannon fodder" for clashes with police. The *Calgary Sun* described the would-be protesters as "groups of noisy malcontents" and suggested they should pay for their own policing costs. Oil-patch insiders were more blunt. "What I'd like to do is arrest them all on opening day and drive them all to Vancouver in transport vans," said one who asked to remain anonymous. Alberta Premier Ralph Klein confirmed the suspicions of youth activists who believe that protest is tolerated only as long as it has no effect, when he issued a veiled warning: "Make your point — fine, that's what it's all about. But don't get in the way of people doing their day-to-day business and what they want to do."

Once again, the security measures were massive and excessive. Teams of police, bolstered by RCMP forces brought in from all four western provinces, were armed with riot gear, truncheons, pepper spray, tear gas, bean-bag guns, shields, padded armour, and plastic handcuffs. On June 11th, black-suited riot police followed the official march of two thousand people by car, truck, motorcycle, and bicycle, and on foot and, the next day, shadowed about five hundred street protesters, outnumbering them three to one. Other officers were posted with rifles on roofs and in helicopters. Randall Hayes of the Rainforest Action Network said the Calgary police presence was more thuggish than it had been in Seattle. And to Canada's shame, two San Francisco Bay area activists slated to speak at a public event on the human rights and environmental impacts of the oil industry — both people of colour — were detained at the Calgary Airport when they arrived, jailed overnight, and sent back out of the country the next morning in chains and shackles.

J15

In the same month — on June 15th — fifteen hundred young people clashed with riot police at an antiglobalization rally in Bologna, Italy, where the OECD was meeting to promote the interests of small and medium-sized business in the global economy. Italian riot police fired tear gas and used batons against the protesters, who marched through the streets to strains of music by Beethoven, while others staged a sit-in, blocking downtown traffic. Five people were injured, and protesters and local citizens alike said that the police used excessive brutality.

Nevertheless, the protests had an impact. Donald Johnston, OECD secretary general, said he was trying to find ways to involve nongovernmental organizations in the work of the OECD, and Italian prime minister Giuliano Amato acknowledged that globalization presents problems and said that the OECD must work to reduce inequality in society: "We share the demonstrators' concerns that the new technology be used to reduce the gap between the wealthy and the poor," he said. A week and a half after the Bologna demonstrations, the OECD became the target for more antiglobalization demonstrations — during its annual meeting in Paris, on June 27, 2000, where people carried signs that read "OECD — Organization against Democracy and Environment."

J31–A14

The antiglobalization movement was present in strength at both the Republican and Democratic national conventions, held in the summer of 2000 in preparation for the U.S. fall election. They wanted to send a message that, although the two parties claim to be on different ideological terrain, their platforms are almost identical on the major issues of trade, economic growth, and the environment.

In both Philadelphia, where the Republican convention was held at the end of July, and Los Angeles, where the Democrats met in August, security preparations were intense. Philadelphia's seven-thousand-member police force received $5 million to be dedicated solely to security operations for the event. The Los Angeles Police Department prepared for over a year and cancelled all time off and vacations for its 9,600 officers; the FBI patrolled beneath the city, welding shut storm-sewer covers and removing mail and paper boxes from the downtown. One reporter said the LAPD looked "as if they were expecting Armageddon."

On Monday, August 14th, President Clinton was trying to deliver his final farewell speech to the Los Angeles convention, when he was all but drowned out by the antiglobalization anthems. They were being performed live at a concert and legal rally near the convention centre by the band Rage Against the Machine, from their album *The Battle of Los Angeles*. Suddenly, reacting to a few black-clad provocateurs throwing bottles over the fence, riot police charged into the crowd on horseback, pinning many against the wall, and opened fire with rubber bullets and truncheons. As tear gas and pepper spray filled the arena, media witnesses report that mounted officers charged the crowd, randomly and brutally clubbing people's heads and backs. Those who asked for help were repeatedly beaten; people were trampled beneath horses; rubber bullets were fired at the backs of many who tried to flee; and an eleven-year-old girl was struck in the back and fell. Many who lingered to help the injured were beaten.

Inside the Democratic convention, a triumphant President Clinton, convinced of the value of the so-called economic miracle he had left his people, stood beaming as wave after wave of applause swelled up from the part of America that has won in the sweepstakes of economic globalization; their cheers drowned out the cries from the street below.

S11

The World Economic Forum of Davos, Switzerland, a powerful global think tank which promotes economic globalization, held its annual Asia Pacific Summit in Melbourne, Australia, in September 2000, immediately preceding the Olympics. As media magnates Rupert Murdoch and Kerry Packer and other key players in Australia's corporate community prepared to welcome such business luminaries as the heads of Microsoft, Softbank, and Siemens, police in Melbourne braced for the biggest protests in Australia since the Vietnam War. On the opening day of the World Economic Forum's deliberations at the Crown Casino (which lost millions of dollars in gambling revenue because of the disruptions), at least ten thousand protesters surrounded the meeting, blocking traffic, causing chaos in the downtown, and preventing several hundred delegates from entering the meeting. Dozens of demonstrators surrounded the car of Western Australia Premier Richard Court and slashed his tires. Prime Minister John Howard had to be taken to the casino by boat.

The next day, as "The Battle of Melbourne" continued, many delegates and journalists had to be pulled over police barricades to enter the casino, where speeches were drowned out by the chants of the crowd. Baton-wielding riot squads, including some officers on horseback, charged through human chains, bashing heads and breaking teeth. Twenty-two protesters were hospitalized.

In spite of a standoff between demonstrators and the Australian authorities, who were furious at the international press coverage of the event just days before the Olympics were to begin, members of the Forum heard the protest message directly from Vandana Shiva. A leader in the fight against genetically engineered foods, she was one of the few representatives of the civil society movement attending the Forum. To a hushed audience of a who's who of the world's corporate elite, Shiva read the simple words of the common people (see box), who had, for all intents and purposes, prevented them from having their meeting.

S26 — PRAGUE

Security plans to deal with the expected large protests at the September 2000 annual meetings of the World Bank and the IMF in Prague were in place

WHY WE ARE HERE

The reasons for us being here are many but centred on our concern for the increasingly unchecked corporate dominance which defines the world we live in.

We reject the World Economic Forum's argument that you are not a decision-making body. The WEF does not need to be a decision-making body to affect our lives and the lives of the people around the world. The WEF represents corporate interests, not the interests of the people they employ or the state or the land and resources they exploit for their financial gain. We are children, mothers, fathers, workers, unemployed, environmentalists, from religious traditions, and Indigenous peoples, among others.

We are blockading because people across the world are suffering under corporate-defined globalization. We are continuing our non-violent protest today and we will be here tomorrow. We are part of a worldwide movement demanding justice before profits. We are not going to go away.

Signed,
On behalf of some of the thousands of S11 blockaders

(There followed the signatures of leaders
of the groups participating in the protest.)

months in advance, including the deployment of eleven hundred riot police and sixteen hundred soldiers on standby. An alarmed President Vaclav Havel said his authorities appeared to be "getting ready for a civil war." In a peacekeeping effort, he brought together three hundred representatives of the IMF, the World Bank, governments, and NGOs at the Prague Castle in the days preceding the meeting. Senior IMF and World Bank officials at the meeting tried to ward off the demonstrations with an act of contrition. World Bank President James Wolfensohn agreed with the protesters' concerns: "Something is wrong when the richest 20 percent of the global population receive more than 80 percent of the global income." IMF Director Horst Kohler conceded his organization must be "willing to change." Canada's Finance Minister Paul Martin called the protesters "sincere" and "allies of Canada."

But it was too little, too late. In spite of tight security that saw thousands of protesters turned back at the border, over fifteen thousand, organized by the umbrella group Initiative Against Economic Globalization, descended upon the meetings in a hail of police water cannons, dogs, and smoke bombs. While most demonstrators remained peaceful, a handful turned Prague's ancient cobblestone centre into a war zone. Local McDonald's outlets and a Mercedes-Benz dealership were smashed to pieces, and the main square was closed down in a strict curfew. Dozens were injured on both sides and delegates to the meetings were stranded for hours on public transit or in their hotels. Paul Martin and other financial ministers were forced to hold bilateral meetings in their hotel rooms and most left early.

With hundreds of demonstrators wearing gas masks behind them, Italian protesters affiliated with "Ya Basta!" even gained access to the heavily guarded complex — the Palace of Culture — where the meetings were taking place. Many delegates (unhurt) were taken out of the meeting in city ambulances with covered windows. One World Bank official, who asked that his name not be used, told economist and World Bank opponent Walden Bello that the protests totally dominated their deliberations and even press conferences, where delegates found themselves arguing with journalists who were speculating that the World Bank and the IMF were obsolete. (He also said that most delegates abandoned the "useless" meetings in favour of at least fifteen "very, very lavish" parties given by the commercial banks — "the prime events of the conference.")

IMF and World Bank officials hurriedly held closing ceremonies a day early and most left town immediately, forced to use public transportation which had been commandeered for their exclusive use when the streets and highways leading in and out of the city became impassable. The irony was not lost on the protesters. A filmmaker sympathetic to the demonstrators found herself by accident standing beside World Bank President Wolfensohn on the metro. "Now that you are using public services, does that mean you won't force Nonindustrialized Countries to reduce theirs?" she asked him. She was shuffled off immediately by security forces while Wolfensohn muttered, "Give me a break."

Almost nine hundred people, three hundred of them non-Czech, were detained in the city's jails, although only a handful were actually arrested. In addition to this mass denial of legal rights, local journalists and protesters chronicled extensive police abuse of prisoners. Paul Rosenthal from Seattle was held for forty hours in the Olsanska jail. "What is happening inside the Czech jails is more than frightening. Women are being forced to strip in front of male guards and perform exercises. People with serious medical problems have been denied help," he said. Twenty-two people were crammed for over thirty-six hours in one impossibly small cell. Many were denied food, water, and sleep, and there were repeated reports of beatings, broken limbs and teeth, and sexual abuse.

Days after all the delegates had fled the city, protesters issued the "Prague Declaration." While admitting that a few among their number had participated in provocative behaviour, they condemned the "psychological terror and physical repression and overreaction by the Czech police forces. We particularly express our grave concern over reports of brutalization of those held in Czech prisons." In their declaration, the protestors claimed victory for the antiglobalization movement, a statement that has not been countered by the World Bank or the IMF. "We believe that the cancellation of the final day of meetings reflects the institutions' recognition of their own lack of credibility," the declaration said. "Confronted with vigorous protests from organizations like ours and a refusal to accept the empty rhetoric of 'poverty reduction' and 'debt relief' offered in response to assertions of their responsibility for decades of economic malfeasance, they have, at last, wisely chosen silence over more lies."

A BATTLE FOR HEARTS AND MINDS

When the smoke from these monumental struggles clears, each side retreats to ponder what just happened and, more importantly, to gauge the reaction of the public. For, more than anything, the current civil society movement is in a battle with the forces of rampant corporate globalization for the hearts and minds of ordinary citizens around the world.

In a post-Seattle article, headed "Citizens' groups: The Non-Governmental Order," the usually conservative *Economist* magazine admitted that "national governments no longer have a monopoly of information or an unequalled reach, compared to corporations and civil society. . . . If the power of NGOs has increased in a globalized world," it went on, "who has lost out?" It remained silent on the implications of the increased power of global corporations, however, and in a previous article described civil society demonstrators as "militant dunces [parading] their ignorance through the streets of Seattle."

Some insight into the hearts and minds of ordinary citizens was gained through a September 2000 *Business Week* poll, and a number of those revelations were startling. While many Americans credited private business with helping to create wealth and jobs, a surprisingly large number of them were also concerned about what they saw as insensitive corporate behaviour. In a cover story entitled "Too Much Corporate Power?" the magazine reported that only 47% of respondents thought that what was good for business was good for Americans; 66% thought that large profits were more important to big companies than developing safe, reliable products for consumers; 72% said that business had too much power over too many aspects of American life; 73% saw corporate CEO pay packages as excessive; and 74% thought that big corporations had too much political influence. When asked whether corporations should have only one purpose — to make the most profits for their shareholders — or more than one purpose, recognizing that they owe something to their employees and the communities in which they operate, 95% chose the latter!

Importantly, *Business Week* reports, this trend also applies to the other pillar of globalization, free trade. Here, however, as another American poll shows, reaction is divided along class lines. According to the Pew Research Center, among American families earning less than fifty thousand dollars a year, only 37% have a positive view of global free trade, compared to 63% for families earning over seventy-five thousand. In Canada, several recent polls have confirmed declining support for free trade. A January 1999 Environics poll found that Canadians in every region felt that NAFTA has done more harm than good, and an Angus Reid/*Economist* poll taken at about the same time demonstrated that support for free trade in Canada had slipped by 13% in one year, down to about 45%. In the area of public services, a November 1999 Vector poll showed a strong majority of Canadians opposed to allowing those services to fall under the discipline of the WTO.

Corporations and financial institutions promoting and participating in unbridled global free trade are under attack, and mainstream economists have noticed the polls that indicate this trend. These power elites are in trouble and they know it. They are trying to reform their image and the reputation of their institutions by numerous means — ranging from the benign to the dangerous.

Seeking respectability from an institution they have usually castigated, a number of large transnational corporations have recently entered into a voluntary "Global Compact" with the United Nations, to show that they are serious about human rights and the environment. The World Bank and other bank bodies, says the *Prague Post*, "who rely on safe exchanges of capital and the implicit approvals conferred by the populations of rich states, are deeply unhappy to find they are increasingly disliked," and are "growing a conscience." World Bank officials are giving speeches about the plight of the world's poor and setting up "multistakeholder dialogues" with selected NGOs (dubbed CONGOs by some — co-opted NGOs). But in other contexts, they have a different way of expressing themselves.

BACKLASH

At an August 2000 meeting in Jackson Hole, Wyoming, organized by the Federal Reserve Bank of Kansas City, senior economists and central bankers met with Federal Reserve chairman Alan Greenspan and WTO Director General Michael Moore to share their concerns that governments of Industrialized Countries, cowed by angry street demonstrations and opinion polls unfavourable to corporations, will abandon the trade liberalization policies they have followed for fifty years. "Despite the extraordinary prosperity, the ability to move forward on various trade initiatives has clearly come to a remarkable halt," said Greenspan. "We all need to press very hard on the political process to maintain the role that we have played to see this major advance in civilization." Moore, who called the Seattle protesters "an umbrella for everything wrong with the twenty-first century," said that governments in industrialized countries have lost "political will." Nicholas Stern, the World Bank's chief economist, called the WTO's failure in Seattle "disgraceful."

While WTO and World Bank officials and corporate CEOs wine and dine the representatives of selected NGOs, attempting to enlist their support, they have far more sinister ways of dealing with those who won't go along with these methods. In some cases, they seek to discredit their opponents; in others, they actually seek to criminalize them. After the defeat of the Multilateral

Agreement on Investment, the International Chamber of Commerce hinted at a backlash strategy by questioning the legitimacy of anti-MAI groups, a suggestion now echoed in newspaper editorials. Who gave these "unelected" groups the right to stall economic progress? they ask, neglecting to mention that business editors and World Bank officials hardly qualify as elected officials either.

After Seattle, corporate consultants Burson Marsteller — a firm that handles public relations for Monsanto — published a "Guide to the Seattle Meltdown," in which the company listed most of the groups responsible for the demonstrations, along with their addresses and websites. The report, which the company called an "alarming window on the future," was produced to allow Burson Marsteller's corporate clients to "defend" themselves against attack. (Just months before this report was distributed to clients, Burson Marsteller paid a Baptist church from a poor neighbourhood in Washington, D.C., several thousand dollars to bus a group of one hundred African-American "demonstrators" to attend a street protest against biotech organized by a coalition of family farm, food safety, and environmental groups.)

How to deal with these troublesome groups was the subject of a top-level seminar held in Washington on March 29, 2000, sponsored by the Cordell Hull Institute, a Washington-based think tank dedicated to rebuilding public support for free trade. Entitled "After Seattle: Restoring Momentum to the WTO," it was attended by a who's who of about fifty present and former international trade officials from the U.S. government and Congress, representatives from embassies of major U.S. trading partners, and lawyers and consultants representing transnational corporations involved in trade disputes. The speakers included Clayton Yeutter, former secretary of agriculture and former deputy special trade representative under Ronald Reagan who oversaw the Canada–U.S. Free Trade Agreement; Robert Litan, former associate director of the Office of Management and Budget under President Clinton; Lawrence Eagleburger, former secretary of state under President Reagan; and Luiz Felipe Lampreia, foreign minister of Brazil.

Only one representative of an NGO was invited. Bruce Silverglade of the Center for Science in the Public Interest wore a dark suit to "blend in" and hoped that, in light of President Clinton's Seattle speech promising to "open the meetings," a real dialogue with civil society was about to begin. Instead, he reports, the seminar turned out to be a strategy session on how to defeat those opposed to the World Trade Organization. The gloves came off right away.

Lord Parkinson, former secretary of state for trade and industry under Margaret Thatcher, slammed groups like Friends of the Earth International and the Sierra Club (who, between them, have hundreds of thousands of members) for being undemocratic and therefore having no right to criticize the WTO. He called President Clinton's speech acknowledging the protesters' concerns "disgraceful" and said that no future WTO meetings should be held on American soil because security wasn't tight enough there. He stated that the staff of the WTO Secretariat should not be balanced with people from Third World Countries just "because of the colour of their skin" and added that he hoped he hadn't offended anyone.

"How can we delegitimize the NGOs?" was the first question from an American participant who suggested they should convince funding foundations to cut off money sources to any participating nongovernmental organizations (a tactic that has already sent a funding chill through the American NGO community). Robert Liton came up with the idea of giving them "other sandboxes to play in," such as the International Labour Organization, because it lacked the enforcement measures available to the WTO. Clayton Yeutter concurred with his British colleague's suggestion of holding the next WTO meeting somewhere outside the U.S., in a place where "security can be secured." He further suggested that the WTO give the public "little advance notice" of where the meeting would be held to "keep the protesters off balance."

At the cocktail party following, a senior South American official, holding a glass of good wine in one hand and a dessert in the other, lamented that if the next WTO meeting had to be held in an out-of-the-way venue, he preferred that it be on a cruise ship. He then gave an impassioned speech opposing labour standards in the WTO and defended child labour by describing how in one region of Brazil, more than five thousand children "help their families earn a little extra money" by hauling bags of coal from a dump yard to a steel mill. His remarks, notes Silverglade, were greeted by a hearty round of applause.

THE CRIMINALIZATION OF DISSENT

According to the Southern Poverty Law Center, a well-respected American civil rights watchdog organization, the FBI and other law enforcement agencies in the United States have shifted their focus from far-right political dissidents to the global civil society movement. The change occurred just before Seattle, when news of the planned protests started to show up on the Internet. According to the *Seattle Weekly*, the Pentagon's top-secret Delta Force — the same unit that was covertly sent to the Waco standoff — set up a command post in a downtown Seattle hotel and sent out undercover operators, dressed as protesters. Activists preparing for Washington found their meetings infiltrated, their public gatherings disrupted, their phones tapped, and police posted outside their homes and offices.

USA TODAY reported that government agents were going undercover to thwart World Bank protesters, monitoring seventy-three Internet sites and sometimes posing as protesters themselves. The article went on to say that Washington police circulated a flyer urging teachers and students in local high schools and universities to watch for "political mobilizing material" and to report any information on such activities to the police. Officers in Calgary actually visited local high schools in the days before the World Petroleum Congress annual meeting, warning students to stay away from protests. Police in Windsor visited the homes of labour and civil society leaders in advance of the OAS meeting, asking intimidating questions, and a site rented months before for over fifty human rights NGOs from all over the hemisphere was suddenly withdrawn.

Canada's spy agency, the Canadian Security Intelligence Service (CSIS) released a study entitled *Anti-Globalization — A Spreading Phenomenon* in August 2000, in which it called critics of unregulated capitalism "militant anarchists" and linked legitimate protest with terrorism. The Pentagon has coined the term "social netwars" to describe nonviolent conflicts between civil society groups and global financial institutions. So concerned is the Pentagon about the increased power of NGOs and their use of the Internet that it commissioned a study of the movement by the Rand Institute, a leading U.S. government-funded think tank with close ties to the White House.

In its report to the Pentagon, the Rand Institute claimed that the "information revolution" is shifting power away from nation-states toward new nongovernmental alliances and networks in civil society and warned about the "threat" this poses to established regimes. David Ronfeldt and John Arquilla, the authors of the study, describe netwar as information-related conflict, which uses the Internet to "disrupt or damage what a target population knows, or thinks it knows, about itself and the world around it." In other words, netwar is a war waged to influence public opinion. The authors coined the term "NGO swarm" to describe the phenomenon of amorphous groups of NGOs, linked by the Internet, coordinating campaigns. Such swarms are difficult for governments to deal with, says the report, as they have no central leadership or command structure and are "impossible to decapitate." Beware, warn the authors; an NGO swarm can "sting a victim to death."

The Washington-based National Lawyers Guild is sounding alarms from the other side of the debate — identifying what it calls "the thinning lines between law enforcement and the military" in the U.S. In a report on Seattle and other recent civil society protests, the Guild says that police in these situations are acting without proper controls. They are exposing the public and themselves to dangerous chemicals, keeping detained protesters in conditions "often resembling torture," and operating masked and unmarked. The report adds that the U.S. is now operating under a wartime economy; since the collapse of the Soviet Union, many resources that were devoted to the military have been redeployed to law enforcement, with major military contractors building prisons and designing "less legal weapon systems" to be used on domestic political dissent, which is seen as a form of warfare.

What is motivating governments and global capital to criminalize political dissent? The only possible answer is that the global civil society movement is rocking the very foundations of unregulated capitalism itself, and in the view of these power brokers, must be stopped. It is one thing to make changes around the edges — to sign a voluntary code here or to raise a wage there. But the new antiglobalization movement will not be content with cosmetic changes, and the power elites of the world know it. In increasing numbers, they are using their domestic security forces against their own citizens to enforce the corporate interests upon which they have become dependent for survival. Some countries, such as the Philippines, are going so far as to pass laws allowing corporations to use their own private security forces to protect their assets.

George Monbiot of the *Guardian* says that we are entering an age of totalitarian capitalism, a political and economic system which, by seizing absolute control of fundamental resources, impoverishes everyone it excludes. If this is true, then a global corporate security system to protect the few winners is absolutely necessary for its survival. The stakes are very high indeed. The world's social security systems are up for grabs (although Lockheed Martin, the world's biggest weapons manufacturer, already delivers welfare in some U.S. states), as are water, air, seeds, and the human genome. The fight for "the commons" and the democratic right to control them is shaping up to be one of the most important showdowns in history.

Dismantled Democracy

*How corporate interests eroded
the institutions that protect
democracy and justice*

*The setting was unusual. Fifty of the most powerful CEOs in the world were
jostling for the attention of the international media at the New York headquarters of the United Nations, an institution they had dismissed or actively
undermined for years. The day was July 26, 2000. The event was the signing
of a "Global Compact" between the UN and some of the world's largest
transnational corporations, many of which have drawn serious charges from
organizations such as the highly respected TRAC (Transnational Resource and
Action Center). Posing alongside Royal Dutch/Shell, still reeling from charges of
human and environmental atrocities in Nigeria; Rio Tinto, a British mining
company that stands accused of human rights and labour violations in at least
a dozen countries; and Nike, itself on the receiving end of NGO allegations that
it uses sweatshop and child labour in the Third World, was UN Secretary
General Kofi Annan, beaming and clearly pleased to find himself the centre of
their attention.*

Never mind that the "guidelines" they signed, promising better labour and environmental standards, were voluntary and unenforceable (in fact, at the press conference, Annan admitted that the UN has no capacity even to monitor compliance) or that dozens of NGOs (many more than the few that signed) had denounced the process as a way for these corporations to "bluewash" their image by wrapping themselves in the flag of the United Nations; Kofi Annan had decided that it was time the United Nations, having fully embraced the basic precepts of economic globalization, became a player in making the system work. He promised at the launch of the Global Compact to "continue to make a strong case for free trade and open global markets" by "putting a human face" on the system.

Other UN agencies have also entered into recent "partnerships" with transnational corporations. Former high commissioner on refugees Sadako Ogata has cochaired several meetings called the Business Humanitarian Forum with John Imle, president of Unocal, a company believed by NGOs to be complicit in human rights violations in Burma. UNESCO (the United Nations Education, Science, and Culture Organization) has formed partnerships with a number of corporations, allowing them the use of its logo, and in spring 1999, it collaborated with The Walt Disney Company, accused by activists of subcontracting to sweatshops in Haiti, at the company's Youth Millennium Dreamer Awards held at Disneyland. UNICEF (the United Nations Children's Fund) also has extensive interactions with corporations: it co-sponsors UNAIDS, a partnership between the UN, the World Health Organization (WHO), and five major pharmaceutical companies, including Johnson & Johnson and others charged by the International Food Action Network with violating the WHO's infant formula code. The United Nations Development Program (UNDP) touts its partnerships with BP Amoco, criticized by Greenpeace and Friends of the Earth for its intention to drill for oil and gas in the sensitive Alaska-Yukon corridor, and Chevron, alleged to be implicated in environmental abuses in Nigeria, Texas, Indonesia, and California.

BLUEWASHING AND THE UNITED NATIONS

The United Nations' flirtations with the business community started almost a decade before this announcement. In 1992, within a month of taking office as UN secretary general, U.S.-backed candidate Boutros Boutros Ghali was already in the midst of developing a code of conduct for multinationals and had virtually eliminated the UN Center on Transnational Corporations (CTC), which had been established to help Nonindustrialized Countries monitor and negotiate with large companies. The downsized CTC was incorporated into a new division and became an instrument to help match corporations with countries as a way of supporting foreign investments. The *Economist* triumphantly noted that the UN, "which spent decades tut tutting about these firms and drawing up codes of conduct to control corporations, now spends much of its time advising countries how best to seduce them." This change had been an objective of many corporations and right-wing corporate lobby groups, like the Heritage Foundation. As Josh Karliner and Kenny Bruno of the San Francisco–area Transnational Resource and Action Centre report, in virtually every international environmental negotiation since that time, business has played a prominent and aggressive role.

On another front, Maurice Strong, the secretary general of the 1992 UN Earth Summit in Rio, formed a business group called the Business Council for Sustainable Development to promote private-sector involvement in international environmental agreements. In Rio, this Council, along with the International Chamber of Commerce, succeeded in having references to mandatory environmental regulations entirely eliminated from the Summit's Agenda 21 document, placing the emphasis instead on the role of multinationals in "self-regulation." Between them, these two powerful corporate lobbies ensured that few real commitments were made at Rio. Say Karliner and Bruno, "Corporate influence is rampant at negotiations of UN-sponsored international treaties and conventions to protect the global environment."

In recent decades, the position of big business consistently has been to maintain an overall agenda of undermining the UN itself, cutting away at attempts to establish international standards governing human rights, the environment, and labour. And when he became secretary general, Kofi Annan took over where Boutros Boutros Ghali left off in courting the favour of big business. In June 1997, Annan invited the CEOs of ten transnational companies to meet with senior UN officials to chart a formalization of corporate involvement with the UN. Over lobster in the secretary general's private dining room, CEOs from the World Business Council on Sustainable Development heard Larry Summers, then deputy secretary of the U.S. Treasury, tout the virtues of privatization, including the private ownership of the environment.

In February 1998 (just around the time, not coincidentally, that the MAI was foundering), a UN delegation led by Annan met with the International Chamber of Commerce in Paris, as a first step in a "systematic dialogue" between the two global actors. The ICC delegation — which included captains of industry from Coca-Cola, Goldman Sachs, McDonald's, Rio Tinto, and Unilever — issued a joint statement with the UN, declaring that the "new-found allies" agreed to "forge a close global partnership to secure greater business input into the world's economic decision-making and boost the private sector in the least developed countries." Several months later, the ICC convened the Geneva Business Dialogue, chaired by ICC President Helmut Maucher, also CEO of Nestlé. In addition to top-level representation from the UN, participants included the European finance commissioner, WTO Director General Renato Ruggiero, high-ranking World Bank officials, senior politicians and bureaucrats from Europe and the U.S., and 450 global business leaders.

During the meeting, ICC chief Maucher said the Geneva Business Dialogue was intent upon achieving concrete results: specifically "action points for how to establish rules for an ordered liberalism." Explaining that global problems require the delegation of power to the global level, Maucher called for both a strengthened WTO and an overhaul of the UN's structure in order to facilitate stronger involvement of business. "A strong UN is good for business," he added, and Kofi Annan agreed, pledging to work more closely with the ICC.

DIFFERENT BEGINNINGS

It was not always thus. The United Nations was established to bring peace and stability to the world through negotiated dispute settlements between nations; the institution belonged to governments and their citizens right from the beginning. Dozens of civil society organizations, including women's and human rights groups and labour unions, participated in the drafting process for the original UN Charter more than fifty years ago in San Francisco.

Crucially, the United Nations was formed after one of the bloodiest armed conflicts in history, a war during which humans visited upon one another unimaginable horrors. One of the first acts of the newly minted United Nations was to adopt a safeguard against such horrors, the Universal Declaration of Human Rights. Never again, vowed the UN, would the world's citizens be subjected to such barbarous violations of their fundamental rights. The Declaration marked a watershed in the long international quest to assert the supremacy of human and citizen rights over political or economic tyranny of any kind.

THE 1948 UNITED NATIONS UNIVERSAL DECLARATION OF HUMAN RIGHTS:

- Granted freedom, equality, life, liberty, and security to every person on earth without distinction according to race, colour, sex, language, religion, political opinion, national or social origin, property, birth, or other status.
- Banned slavery, torture, arbitrary arrest, detention, and exile.
- Affirmed the rights of nationality and of freedom of thought, expression, and assembly; the right to vote; the right to freely participate in the cultural life of the community; and the right to marry and rear a family.
- Declared equal rights for every person before the law and established the right of presumed innocence and a fair trial.
- Secured the rights of freedom of movement and of asylum from persecution.
- Affirmed the right to work, to just conditions of work, to equal pay, to just and favourable remuneration worthy of human dignity, to membership in a trade union, to rest and leisure, and to protection against unemployment.
- Guaranteed a standard of living adequate for the health and well-being of the whole family, including food, clothing, housing, and medical care; guaranteed the right to security in the event of unemployment, sickness, disability, or old age; and guaranteed the right to free, compulsory education and to equal social protection for all children, regardless of family status.

The United Nations also created the International Covenant on Economic, Social, and Cultural Rights, and the International Covenant on Civil and Political Rights, which, between them, bound member-states to accept the moral and legal obligation to protect and promote the human and democratic rights delineated in the Declaration. The individual rights and responsibilities of citizens as established in the Declaration, together with the collective rights and responsibilities of nation-states as established in the Covenants, came to represent the foundation stones of democracy in the modern world — a kind of twentieth-century Magna Carta. They became the basis for a global crusade for universal health care and education and for the battle against child poverty and disease, and they led to further declarations on the rights of women, children, and Indigenous peoples.

Parallel to this process, a historic meeting was held in the small New Hampshire town of Bretton Woods in 1944, between the governments of Great Britain and the United States to establish postwar conditions for global economic recovery. There, they set up the World Bank, to help with reconstruction after the war and to assist Third World Countries with long-term development programs. They also instituted the International Monetary Fund (IMF), to promote currency stability and oversee international financial and monetary order. Both the World Bank and the IMF were mandated to alleviate global poverty. The Bretton Woods Institutions, as they came to be known, were originally placed under the control of the Economic and Social Council of the United Nations (ECOSOC) and were supposed to be based on UN values of poverty alleviation, human and social rights, and full employment.

Similarly, in 1947, a new trade body — the International Trade Organization — was created to promote orderly global trade, but under the jurisdiction of the UN and within its social mandate. In the original drafting of the ITO, there were rules against dumping, rules to stop global monopolies, and provisions to put a stop to anticompetitive global business practices of corporations. The new ITO would even have allowed a country to expropriate the assets of a foreign company for reasons of national economic sovereignty if this was necessary to maintain the goals of full employment and social security mandated in the Declaration and the Covenants.

In a 1994 report marking the fiftieth anniversary of the United Nations, former UN official Erskine Childers noted that it had always been the intention of the UN to set macroeconomic policy through the General Assembly, thus maintaining democratic control over both trade and finance policies and the Bretton Woods Institutions.

THE WASHINGTON CONSENSUS

However, there were other, powerful players at work. After World War II, the U.S. found itself with a highly industrialized infrastructure, producing more goods than it needed for its own consumers. It wanted to use the new Bretton Woods Institutions to open up global markets to American goods and promote American free-market systems and values around the world. At the same time, postwar America was becoming increasingly anticommunist, with the Soviet threat rapidly replacing the Nazi menace in its collective consciousness. The stage was being set for an emerging global regime based on a model of development rooted in the belief that liberal market economics constitute the one and only economic choice for the whole world, including poor countries. This ideology took hold over the decades, and finally came to be known as the "Washington Consensus" — a term coined in 1990 by John Williamson of the Institute for International Economics, a conservative Washington-based think tank.

Led by American business interests, the free-market doctrine would eventually force most governments in the world to give up controls on foreign investment, liberalize trade, deregulate their internal economies, privatize state services, and enter into head-to-head global competition. Economist Paul Krugman explains that the Washington Consensus now defines "not only the U.S. government, but all those institutions and networks of opinion leaders centred in the world's de facto capital — think tanks, politically sophisticated investment bankers, and world finance ministers — all those who meet in Washington and collectively define the conventional wisdom of the moment."

While the Washington Consensus model was only in its embryonic stages in the late 1940s, American private-sector interests were sufficiently influential for some powerful U.S. politicians and corporate leaders of the day to see the United Nations as a potential threat. In 1947, under intense pressure from the United States and without a General Assembly vote, the UN approved the separation of the Bretton Woods Institutions from the United Nations, thereby splitting their mandates. That same year, the U.S. undermined the UN's ITO project, refusing to even present its new-formed charter to Congress, thus sounding its death knell. Instead, it created the GATT (the General Agreement on Tariffs and Trade, which would come under the jurisdiction of the World Trade Organization when the WTO was created in 1995) to reduce restrictions on trade in goods and services. Not surprisingly, under the new structure, the new GATT, like the IMF and the World Bank, was not answerable to the United Nations or its member-governments.

The WTO and the Bretton Woods Institutions all operate out of Geneva, where they have large secretariats paid for by their member-states. The governing bodies of the IMF and the World Bank raise money directly from those governments, based on a set formula, and by issuing bonds. The U.S., by far the biggest donor, appropriates these funds annually from Congress amid much heated debate. Canada's contribution is buried in a line-item in the annual budget and is never subjected to discussion. Much of the work of the Bretton Woods Institutions is done by subcommittees about which very little is known.

For instance, the French Treasury in Paris houses a small secretariat for a powerful institution called the "Paris Club," about which it is next to impossible to find any literature or even a phone number or address. But the Paris Club decides the fates of small nations. Here, at specific meetings called around particular debt crises, Third World debtors and their creditors from rich countries get together with IMF and World Bank officials to set rigorous conditions for debt relief. At these meetings, says one insider, the Nonindustrialized Countries get "beaten up." The Club gives a great deal of power to the IMF and the World Bank, as its process replaces one-on-one negotiations between the debtor countries and their creditor countries, through which less onerous conditions might have been set. Similar negotiations between poor nations and their private bank creditors take place at the "London Club," another secretive group with no permanent address.

As Victor Menotti of the International Forum on Globalization notes, the separation of the Bretton Woods Institutions from the UN paved the way for today's international system, which institutionalizes corporate rights over the universal social and citizen rights embodied in the UN. As the World Bank and the IMF became more powerful and wealthy, slowly consolidating their alliance with American and European corporations over the coming decades, the UN had to fight for budgets for various programs and struggled under tight budgets, unenforceable mandates, uneasy relations with big business, and sporadic political support in Washington.

THE BRETTON WOODS INSTITUTIONS AT WORK

As the demonstrations of the year 2000 in Washington and Prague suggested, the World Bank and the IMF have come to be seen as global institutions that embody all the worst traits of power and enforce all the worst characteristics of the global economy. The World Bank now employs over eleven thousand people, has offices in sixty-five countries, and lends more than U.S.$20 billion a year. Countries have voting power in the Bank relative to the amount of money they contribute every year; accordingly, the U.S. and several other wealthy countries dominate the decisions about who receives financial aid, how much they receive, and what conditions they must agree to meet. During the Cold War, reports the Institute for Policy Studies (IPS), a respected Washington-based think tank, the United States frequently used the World Bank as an arm of U.S. foreign power to aid allies and punish enemies.

Most of the World Bank's lending goes to fund "Developing Country" projects — long-term, low-interest loans to build dams and power plants and to "modernize" food production methods. However, the Bank's Articles of Agreements state that one of its principal goals is "to promote foreign private investments." In fact, says the IPS, the U.S. Treasury promotes U.S. government funding of the World Bank as a way to boost American firms. A top Treasury official bragged to Congress that for every dollar the U.S. contributes to the World Bank, American corporations receive $1.30 back in contracts.

PROFITABLE POISONS

What might have become a development institution has largely evolved into a facilitator of global corporations' overseas investments, often with devastating consequences for the environment, for communities, and for workers. None have benefited more than agribusiness and energy firms; more than two-fifths of World Bank loans during its over half-century existence have gone to these two sectors. For decades, the World Bank has been the world's largest promoter of chemical-intensive agriculture. Agrochemical firms from the United States and Europe have been the prime beneficiaries.

World Bank projects have become major contributors to green-

> house gas emissions; World Bank oil, gas, and coal projects initiated
> between 1992 and 1998 added an amount of carbon to the earth's
> atmosphere equivalent to one and a half times that emitted by all
> the world's countries in one year. These energy projects invariably
> provide electricity to export-oriented firms and seldom meet the
> growing energy needs of the world's poorest, two billion of whom
> live without access to electricity.
>
> Institute for Policy Studies, Washington, D.C., *Field Guide to the Global Economy*

The International Monetary Fund, supposedly mandated to offer short-term financing to ailing countries and to prevent currency crises, now focuses on ensuring that private investors and banks are shielded from large losses when their Third World investments go bad. During the 1960s and 1970s, transnational banks lent hundreds of billions of dollars to poorer nations, often for giant ecologically damaging projects such as dams, nuclear power plants, or tourist resorts. In Brazil, the Polonoreste Road and Colonization Project caused massive deforestation and displacement. In India, the Narmada Dam Project forced the resettlement of millions of tribal and other poor people. Much of the money ended up lining the pockets of corrupt dictators or entrepreneurs. And to add insult to injury, by the early 1980s, after interest rates had skyrocketed, many countries found themselves unable to pay back the loans to which they had become chained in order to build these boondoggles.

STRUCTURALLY ADJUSTED LIVES

In the guise of a solution to their problems, the IMF and the World Bank made an offer these countries could not refuse: agree to implement a set of "Structural Adjustment Programs" (SAPs) and we will renegotiate the terms of your debt and lend you even more money in the form of "balance-of-payment" loans as a reward for compliance. About eighty countries were forced to weaken their tools of national sovereignty and adopt the "Washington Consensus" package: deep cuts to government spending, particularly on education, health, and welfare; deregulated transportation, energy, and telecommunications regimes; reduced real wages and lower labour standards; liberalized financial markets; export-oriented agriculture; increased interest rates to attract foreign capital; and the dismantling of protections for domestic industries.

The effects were devastating. As transnational corporations moved in to reap the benefits of the newly deregulated environment, they displaced millions of domestic jobs; millions more found themselves with no access to basic health care, education, or clean drinking water; natural resources were plundered for massive exports; the cost of local food and fuel skyrocketed. Spending on education in the poorest thirty-seven countries declined by 25 percent in a decade. In sub-Saharan Africa, attendance at school plunged as costs soared, the cost of a student textbook sometimes being as high as the equivalent of six years of a teacher's salary.

Jubilee 2000, the ecumenical movement working for the cancellation of Third World debts, conservatively estimates that nineteen thousand children die every day as a result of the restructuring proposed and imposed by the IMF and the World Bank. Leading Philippine academic Walden Bello says the lenders' policies have merely propped up dictators friendly to Western capital. The World Bank poured U.S.$40 million into Indonesia during the Asian crisis of 1997 in support of former President Suharto and his oppressive regime — apparently to improve that country's economy. However, in exchange for the money, the Bank attached a list of over one hundred conditions, many of them devastating to the local economy. "The people of Indonesia will never forget this," says Bello.

THE SAPS' DUBIOUS TRACK RECORD

- In Senegal, touted by the IMF as a success story because of increased growth rates, unemployment increased from 25 percent in 1991 to 44 percent in 1996.
- Zimbabwe's SAP forced the reintroduction of school fees, leading to declines in attendance, especially for girls, while a one-third cut in health spending in that country has been linked to a doubling of deaths of women during childbirth.
- Costa Rica, the first Central American nation to implement a SAP, saw real wages decline by 16.9 percent between 1980 and 1991, and a 35 percent cut in health programs led to a dramatic increase in infectious disease rates and infant mortality.

> • **During the first four years of Hungary's SAP, unemployment rose from 0 percent to 13 percent. Between 1989 and 1996, the value of wages fell by 24 percent.**
>
> Institute for Policy Studies, Washington, D.C, *Field Guide to the Global Economy*

In spite of these monumental sacrifices, debt in the Nonindustrialized World has grown by over 400 percent since 1980; countries of the South now send more money to the North in debt repayment than they receive in foreign aid and export earnings combined. Even the World Bank admitted in its 1999 operations evaluation that much is not right with its programs. In countries it has "aided" through structural adjustment, 54 percent of the people have experienced stagnating per capita income, rising poverty, and declining life expectancy. As a result, the Bretton Woods Institutions have entered the public relations field.

KINDER, GENTLER SAP

Bretton Woods analysts Nancy Alexander and Sara Grusky of the Globalization Challenge Initiative say that the World Bank and the IMF now have a new mandate — a "shadow side" — to cushion the blows of globalization. The World Bank has beefed up the department that deals with world poverty, and in September 2000, it released a two-year, two-volume survey of twenty thousand people who live on less than a dollar a day. Both institutions now often cast themselves as the allies of poor countries against the United States and Europe and give public lectures about the world's poverty crisis on a regular basis.

They have also started to reinvest in social security, water delivery, and sanitation programs. They seem to be operating according to the philosophy of the chief economist of the Inter-American Development Bank, who has pointed out that it is important to send in the "ambulances" (social programs) after the "tanks" (SAPs) have rolled through the country. However, there are deep flaws in the new-found scruples of the IMF and the World Bank.

For one thing, both institutions maintain their central mandate to promote economic globalization policies around the world and shut down debate, based on the free-market assumptions of the Washington Consensus. Along with the World Trade Organization, for example, the Bank leads a Global Facilitation Partnership, which coordinates government and corporate efforts to build and maintain a constituency supporting trade liberalization in the Third World. Both have also retained their strong links with transnational corporations and their lobby and industry groups, including the International Chamber of Commerce and the World Economic Forum. Their future security is still intimately tied to how well they perform for these interests. Perhaps most important, however, is the fact that both institutions still promote the very policies of deregulation and privatization that have depleted the commons, leaving billions without basic services.

When the World Bank and the IMF open their coffers to provide social programs and health services, they do so by promoting private-sector models. In many countries, they are prepared to pay for water service infrastructure and delivery, but only if the beneficiary nations agree to open their doors to for-profit megacorporations that deal in water. This approach poses multiple problems. Private water projects brokered by the World Bank have minimal disclosure requirements. One water corporation executive who spoke at the March 2000 World Water Forum in The Hague encapsulated the thinking undergirding this erosion of citizens' right to know how basic services are being delivered. As long as water was coming out of the tap, this executive said publicly, citizens had no right to any information as to how it got there. Further, the World Bank is underwriting giant corporations with public money, often incurring the risk while the company reaps the profit.

And the governments that supposedly benefit from the entire enterprise are forced to ensure a return to company shareholders. In one recent water privatization project, for instance, Chile was required to guarantee a profit margin of 33 percent to Suez Lyonnaise des Eaux as a World Bank condition — regardless of how well the company eventually performed. And there are political goals as well. In documentation connected with a World Bank water loan to Budapest, the aim was written explicitly: one of the purposes of the financial assistance, the statement said, was to "ease political resistance to private sector involvement."

WHO TURNS THE TAP?

Water privatization is a crucial issue for public debate. Human lives depend on the equitable distribution of water resources; the public should be given a voice in deciding whether an overseas-based transnational corporation whose primary interest is profit maximization should control those critical resources. Water is a life-giving scarce resource which therefore must remain in the hands of the community through public-sector delivery. Water must not be provided for profit, but to meet needs.

South African Municipal Workers' Union, "Your Water," 1998

GLOBAL CASINO

Nowhere has the effect of the Bretton Woods Institutions been so pernicious as in the facilitation of currency speculation — the close to Can$2 trillion in rapidly expanding pooled mutual and portfolio funds that roam the world every day, preying on real or perceived weaknesses in national economies.

Unlike the "real" economy, which produces actual goods and services, the "money" economy, which is at least a hundred times larger, is based on that ephemeral phenomenon known as "casino capitalism." Ninety percent of all foreign exchange transactions are short-term speculations, completed in less than a week. Most foreign capital that flows into a country never finds its way into the real economy of manufacturing or agriculture; it simply substitutes foreign for domestic ownership and provides the money to finance capital flight, leaving local industries hollowed out. In other words, providing jobs and investing in local communities have never been goals associated with this capital; the point has generally been to rob local resources and economies in order to provide overseas profit.

This currency speculation is aided and abetted by the world's one hundred or so major private banks, who, together, have assets totalling more than U.S.$21 trillion — the equivalent of three-quarters of all the economic activity taking place in the world. The IMF and the World Bank, assisted by the banks, work to ensure easy mobility for this capital, allowing financial speculators to freely enter and exit a country with minimal risk. Because of this, investors are able to easily flee a situation if they become concerned about potential profits or losses.

In 1997, nervous Western investors began pulling billions of dollars of short-term "hot money" out of Asian countries. Those nations had been burdened with huge debts after following to the letter the IMF–World Bank prescription of "fast-track capitalism." They had liberalized their financial sector, maintained high interest rates, and pegged their national currencies to the U.S. dollar to reassure foreign investors of low risk. When investors began pulling out dollars, dollars naturally became scarce and their value increased, thus forcing down the value of the Asian national currencies.

CAPITAL OFFENCES

Once the Asian economies had begun to "deregulate" and were standing in the world marketplace more or less naked, the "hedge funds" were let loose on them. These funds are actually huge concentrations of capital owned by very wealthy Western white men, who manipulate bewilderingly complex financial instruments called "derivatives." They usually locate their offices in offshore tax havens like the Cayman Islands and do everything in their power to avoid regulators or tax collectors in the so-called free market democracies. The funds easily raped Thailand, Indonesia, and South Korea and then turned the shivering survivors over to the IMF, not to help the victims but to ensure that no Western bank was stuck with "nonperforming" loans in the devastated countries. The IMF is also the U.S. government's chosen instrument for "reforming" these countries to make them look more like New York.

Chalmers Johnson, president of the Japan
Policy Research Institute in San Diego, California

In the midst of the crisis, the U.S. Treasury Department worked closely with the IMF and private banks to pony up a bailout of U.S.$121 billion — much of it to hedge fund speculators, prompting financier George Soros to muse that these days, presidents and prime ministers court financiers and industrialists, not the other way around. The banks that made the bad loans in the first place fared extremely well that year.

Meanwhile, the crisis led to a chain reaction of currency devaluation throughout the region and into South America, which by the World Bank's own conservative estimate, plunged 10 million people into "extreme poverty" (a dollar a day or less) and 24 million into "poverty" (under two dollars a day) and left an estimated 27 million workers without jobs in the five countries most severely hit. In spite of some recovery since — seen by many analysts as temporary — the living conditions of the peoples of the region never recovered. In fact, the gap between rich and poor in Asia Pacific has hit historic highs.

Even Japan has been deeply affected by the region's crisis and by adopting many of the practices of economic globalization. The most striking sight to recent visitors is the number of homeless people walking the streets in Tokyo. In train stations, in parks and gardens, and all along the waterways, thousands of men, many in suits, are living in pitched tents or right on the pavement. Japan has abandoned its policy of providing lifelong employment, and since 1997, one million people a year have been "restructured" out of their jobs. In Tokyo alone, suicides have risen by 53 percent since 1991 — and they have usually been the result of shame over losing a job. Economic stagnation, growing debt, suicide, record unemployment, youth violence, and homelessness are the hallmarks of the new Japan. Its deep economic slump has analysts asking whether this is a signal that the global expansion has peaked.

WOUNDED BEAR

The IMF, the World Bank, and the American government are so sure that fast-track capitalism is the only medicine for ailing economies that they consistently ignored the many signs that Russia's economy was collapsing throughout the 1990s. Instead, they waited patiently for the free-market miracle they were sure would come to the former communist nation. In her powerful new book, *Contagion: The Betrayal of Liberty — Russia and the United States in the 1990s*, journalist Anne Williamson tells a chilling story. After the fall of the Soviet Union, American economic "advisors," backed by the Clinton administration and billions of dollars from private American banks and the IMF (who sent a staff of 150 into Russia to oversee the project), administered "shock therapy" to the Russian economy. The plan assigned control of Russia's mightiest state-owned industries to a handful of Boris Yeltsin's cronies. The wealth they received included the assets of the country's giant oil, gas, electrical, and telecommunications industries; some of the world's largest paper, iron, and steel factories; a number of the world's richest gold, silver, diamond, and platinum mines; and a cluster of automobile and airplane factories.

These plunderers then sold the shares of their new properties back to the Western banks and investors at bargain basement prices and pocketed the profits, while retaining control of the companies. Led by Yegor Gaidar, head of the Moscow-based Institute for Economics in Transition, they became instant millionaires and billionaires and left millions of Russian workers virtual slaves to their new foreign-investor masters.

By 1999, Russia was a financial basket case, and billions of U.S.-taxpayer-backed IMF loans had vanished into the secret bank accounts of both Russian and American gangster capitalists. In a scathing October 2000 article written for *The Nation* magazine, Stephen F. Cohen, professor of Russian studies and history at New York University, charges the U.S. and Western media with having committed malpractice by not telling this story, choosing instead to become missionaries for the American administration. He reports that Russia is now afflicted by the worst economic depression in modern history, corruption so extensive that capital flight exceeds all foreign loans and investment, and a demographic catastrophe unprecedented in peacetime.

Astonishingly undeterred by this and other fiascos, the IMF moved in 1998 to expand its authority over capital movements within its member countries. Rather than heeding the call from Nonindustrialized Countries and NGOs all around the world to re-regulate global capital flows, the IMF declared its intention to prevent governments from imposing controls on portfolio and foreign direct investments altogether. Only rigorous protests from many NGOs around the world have stalled the plan for now.

THE WORLD TRADE ORGANIZATION

The World Trade Organization was formed in 1995 at the conclusion of the "Uruguay Round" of GATT negotiations. It did not cancel out the GATT; rather, the WTO began to enforce the agreement, using its status as a permanent institution with a huge secretariat. Since the actual creation of the GATT in 1948, there have been eight rounds of negotiations, each consisting of a series of meetings spread out over several years to negotiate a fixed agenda of issues. The first six rounds concentrated exclusively on tariff reductions. But the seventh, the "Tokyo Round" (1973–1979), coincided with the emergence of what later became known as the Washington Consensus as a global economic model and the rise of the giant transnational corporations. These companies had escaped nation-state regulations because they had become global operations and now wanted international deregulation as well. Almost exclusively based in the Industrialized Countries of the North, the corporations wanted more access to unregulated labour and consumer markets and an expanded supply of natural resources. So it was obviously in their interests to dismantle the regulatory regimes many Nonindustrialized Countries had built up to protect their own workers, industries, and resources.

Influenced by this economic climate, it was at the Tokyo Round that the GATT first began to deal with "non-tariff barriers" — the rules, policies, and practices of governments, other than those pertaining to tariffs, that can have an impact on trade. Since non-tariff barriers can potentially apply to everything governments do, including delivering social services and protecting health and the environment, citizens' groups, particularly in the Third World, began to monitor the GATT for the first time.

The Uruguay Round of negotiations (1986–1994) expanded the scope of the discussion dramatically, tabling issues concerning agriculture and services — another first for the GATT — and covering areas not normally associated with trade. These so-called "trade-related" items eventually gave rise to a controversial body of rules on intellectual property rights and investment measures. The "Millennium Round" scheduled for Seattle was to greatly accelerate trade liberalization in existing areas like agriculture and intellectual property rights and expand into whole new sectors in services, investments, genetically engineered foods, and forests.

THE LEVERS OF POWER

Operating out of Geneva, Switzerland, with an administrative staff of five hundred, the WTO enforces more than twenty separate international agreements, using international trade tribunals that adjudicate disputes. Although on paper all countries are equal under the WTO, in reality, the larger countries have the economic power to withstand trade sanctions from smaller countries, whereas smaller countries are always at a disadvantage in a dispute with a larger country. The agreements include:

- The General Agreement on Tariffs and Trade (GATT), whose mandate is to eliminate all remaining tariff and non-tariff barriers to the movement of capital and goods across nation-state borders. The GATT contains the two core WTO articles: National Treatment, whereby imported and locally produced goods and services must be treated equally, regardless of the conditions in which they were produced and regardless of whether such treatment will displace local farmers or workers; and Most Favoured Nation Status, whereby each member country must treat the imports of all member countries equally, regardless of the nation's human rights records, environmental conditions, or workplace standards;
- The General Agreement on Trade in Services (GATS), the first multilateral, legally enforceable agreement covering trade in services such as banking, insurance, data management, communications, and financial services. Negotiations are now underway to expand the scope of the GATS to cover *all* services, including health care, education, social security, culture, and environmental services, including water;
- Trade Related Intellectual Property Measures (TRIPS), which sets enforceable global rules on patents, copyrights, and trademarks, and permits the patenting of many plant and animal forms, as well as seeds. Recently, transnational pharmaceutical corporations have invoked TRIPS to stop Third World Countries from providing generic, cheaper drugs to AIDS patients;
- Trade Related Investment Measures (TRIMS), which dictate what governments can and cannot do in regulating foreign investment. Many corporations want to use TRIMS to introduce elements of the foundered Multilateral Agreement on Investment (MAI) directly into the World Trade Organization so that private corporations could sue foreign governments for legislation causing them lost future profit;
- The Agreement on the Application of Sanitary and Phytosanitary Standards (SPS), which sets constraints on government policies relating to food safety and animal and plant health, ranging from those governing pesticide use and biological contaminants to policies related to food

inspection, product labelling, and genetically engineered foods. The SPS oversees the Codex Alimentarius, an agreement mandated to harmonize worldwide food quality standards, largely controlled by big food and agribusiness corporations;

- The Financial Services Agreement (FSA), established to remove obstacles to the free movement of financial services corporations, including banks and insurance companies. This is opening the door to mega-mergers in the financial sector and the loss of local economic control in many countries;

- The Agreement on Agriculture (AOA), which sets rules on the international food trade and restricts domestic agriculture policy, extends right down to the level of governments providing support for their own farmers, maintaining emergency food stocks, setting food safety rules, and ensuring that their citizens have an adequate food supply. This agreement has been roundly criticized for intensifying resource exploitation and corporate farming and for rolling back environmental protections;

- The Agreement on Subsidies and Countervailing Measures (ASCM), which sets limits on what governments may and may not subsidize and contains many loopholes favouring wealthy countries and agribusinesses;

- The Agreement on Technical Barriers to Trade (TBT), set up to ensure that nations do not have regulations (non-tariff barriers), such as environmental laws, that would interfere with trade liberalization;

- The Agreement on Government Procurement (AGP), which sets limits on what guidelines or restrictions governments are permitted to use when purchasing goods, such as "domestic content" or community reinvestment rules.

GLOBAL GOVERNMENT

From the outset, the WTO was crafted like no other international agency. The architects of the final agenda for the Uruguay Round put in place not only a body of rules governing the global economy but also the powers and tools of a global government. Unlike the GATT, which was effectively a business contract between nations, the WTO has been given "legal personality." It has international status equivalent to the United Nations, but unlike the UN, it has enormous enforcement powers. Over the past six years, the operations of the WTO show that, through its disputes adjudication and enforcement process, it has acquired the judicial, legislative, and executive powers of a global governing body.

Judicial Powers

Under the WTO's dispute settlement mechanism (expressed through its Dispute Settlement Body), member-countries, acting on behalf of their own corporate clients, can challenge the laws, policies, and programs of any other country as being in violation of WTO rules. Panels of unelected experts have the power to adjudicate claims of alleged violation of these rules and to hand out punishments. The losing country has three choices: change its law to conform to the WTO ruling; face harsh, permanent economic sanctions; or pay permanent compensation to the winning country.

Because their only task is to judge whether or not a country's policy is a "barrier to trade," the panels do not have to consider other factors, such as public health, economic justice, or democratic sovereignty. Nongovernmental organizations and other noncommercial interests are entirely excluded from the process. No conflict-of-interest rules govern the choosing of panelists; many of them come from law firms specializing in trade disputes or that receive lucrative government contracts. What's more, the panels operate in secret, with all documents, hearings, and briefs kept confidential.

Legislative Powers

In turn, these WTO tribunals have the authority to, in effect, strike down domestic laws, policies, and programs of member-states judged to be in violation of WTO rules and to require countries to establish new laws, policies, or programs that conform with WTO rules. The panelists have little or no concern for the domestic laws of other countries, let alone respect for the social obligations of governments toward their citizens. As a result, in rulings administered to date, the WTO has invariably favoured the interests of corporations over the rights of nations and democratic laws created in the public interest. All but one of the dozens of domestic environmental and health laws that have been challenged through the Dispute Settlement Body have been struck down. Panel decisions can be appealed, but even if an appeal resulted in a decision against the WTO, only a unanimous vote of all 134 nations would be able to overturn a WTO ruling.

Because sanctions are imposed by the winning country, WTO rulings invariably favour larger economies. Nonindustrialized Countries cannot afford to pay compensation for going against any ruling, and if they were to try to impose a sanction against a superpower, it would have little effect. However, if a powerful Industrialized Nation transgressed a WTO ruling, it would be in a position to pay compensation or withstand sanctions. It is no surprise that of the 117 WTO challenges to date, the United States has initiated 50.

Executive Powers

Although official WTO decisions are made by vote or by consensus in the 134-member General Council, real decision-making powers are now increasingly vested in what has become known as "the QUAD" — the U.S., the European Union, Japan, and Canada. The QUAD convenes separately several times a year between General Council meetings, repeatedly making key decisions on what the WTO will do on major agenda priorities. These QUAD meetings take place behind closed doors without the participation of other member-countries, and although the QUAD is not formally recognized as the WTO executive, it is by its composition able to informally exercise executive powers. If countries balk at their decisions, they are threatened with being abandoned by the global trading system and with reduced access to IMF loans and World Bank aid.

No other international agreements (with the exception of NAFTA, see Chapter Five) have the legal and enforcement powers of the World Trade Organization. WTO rulings are so powerful that they take precedence over Multilateral Environmental Agreements (MEAs), such as the Convention on Biological Diversity; human rights agreements like the UN's Universal Declaration of Human Rights; and international labour codes, such as those of the International Labour Organization (ILO). WTO rulings also apply to laws at every level of domestic governance — federal, provincial, state, regional, or local. If a law or regulation is challenged at the WTO and found to be trade illegal, it has to go, no matter who passed it or why.

With judicial, legislative, and executive powers stronger than those of many nations, the World Trade Organization is poised to exert despotic control over people whose interests have nothing to do with the aims of this monolithic booster of megabusiness.

4

Global Governance

How the World Trade Organization
and allied institutions operate as
a global corporate government

*T*he U.S.-based Motion Picture Association is one of the major corporate forces
that has pressured politicians to support both NAFTA and the WTO. The attitude that motivates groups with such interests was summarized neatly by Jack
Valenti, the association's president. "The prospect of pain must be inserted into
the equation," he once said of free trade negotiations, "else the solution will
never be suitable." In the popular fall 2000 blockbuster, The Art of War,
Donald Sutherland plays the secretary general of the UN. He has been persuaded
to use covert operations, headed by Wesley Snipes' character, to broker a
UN–China trade deal. (Without explanation, the movie unashamedly shifts
responsibility for trade deals from the unpopular WTO to the benign UN.) The
movie presents free trade as the economic panacea for the whole world, China
included, and anyone who disagrees is criminalized. Triads, snakeheads, and
right-wing extremists oppose the UN–China trade agreement; the dead bodies of
would-be immigrants on a container ship are the result of a plot to kill the deal.

The movie includes a superb one-liner about the current position of the United Nations on the world stage: "You know," says Donald Sutherland's character, "if this treaty with China could just go through, the United Nations could possibly become a world power." The pending entry of China into the WTO has the industry salivating, and China is bracing for the invasion of American movies. Already, the ten American films permitted to enter the country every year have come to dominate the market.

CORPORATIONS RULE THE WTO

Sweeping WTO powers are needed if global capital is to have the freedom to operate on a "level playing field" of worldwide deregulation. Transnational corporations and their domestic and international associations know this, so from the beginning, they have worked to obtain a direct voice in creating and shaping the WTO. As for civil society groups, they have had no impact on its development. A senior WTO official once confessed to the *Financial Times* that this was true. "The WTO," he said, "is the place where governments collude in private against their domestic pressure groups."

In the United States, more than five hundred corporations and business representatives have been officially credentialed as security-clear trade advisors, including the U.S. Chamber of Commerce; numerous Fortune 500 companies; the Business Roundtable, which represents the country's two hundred largest corporations; and a host of industry-specific lobby groups. The ongoing President's Advisory Committee for Trade Policy Negotiations, for example, is composed of representatives from AT&T, IBM, and Eastman Kodak, among others. The WTO has no similar access to the good counsel of nongovernmental organizations representing the environment, labour, human rights, or social justice.

In Japan, direct links between Japanese megacorporations and the government are firmly institutionalized through the Keidanren, the Japan Federation of Economic Organizations. The Keidanren is organized into public policy committees, and these are chaired by the CEOs of major Japanese corporations. The Committee on Trade and Investment, for example, is chaired by the CEO of the Mitsubishi Electric Corporation, and the Committee on Environment and Safety is chaired by the CEO of the Nissan Motor

Corporation. The Keidanren regularly presents its policy platform to the Diet and the highest levels of the Japanese government.

In Europe, the Commissioner of the European Union on WTO Policies and Administration maintains direct links with the European Round Table of Industrialists (ERT), which is composed of representatives of the fifty largest European-based corporations, including Nestlé, Unilever, Siemens, Bayer, and Philips. The ERT has been pushing hard for an "acceptable MAI" in the WTO in the wake of the failed OECD attempt to adopt a global investment treaty. The International Chamber of Commerce (ICC), also a major proponent of a renewed MAI, is the international business grouping with the closest link to the WTO Secretariat.

A COZY BUSINESS

We've always had, throughout the years, a very close working relationship with the WTO, because obviously they deal with issues which are central to business interests. The ICC has always been a vector for business input into WTO work, since its creation and since the creation of the WTO and the beginning of the multilateral trade negotiations.

Stefano Bertasi, Coordinator, ICC Working Group on Trade and Investment

In Canada, the fourth member of the QUAD, corporate-government links have also been forged through the Business Council on National Issues (BCNI). Modelled after the U.S. Business Roundtable, the BCNI represents the 150 largest corporations in Canada and has been the most influential champion of free trade, privatization, deregulation, and tax breaks for corporations. The Canadian government regularly consults the BCNI and its members through various trade and investment working groups and industry associations who were present in force during the Seattle talks (see Chapter Five).

As well as having an enormous influence within their own governments, these corporations and corporate associations work across borders to promote joint interests. The European-American Business Council (EABC) is one new industry group made up of eighty-five transnational corporations with headquarters based in either Europe or the United States. It worked closely with the more than one hundred corporations involved in the Transatlantic

Economic Partnership. (This government-corporate cooperative effort was established in 1998 by the European Union and the U.S. government to start negotiations to remove barriers to transatlantic trade, with the ultimate goal of jointly influencing the agenda of the WTO before the Seattle meeting.) The EABC favoured an ambitious stepped-up agenda, including new provisions governing services, agriculture, and investment.

As described in Chapter One, American transnational corporations played a significant role in Seattle, both in hosting the event and in setting the agenda. All transnational corporations are considered equal partners with governments at APEC, and host countries offer them exactly the same VIP status as politicians and trade negotiators. Big business was, of course, behind the creation of NAFTA (see Chapter Five), and the drive to expand free trade even further by creating a Free Trade Area of the Americas (FTAA), covering all the countries of North, Central, and South America. Similarly, Asian and Australian corporations are behind the push to establish a real free trade agreement in Asia Pacific, including an investment treaty, starting with Singapore and Japan, but moving to embrace all the countries of the region within a decade.

During the winter of 2000, the U.S. Congress debated the inclusion of China in the WTO, and as the *Wall Street Journal* reported, American big business pulled out all the stops to see that the trade deal went through. Top business executives issued a stern warning to federal lawmakers: vote against the deal with China and we will hold it against you when it comes time to write cheques for your campaigns. Phil Condit of The Boeing Company and Robert Burt, CEO of FMC Corp., publicly warned each member of Congress that their "friendliness to business" would be assessed by how they voted on this bill. "We aim our donations at people who support free enterprise and what we see as the free enterprise system," they said in a written statement. "Free trade is certainly one element that goes into that."

In February 2000, members of the mighty Business Roundtable held a breakfast strategy meeting with U.S. Treasury Secretary Larry Summers (former chief economist with the World Bank), Commerce Secretary William Daley, White House advisor Gene Sperling, and U.S. Trade Representative Charlene Barshefsky to press their case on China, and in the ensuing weeks they fanned out on Capitol Hill to lobby individual senators and Congress representatives. Executives of these Roundtable member-companies also encouraged their employees to climb on the bandwagon, lobbying their members of Congress to "save American jobs" by opening trade with China. Boeing contributed almost $2 million to candidates and parties in the 1998 Congressional elections and promised more for candidates who voted "right" on China.

THE TOOLS OF RULE

In their persistent efforts to control world markets, transnational corporations have attempted to equip themselves with levers of power by altering legislation governing intellectual property, financial services, and foreign investment. On the intellectual property front, several leading U.S. corporations — including Bristol-Myers Squibb; DuPont; Pfizer; Monsanto (now a wholly owned subsidiary of Pharmacia Corporation), and General Motors — constituted themselves as the Intellectual Property Rights Committee and, in collaboration with Japanese and European corporations and industry groups, they successfully lobbied for, and effectively wrote, a global agreement on intellectual property rights that was adopted during the Uruguay Round of GATT negotiations.

As a result, the TRIPS agreement (Trade Related Intellectual Property Measures) is forcing country after country to adopt U.S.-style laws, including legislation granting monopoly sales rights to patent holders for extended periods of time. The main victims, not surprisingly, have been the countries of the Nonindustrialized World, where up to 80 percent of patents for technology and products are held by transnational corporations. Millions of people in those nations have been denied access to cheaper, generic drugs.

On another front, the world's leading financial institutions have been demanding that all countries remove restrictions on foreign access to, and foreign ownership of, their banking, insurance, investment, and securities firms. With global bank assets estimated to be over U.S.$41 trillion, the stakes are high for the big financial conglomerates. After several unsuccessful attempts to negotiate an international financial services agreement, major American and European Union financial corporations formed the Financial

Leaders Group, which included Barclays, Chase Manhattan, Bank of America, ING Group, Dresdner Bank, Citigroup, Goldman Sachs, Ford Financial Services Group, the Royal Bank of Canada, and over fifty other leading bank, insurance, and investment corporations.

These companies prepared their own version of an international financial agreement and worked hand-in-glove with U.S. and European government officials to exert enormous pressure on Asian and Latin American countries to endorse it. By December 1997, seventy WTO member countries from all over the world, including Canada and many Asian and Latin American countries, had signed on, thereby diminishing their sovereignty over their financial sectors to foreign-based banks and insurance and securities corporations.

The corporate giants have also been calling for a global investment treaty that would guarantee and protect the entry and establishment of their production operations in all nations. Since the attempt to negotiate the Multilateral Agreement on Investment at the OECD was shot down in 1998, deliberate steps have been taken to revive the MAI at the WTO. Originally crafted by the International Chamber of Commerce and supported by the Fortune 500 corporations, the blueprint for the MAI would have provided transnational companies with a set of power tools that could have been used not only to guarantee protection for their investments and operations in other countries, but also to ratchet down any government laws, policies, and programs that might have impeded their ability to rake in the profits. Moreover, the "investor-state" mechanism of the proposed treaty would have given global corporations the right to sue governments directly for alleged violations of the MAI. Prompted by leading European multinationals like Nestlé, Shell, and British Petroleum, the European Union is determined to bring investment negotiations back to the WTO.

THE WTO'S THREAT TO THE ENVIRONMENT

There is no environmental agreement within the World Trade Organization itself; however, most aspects of the WTO adversely affect the environment and constrain the rights of citizens and their governments to maintain good environmental rules or standards. As Canadian legal trade expert Steven Shrybman explains, "In the simplest of terms, the essential goal of WTO rules is to deregulate international trade. All WTO agreements set out detailed rules intended to constrain the extent to which governments can regulate international trade, or otherwise 'interfere' with the activities of large corporations. The WTO agreements provide extensive lists of things that governments can no longer do."

The key GATT articles affecting environmental rules — the National Treatment and Most Favoured Nation Status clauses — prevent governments from setting standards that favour goods that have been produced or harvested in an environmentally sustainable way. These clauses stipulate that countries must treat "like" products from one country as favourably as those from another, that no distinction can be made between foreign and domestic "like" products, and that quotas or bans imposed for environmental reasons can be challenged as forms of protectionism. Hence, objections to methods of production (called "production and process methods," or PPMs in trade jargon) cannot be used to ban a product. This suddenly legalizes a whole host of terrible and inhumane environmental practices.

For example, these clauses of the WTO were successfully used to strike down the U.S. Marine Mammal Protection Act because it banned the import of tuna caught in Mexican and European drift nets that also slaughter dolphins (at an estimated annual rate of 150,000). The articles were also used to override the U.S. Endangered Species Act when the WTO ruled against its requirements that shrimp farmers, both domestic and foreign, must equip their nets with inexpensive turtle-excluder devices in order to protect endangered Asian sea turtles.

Another WTO provision, Article XI, prohibits the use of export controls for any purpose and eliminates quantitative restrictions on imports and exports. This dangerous provision effectively eradicates a nation's right to allocate its natural resources and means that no limits are placed on the quantities of any natural resource that can be exported or imported. The implications for trade in water and other essentials of life are clear. As transnationals gear up to privatize the world's diminishing supplies of fresh water in preparation for the bulk water trade (see Chapter Six), human life and health are at risk of being put on the auction block. Since this precious resource is included in the WTO's GATT agreement as a tradeable "good," quotas or bans on the export of bulk water by ecologically damaging supertankers or megatechnology diversion projects could be challenged as a form of protectionism.

National environmental protections are also in danger of being eroded by the WTO's Agreement on Technical Barriers to Trade (TBTs). Under this agreement, a nation must be prepared to prove, if challenged, that its environmental standards are both "necessary" and have been established in the "least trade restrictive" way to achieve the desired goals of conservation, food safety, or high health standards. This means that a country bears the burden of proving a negative — that no other measure consistent with the WTO is reasonably available to protect environmental concerns. The positive alternative, the Precautionary Principle, a central operating principle of the environmental movement, says that environmental and health concerns must always be given the benefit of the doubt. This means that a country would not have to prove its methods were completely conducive to international trade as long as they met the country's environmental and health standards.

In addition, the term "least trade restrictive" is unclear and open to arbitrary determination by WTO panels, thus creating a "chill effect" whereby countries, especially smaller ones, tend to avoid even enacting standards just in case they might be challenged before a WTO tribunal. For instance, because industry groups have lobbied hard against eco-labelling at the WTO, many countries are reluctant to begin the practice, for fear of WTO challenges.

Defenders of the World Trade Organization's tactics point to Article XX of the GATT, the clause that provides for "General Exceptions" to WTO rules by allowing countries to protect "human, animal, plant life or health . . . [and] the conservation of exhaustible natural resources" if the restrictions apply equally to domestic producers and consumers. However, by adding the provision that Article XX must be interpreted in such a way that environmental standards and regulations are least trade restrictive, the WTO has rendered the general exemption almost useless. This observation has been confirmed by a comment from the American Electronics Association. In response to new European environmental guidelines relating to electronic products, the association remarked that "so far, no panel called to apply Article XX has accepted the necessity of a measure otherwise inconsistent with other GATT provisions." In other words, all panels have noted that Article XX is inconsistent with other GATT provisions, so it has been dismissed. (The sole exception to this practice so far, is the Canada-France asbestos case, described in Chapter Six.)

Finally, the World Trade Organization has undermined progress made in Multilateral Environmental Agreements (MEAs) — agreements between nations concerning endangered species, global warming, and other issues. It has conveniently leapfrogged these pacts by building "WTO Superiority Clauses" into the agreements, whereby, in any case of conflict, the WTO takes precedence. If one nation claims that its MEA should actually supersede the WTO, the superiority clauses can be used to override their position. When opposed, the WTO can enforce rulings that are legally binding, even if they contravene MEA agreements. MEAs, on the other hand, contain no such enforcement measures. Even when an MEA appears compatible with the WTO, other rules often conflict with these obligations. For example, as the International Forum on Globalization explained in their pre-Seattle publication *Invisible Government*, edited by Jerry Mander and Debi Barker, the rules of the Convention on Biological Diversity (CBD), signed at the Earth Summit in Rio, are being undermined by the WTO in three ways.

First, the CBD was formed to preserve biodiversity and to protect species from extinction; yet global free trade promotes industrial agriculture and forestry, which in turn promote monoculture, leading to the destruction of biodiversity and pushing millions of species to extinction. Second, the CBD calls for the protection of Indigenous knowledge. However, the TRIPS agreement promotes the patenting of Indigenous knowledge by corporations, a process called "biopiracy," whereby countries are forced to recognize foreign patent rights over their genetic heritage. Third, the agreement contained provisions for an international Biosafety Protocol. Although the Protocol was ratified in Montreal early in 1999, the United States did not sign it and maintains that the WTO takes supremacy over it.

MEGABUSINESS MELTDOWN

Given current corporate practices, not one wildlife reserve, wilderness, or Indigenous culture will survive the global economy. We know that every natural system on the planet is disintegrating. The land, water, air, and sea have been functionally transformed from life-supporting systems into repositories for waste. There is no polite way to say that business is destroying the world.

Paul Hawken, *The Ecology of Commerce: A Declaration of Sustainability*

THE WTO'S IMPACT ON FOOD SECURITY AND FOOD SAFETY

The WTO Agreement on Agriculture (AOA) is one of the most complicated of all the WTO agreements. Ostensibly introduced to remove subsidies around the world, it has worked largely to the benefit of large agribusiness corporations, no matter what their country of origin. The prime AOA goal of reducing or eliminating agricultural import tariffs has allowed cheap, subsidized products from the North, particularly Europe and the United States, to flood Third World countries that have already been forced to eliminate subsidies to their own farmers — or to reduce them to levels consistent with or below U.S. and European levels. Subsidized meat imports from Europe, for example, have helped to wipe out the pastoral economies and cultures of West Africa.

Family farms and small agricultural operations all over the world have been destroyed by free trade in agriculture. Even in the North, it is almost impossible to guarantee a fair return at the farm gate because of the global flood of cheap imported products produced under deteriorating conditions and declining standards. Farmers are finding it increasingly difficult to negotiate prices for products collectively, with either domestic or foreign buyers, and the actual and proposed elimination of domestic agriculture price supports to protect farmers has left them at the mercy of international prices. The reduction and eventual elimination of supports in an area already traditionally subject to the unpredictability of weather and lack of much-needed labour adds just one more element of chaos to the mix. When small farm operations lose profits because of worldwide fluctuations in commodity prices, they can be wiped right off the map. Only huge operations, with investment support from megacorporations, can be sure to survive.

The AOA assault on non-tariff measures such as environmental standards and supply management programs has been used to downgrade numerous safeguards to public health and protections for farmers. To take just one case, the United States, through the WTO, has successfully challenged Japan's health-related pesticide-residue testing requirements for agricultural imports, and as a result, dozens of Japanese pesticide bans have been lifted over the past few years.

AOA requirements also mean that sovereign nations are now in the ludicrous position of being unable to maintain emergency food stocks in anticipation of drought, crop failure, or war. They are now forced to buy everything they need on the open market. "Food self-sufficiency" now means having the money to buy food, not the domestic ability to produce it. It is clear how this penalizes poorer countries and poor people: they do not have ready, steady currency to buy food, and because they are closer to the starvation line, they may have a greater need to set up emergency food stocks during relatively good years.

Even in countries that are currently less likely to suffer from famines and food shortages, citizens are at greater risk of eating unsafe food because of the WTO/SPS agreement. Canada and the United States, for instance, successfully used the SPS to strike down a European ban on North American beef containing harmful, possibly cancer-causing hormones. Deeply sensitive to lingering concerns about mad-cow disease after an outbreak of the illness in the U.K. in the mid-1990s, the European Union implemented a ban on nontherapeutic use of hormones in its food industry, citing many studies linking them to illness.

The WTO panel, in its self-styled wisdom, demanded "scientific certainty" that these hormones cause cancer or other adverse health effects. This ruling has frightening implications for the ability of governments to set high standards to protect public health. Instead of ensuring that their citizens have access to the healthiest possible food, governments are now being put in the position of allowing entry to foods that may be as unhealthy as possible.

BIGGER AND BETTER GRUB AND BUGS

The free trade vision expressed by the WTO Agreement on Agriculture is of an integrated global agricultural economy, in which all countries produce specialized agricultural commodities and supply their food needs by shopping in the global marketplace. Food is grown, not by farmers for local consumers, but by corporations for global markets. The implementation of this global model has already spelled disaster for the food security of poor countries, as subsistence farms are lost to export producers.

Taken together, the different agreements of the WTO set the stage for the next "Green Revolution": the spread of biotechnology in the form of genetically engineered foods; terminator genes that prevent seeds from producing, so farmers have to buy rather than grow their

> **own seed-stocks; vegetables that are lethal to the insects that eat them; and plants that are virtually immune to pesticides, which therefore can be dosed with more pesticides with immunity.**
>
> Steven Shrybman, *The World Trade Organization, A Citizens' Guide*

THE WTO'S THREAT TO SOCIAL SECURITY

In spite of the obvious rejection of the Seattle Millennium Round, WTO officials have launched an ambitious new round of talks on services under the General Agreement on Trade in Services (GATS). Their aim is to radically restructure the role of government worldwide by subjecting an ever-greater degree of governmental decision making to the discipline of the WTO. The GATS is extraordinarily broad, explains Scott Sinclair, a trade expert with the Canadian Centre for Policy Alternatives, and deals with every service imaginable. It applies to all levels of government, not only in the domain of cross-border trade, but also in the area of domestic policies governing the environment, culture, natural resources, health care, education, and social services. The current round of GATS negotiations has put every single social service on the table and is only the first of many rounds whose ultimate goal is the full commercialization of all services.

The service sector represents the fastest-growing "market" in international trade, and of all services, health, education, and social security are shaping up to be the most potentially lucrative. Global expenditures on education now exceed U.S.$2 trillion, and in health care, they exceed U.S.$3.5 trillion. Public education, health care, and welfare have been targeted by predatory and powerful transnational corporations which are aiming at nothing less than the complete dismantling of these public systems. To bring this situation about, all they need to do is to subject government-run public services to the rules of international competition and the discipline of the WTO — the same institution that has knocked down domestic standards in the areas of culture, the environment, and fair trade.

Governments seem to understand that GATS is a corporate agreement; on its website, the European Commission calls the General Agreement on Trade in Services "first and foremost an instrument for the benefit of business." Created in 1994, the GATS at first dealt only with items on a "request" basis, allowing countries to exempt whole areas from its reach. A country or several countries could request that a sector, such as e-commerce, be negotiated, and other countries would agree or not to the offering. Under this system, countries were able to exempt social programs, including health and education. However, in the lead-up to Seattle, an aggressive campaign was launched by the U.S. to have the GATS automatically include every conceivable item that might be considered a service — targeting education, health care, and social security in particular.

U.S. Trade Representative Charlene Barshefsky asked the powerful American lobby group, the Coalition of Service Industries, what it would like to see included in a comprehensive GATS agreement. The Coalition came back with a thirty-one-page list. This group and its counterpart in Europe have identified the following areas for trade liberalization: health care; hospital care; home care; dental care; child care; elder care; education — primary, secondary, and post-secondary; museums; libraries; law; social assistance; architecture; energy; water services; environmental protection services; tourism; postal services; publishing; and broadcasting — among many others.

The current GATS rules already threaten the rights of citizens to social security delivered publicly and equitably by their governments, thus contravening the guarantees of the UN's Universal Declaration of Human Rights. Although governments are now technically allowed to exempt social security measures and social programs, under the GATS, these measures have to be totally free from commercial provisions to qualify, and there are very few countries in the world that don't allow some level of commercial activity in these areas. In the new GATS negotiations, however, even the existing allowances for exemptions are up for grabs. The WTO's member-nations have agreed that everything is "on the table," which feeds into the WTO's long-term goal of ever-increasing expansion of the GATS' powers.

Most distressing to the world's citizens, member-governments have agreed to take the first steps toward giving the GATS more levers of influence. These are the goals they have approved: to expand the area and number of services covered and to constrain governments' regulatory authority in services; to discuss adding "national treatment" to the GATS provisions, which would allow foreign for-profit corporations to enter every country in the world and become eligible for public subsidies that would help them set up services; to grant "commercial presence" to foreign for-profit social service corporations, thereby giving them influential investment rights; and to subject sovereign governments to a regime of "domestic regulation" (read: domestic *de*regulation) by the WTO, which would severely limit their ability to enact and enforce environmental, health, and social security rules and standards.

> ## CURTAILING THE COMPETITION
> **Global business interests are seeking binding, global, and irreversible rules on services. It should come as no surprise that multinational corporations, as they expand and extend their global reach, increasingly have a strong interest in reducing the cost of complying with the regulations they face in different countries. They also benefit by reducing competition from domestic, sometimes publicly owned, firms and from the privatization and commercialization of public enterprises that allows them to expand their market share. Adopting global rules to reduce or eliminate constraints placed by governments on their international commercial activity is understandably a key priority of many global corporations operating in the service sector.**
>
> Scott Sinclair, *GATS: How the World Trade Organization's*
> *New "Services" Negotiations Threaten Democracy*

THE WTO'S ROLE IN MILITARY REPRESSION

The Peace Research Institute in Oslo has studied the major wars of the 1990s (overwhelmingly civil wars, not inter-country wars) and found that they share certain characteristics: they have taken place in countries with high levels of poverty and land degradation, low fresh water availability, high external debt, falling export income from primary commodities and a history of vigorous IMF intervention — all conditions heightened, if not totally caused, by the World Bank, the IMF, and the WTO.

Through one of its clauses, the WTO also plays a special role in promoting the pernicious global arms trade. As Steven Staples of the International Network on Disarmament and Globalization explains, a little known but highly significant provision of the GATT — Article XXI — exempts activities in the military sphere, including massive government research and export subsidies, from challenge. Every country may maintain measures it "considers necessary for the protection of its essential security interests, relating to the traffic in arms, ammunition, and implements of war." This national security exception (which is also contained in NAFTA), provides a blanket exemption for military spending for any reason related to national security, based on the premise that the fundamental role of government is to provide for a military to protect the country and a police force to maintain security within it.

It is a very powerful exception because it permits governments to define for themselves their "essential security interests." The United States, for example, maintains domestic control over broadcasting, because the U.S. government considers it necessary for national security, even while that same government uses the WTO and NAFTA to attempt to force Canada to open up its broadcasting sector to international competition.

Because the security exception shields the war industry from challenges by the WTO, it actually spurs government military spending, as government exports associated with the military are the only ones to which subsidies may be applied. Several recent WTO challenges, such as those related to Canada's subsidization of nonmilitary aerospace technology, have forced governments to shift to "WTO-compliant" subsidies, thus increasing their military spending to support their international nonmilitary high-tech sectors.

Having learned from Canada's "mistake," South Africa is currently undergoing a huge arms-buying spree, purchasing billions of dollars' worth of helicopters, aircraft, ships, and even submarines from European weapons manufacturers. Concurrently, government officials have negotiated an agreement that the corporations will move some of their production for these contracts to South Africa, creating jobs and investment in the WTO-friendly military sector.

The WTO has thus begun to shape a world where governments are being manipulated into placing more value on military defence than on ensuring that their own citizens have access to good education, safe food, and relief in times of economic emergency. And in a further nasty twist, the Nonindustrialized World will lose again. Since two-thirds of global military spending is concentrated in the economies of the QUAD, the security exception gives these countries a competitive advantage over Third World nations. In most cases, their relatively minuscule military budgets will leave them at the back of the pack in the brave new race to material and military glory.

LOSING THE RIGHT TO DO RIGHT

The lesson is clear: under the WTO's rules, local communities and even national governments have lost the right to condition their purchases, investments, and other economic activities to peace, social justice, or human rights principles. Because the security exception shields the war industry from challenges to the WTO, it works to spur military spending by governments. Governments can use the military to promote jobs, new emerging industries, and high-tech manufacturing. It allows governments — most importantly the U.S. and other NATO countries and Japan — to provide protection and subsidies for both their national arms industries and military exports, while being pressured to disinvest in areas like health and social services.

Steven Staples, "The WTO and the Global War System,"
Seattle Symposium, November 1999

Transnational weapons manufacturers are now scouring the world in search of new government subsidies, favourable tax incentives, lower wages, and weak labour standards, all WTO-certified. As Steven Staples reports, recent years have witnessed huge mergers in the military sector. The Pentagon, to maintain its influence in the industry, recently announced that British Aerospace, Europe's largest weapons corporation, will be given national treatment rights in the U.S. — treated as if it is an American company, subject to all the privileges and controls that brings.

Meanwhile, the U.S. Space Command openly boasts that its future mission — to create space as the "fourth medium of warfare" — will be used to protect American commercial and investment interests around the planet. Admitting in its *Visions of 2020* report that globalization will accelerate the widening gulf between "haves" and "have-nots," the agency compares the effort to control space with conflicts engendered centuries ago when the American navy protected U.S. commercial interests by force.

General Joseph Ashy, former commander-in-chief of the U.S. Space Command, has said, "It's politically sensitive, but it's going to happen. Some people don't want to hear this, and it sure isn't in vogue, but, absolutely, we're going to fight in space. We're going to fight from space and we're going to fight into space." Its new mandate, clearly spelled out on its website, links its war mission in space with American commercial interests. "Due to the importance of commerce and its effects on national security, the United States may evolve into the guardian of space commerce."

There, it will be protected by TRIPS and TRIMS and GATS and GATT — the alphabetization of power.

5

National Collusion

How Ottawa plays the game of global
corporate governance through the
Department of Foreign Affairs
and International Trade

*L*ate *in 1998, senior bureaucrats in the Department of Foreign Affairs and
International Trade (DFAIT) sent two detailed memos to then Minister for
International Trade Sergio Marchi, outlining a communications strategy to
promote trade liberalization and counter the critics who had recently and
successfully rallied public opinion against the failed MAI. Called* Trade
Communications: After the MAI *and* Outreach on Trade Liberalization,
*the confidential papers paint a cynical picture of a department embarrassed
by its failure to communicate all the advantages of trade liberalization to
Canadians and determined to rectify the situation by an expensive public
relations campaign enlisting the help of big business.*

*Intended for the Minister's eyes only (he is referred to as "Chief Salesman
for Canada"), the papers outline a bold plan to shift public opinion in the
government's favour. "To counteract charges that trade liberalization is not
necessarily in the interest of Canadians and/or the rest of the world, DFAIT*

will need to draw on . . . work with partners in the private sector and interna-
tional organizations. . . . You plan to announce that you will launch a process
of 'consultation' and 'citizen engagement' on preparations for the new WTO
negotiations. . . . Create a dialogue on the principle of trade liberalization. Leave
the contentious issues — agriculture, labour, and the environment — to the
efforts your colleagues in these respective departments have already begun. . . ."
The authors make no bones about the fact that for DFAIT, "the business
community is our priority audience" and they admit that the department
"devotes extensive resources to serving this largely supportive community. . . ."
The bureaucrats counsel the use of massive public education material —
"building blocks for targeted communications products" — based on the
"format approach of the Business Roundtable in the United States. . . ." And
they recommend seeking sponsorship from business: "BCNI [the Canadian
corporate lobby group Business Council on National Issues], they say, has
already expressed interest and Red Wilson [former CEO of BCE] told me the
idea was worth a discussion."

In these documents, the DFAIT bureaucrats claim that their key objective is
to "position the government of Canada, and particularly the Minister for
International Trade, as an earnest partner in a sustained dialogue with
Canadians on trade issues." But their apparent virtuous motives are undermined by a cynical plan to get public opinion onside with no substantive
change to policy. No real sharing is envisaged, nor do the authors anticipate
that they have anything to learn from civil society. They discuss how to deal
only with those interested in "genuine dialogue with the government," by
giving civil society groups lots of work; as the document puts it: "the more
they are asked to bear some of the load, the less likely the need to deal with
groups not truly interested in dialogue."

CONSULTATION FEVER

As any Canadian NGO can testify, in the months and years since the October
1998 defeat of the Multilateral Agreement on Investment (MAI), DFAIT has
launched an unprecedented round of consultations with Canadians from

coast to coast. Hardly a month has gone by in over two years without some parliamentary committee or departmental consultation on the most minute detail of the government's trade and investment policies. The deluge has been so great that many civil society groups can't keep up with the demand for their involvement. At first glance, one might assume the Canadian government had learned from its past mistakes and started a real dialogue with its citizens. However, the above memos indicate that these meetings are for display purposes only, intended to mask what DFAIT is really up to on the international front. For example, several months after these memos were written, the Investment Trade Policy Division of DFAIT invited a thousand participants to take part in a series of "roundtable discussions" on government procurement, investment, and competition policy, but a breakdown of invitees showed that almost 75 percent were from the business community. Not surprisingly, the government heard few divergent views in this process.

It did hear those opposing opinions, however, when, in the spring of 1999, the House of Commons Standing Committee on Foreign Affairs and International Trade held public hearings on the World Trade Organization's Millennium Round meeting, to be held in Seattle the following November. Hundreds of environmental, labour, farm, social justice, cultural, church, and public sector groups testified before an all-party parliamentary committee. Many were opposed to the WTO altogether and called for Canada to withdraw from negotiations; many others thought that the institution could be reformed to become a more humane, responsible vehicle for a just trade system and called on Canada to play a role in this process. All, however, shared the critique that the WTO, in its current form, contains no minimum standards to protect basic social, human, cultural, and environmental rights and is a threat to world stability.

Yet when the Standing Committee issued its report in June 1999, only lip service was paid to the articulate and well-researched presentations made by civil society groups. As Christine Elwell of the Sierra Club found in a study of the recommendations, the report called on Canada to take a "business as usual" position and, in Seattle, to push aggressively for liberalization in agriculture, services, and investment. So citizens' groups, now working together in a coalition called the Common Front on the WTO and cochaired by the Council of Canadians and the Canadian Labour Congress, rallied and lobbied the Trade Minister himself. To no avail; in early November, with only weeks to go before the Seattle meeting, Minister for International Trade Pierre Pettigrew published the Canadian government's WTO negotiating position paper, basically rubber-stamping the parliamentary committee's report and declaring that nothing was "off the table, a priori," including the "politically sensitive" areas of health and education. Canada went into the Seattle meetings prepared to open up whole new sectors to the discipline of the WTO while not advocating for any of the progressive changes that NGOs had demanded and that DFAIT's wide consultation process had led them to believe would happen.

CANADA IN THE LEAD

Disappointment on the part of civil society groups was beginning to be replaced by anger with the dawning realization that Canada was not just "going along" with the process of economic globalization and the WTO. It was becoming a leading player in its development and acting as a stalking horse for the United States, where public antipathy against free trade has been growing. In fact, Canada has been taking a leading role in the World Trade Organization for well over a decade. During the Uruguay Round of the GATT, remembers then senior Canadian trade negotiator Sylvia Ostry, there was a recognition that the GATT could no longer provide an adequate foundation for the "much more ambitious and comprehensive" new trading system that was being formed. A "fundamental shift in policy template" marked the Round, leading to a "deeper integration agenda" that was clearly intruding on domestic policy space in trade, investment, technology, social regulation, and health and safety measures.

"While the Uruguay Round marked the launch of the deeper integration agenda," Ostry wrote in a 1999 paper for the Washington-based Brookings Institution, "it represented only the first step. The mandate for the first post–Cold War institution was indeed formidable." What was needed was a membership organization with teeth, rather than the existing trade agreement, and a dispute settlement mechanism that would be the "jewel in the crown."

It was Canada that proposed the establishment of the World Trade Organization, an offer quickly endorsed by the European Union.

> ## ON TO WTO GLORY, WITH CANADA FAST BEHIND
> Developments in the substantive negotiations are now demonstrat-
> ing that the Uruguay Round results cannot be effectively housed in a
> provisional shelter. It is also becoming clear that the post-Uruguay
> trade policy agenda will be complex and may not be adequately man-
> aged within the confines of the GATT system as it now exists. . . .
>
> Government of Canada, press release, April 1990

Canada has also been a keen participant in the Asia-Pacific Economic
Cooperation forum, hosting the 1997 meeting in Vancouver that led to the
infamous "pepper-spray" incidents against peaceful protesters and the subsequent inquiry. Security documents since released make it clear that DFAIT
and the Prime Minister's Office had given guarantees to then Indonesian
Dictator President Suharto (conservatively estimated to have been responsible for a million deaths) that he would be shielded from protesters in
Vancouver and that objectors would not even be allowed to get near enough
for him to see or hear them.

Similarly, Canada was an MAI cheerleader from day one. DFAIT worked
with the U.S. State Department and the European Commission to propose an
investment treaty to the first Ministerial Meeting of the newly formed WTO
in December of 1996, where it was roundly rejected by Third World countries
as a form of neocolonialism. Undeterred, Canada and the U.S. took the MAI,
drafted by the International Chamber of Commerce, to a more welcoming
OECD in Paris, where negotiations were already underway. When the MAI
became public and controversial in Canada, then Minister for International
Trade Sergio Marchi attacked critics as "professional doomsayers" given to
"distortions and misunderstandings."

Canada has been an enthusiastic supporter of free trade in North America,
first under Progressive Conservative Prime Minister Brian Mulroney and then
under Liberal Prime Minister Jean Chrétien. Weeks after his election win
in 1984, Brian Mulroney told a blue-chip business audience in New York
that Canada was "open for business" and promised to take down barriers to
American investments and goods in Canada. Years later, in an interview with
journalist Marci McDonald, Peter Murphy, the lead U.S. trade negotiator
for the Canada–U.S. Free Trade Agreement in the mid-1980s (now deceased),

confirmed that Canada wanted the trade deal far more than the U.S.

In Canada, by 1986, talks about free trade had become the most important aspect of the government's economic policy. A huge team of over one hundred trade experts, taken from a number of government departments, were transferred to a new entity called the Trade Negotiations Office — which took up an entire floor of a lavishly furnished downtown Ottawa office tower. External Affairs funded the office and paid Simon Reisman, a retired trade bureaucrat who had spent many years in External Affairs, one thousand dollars a day to run operations there. For the United States, whose delegation of three was housed in a cubbyhole in an old, cramped Washington building, the talks were a sideshow, a stepping stone to the real goal. They were merely an effort to ensure that a new round of GATT negotiations included measures sought by American corporations but resisted by many countries. Canada's capitulation on several controversial issues would be used as a "lever" against Europe in particular.

When Jean Chrétien's Liberals, who had spent nine years fighting Mulroney's free trade policies, came to power, their first act was to ratify the much-contested NAFTA. Many Canadians were shocked at this betrayal of an election promise. But clues had been visible for some time to indicate that the Liberals were adopting an aggressive proglobalization stand. In 1991, the Liberals brought together a hand-picked gathering of "thinkers" to what came to be known as the "Aylmer Conference" in Quebec, where the party clearly embraced the "inevitable reality," as Jean Chrétien called it, of the global economy. The next year, Liberal Trade Critic Roy MacLaren published his controversial paper, *Wide Open*, calling for Canada to become the first country in the world to unilaterally take down all barriers to trade and investment, whether or not other countries reciprocated.

By the time of the 1993 election, as journalists Ed Greenspon and Anthony Wilson-Smith have chronicled in their 1996 book, *Double Vision*, the Liberal party was ready to embrace free trade and sign NAFTA. But such an about-face was politically problematical, so senior advisors from the White House met with senior advisors to Jean Chrétien in the weeks before the election to work out a face-saving plan, including toothless side-deals on environment and labour, to allow the passage of NAFTA. After this first capitulation, the Chrétien Liberals never looked back and became the most determined promoters of continental and hemispheric free trade of any government in the Americas.

Jean Chrétien was on a Team Canada trade mission to Chile when he received news of Pierre Trudeau's death in late September 2000. The irony appeared lost on him in his genuine grief over his mentor's death. But it was obvious. Systematically, through his policies, trade agreements, and trade missions, Jean Chrétien had steadily eroded the cultural and economic policies of Trudeau and Pearson. Trudeau's protégé, a street fighter who had risen through the political ranks on the strength of his belief in Canada, had chosen, as prime minister, to pander to corporate interests and turn his back on the citizens he had been elected to defend.

And the free trade boosting continued. Canada hosted the June 2000 tenth anniversary meeting of the Organization of American States (OAS) in Windsor (see Chapter Two) and is the enthusiastic host of the April 2001 Summit of the Americas, an assembly of all the leaders of all the nations of North, Central, and South America, except Cuba. The Free Trade Area of the Americas agreement (FTAA) is slated to include new provisions on services, agriculture, and investment, incorporating the worst elements of the current NAFTA, the proposed changes to the General Agreement on Trade in Services (GATS), and the defeated MAI.

Perhaps most distressing to learn, however, is the fact that, in spite of Canada's historic commitment to public services and the overwhelming support for universal health care and education among Canadians, the Canadian government assumed leadership in advancing a whole new post-Seattle round of GATS negotiations to liberalize trade in these and other services under the WTO.

SCHOOLS AND HEALTH FOR SALE

I'm not talking exemptions this or that. I want us Canadians to be able to export our competence in these areas [of health and education] to the world.

Minister for International Trade Pierre Pettigrew,
when asked if he would seek another exemption for
health and education in the new round of GATS talks

In January 2000, only months after the failed WTO talks in Seattle, DFAIT set up twenty-six working groups in Ottawa to promote every aspect of the services negotiations, and former Minister for International Trade Sergio Marchi, now Canada's ambassador to the WTO, was named the chair of this round, where he has promoted an aggressive agenda.

Anyone who has followed Mr. Marchi's political career might find his most recent incarnation puzzling. When he was a Liberal backbencher, he was strongly opposed to free trade and a passionate defender of universal social programs. In 1991, he advocated reopening the Canada–U.S. Free Trade Agreement (FTA) to renegotiate the onerous energy provisions. "Who in their right mind would treat Americans as Canadians in times of energy crisis?" he demanded in the House of Commons. Two years later, he called the FTA, NAFTA, and the GST "a crown of thorns for the country." Like other trade ministers around the world, however, he changed his position entirely when he assumed office. In fact, as trade minister, Sergio Marchi was the first to broach the topic of the need for trade rules to apply to education. In a 1997 speech to an "education industry" audience in Toronto, he said: "Education is now an industry," for which we need to identify our "markets" and develop and promote our "products." There was money to be made from the global trade in educational services, he assured his listeners, and he called for enforceable rules to oversee that commerce.

Marchi's successor, Pierre Pettigrew, made a similar about-face. Pettigrew once wrote a book sounding the alarm about economic globalization and opposing free trade agreements that contained no social and environmental safeguards. He changed his position entirely, however, when he assumed office.

TRADE UBER ALLES

Civil society groups are also deeply concerned about the ascendancy of the Department of Foreign Affairs and International Trade (DFAIT) in the Canadian government's policy development. On taking office in 1993, and in keeping with its newfound evangelism in promoting global free trade, the Chrétien government merged the old Department of External Affairs with the Department of Trade, creating DFAIT and giving the Trade Secretariat increased powers relative to both Foreign Affairs and most other departments in Ottawa. By 1977, priorities for the department had been clearly set in favour of trade liberalization and business promotion over the more traditional role of foreign policy.

DFAIT, along with the Departments of Finance and Industry (both of which have also reoriented their mandates to strongly promote international trade), now forms an "unholy trinity" within the government that exercises formidable powers. While other budgets have decreased (for example, Environment's budget has been cut in half from a decade ago), the funds for trade development in DFAIT have almost doubled.

Much of the budget increase goes to cover DFAIT's costs as the new watchdog of other departments, both federal and provincial, to ensure that any and all policy proposals they are considering do not violate trade rules. For the most part, this practice goes unpublicized — the offending proposed regulation or law is just quietly withdrawn and the public never finds out about it. Of course, this also creates a "chill effect" among policymakers, who figure out for themselves that some of their proposals won't pass DFAIT muster, so they don't even bother to bring them forward.

In some blatant cases, however, a policy has been put on the table and Trade has trumped it. In 1991, Finance Minister Michael Wilson overruled then Culture Minister Marcel Masse on policy intended to Canadianize the book publishing industry. In 1997, then Minister for International Trade Art Eggleton set off a firestorm of protest when he openly differed with Heritage Minister Sheila Copps on the future of Canadian culture in a global economy: "The trend to open markets and communications is global and irreversible," he said.

A year later, when Canada was under WTO threat for policies that protected the Canadian magazine industry, Copps' office confirmed that neither the minister nor her staff were party to the negotiations with the American industry; those were being handled exclusively by DFAIT and the new minister, Sergio Marchi. Janet Bax, then director of communications at Heritage, explained that this approach was being taken so her department wouldn't say anything "to jeopardize our negotiating position."

Following an aggressive lobbying campaign in 1992, the giants of the pharmaceutical industry succeeded in winning twenty-year monopoly protection in Canada for their drug patents, later cemented by NAFTA. In 1997, the Liberals held a promised parliamentary review, but rather than giving this work to the Health Committee, they sent it for review to the Industry Committee. Nevertheless, the all-party parliamentary panel recommended several major changes to the law. They had been persuaded to do so by a barrage of well-researched arguments submitted by civil society and health care groups, including evidence that under this legislation, drug prices had skyrocketed, along with profits for the big drug companies. Then Health Minister Dave Dingwall dismissed the Committee's work, saying that because of NAFTA, the government could not "turn back the clock."

So powerful has DFAIT become within government circles that it often operates without consultation or permission from other departments or their ministers. DFAIT's mandate is to promote liberalized trade and investment at home and in international negotiations — *not* to try to balance the needs and rights of Canadians with the imperatives of global trade. So if a sector such as culture is exempted in one agreement, DFAIT attempts to have it included in the next round of negotiations of this agreement or in negotiations for other agreements.

For instance, the cultural exemptions secured in NAFTA, weak as they were, were not repeated in the World Trade Organization negotiations, and Canada has actually put culture on the table in the new GATS negotiations. DFAIT bureaucrats are hired on the basis of their belief and expertise in trade matters, so they don't often stray from the central dogma. When they work with other government agencies, such as Status of Women or Environment, they generally do so only in order to enlist their support for the cause.

In fact, it is not uncommon for other departments, levels of governments, and ministers to be left completely in the dark about what negotiations DFAIT is involved in and what impact those discussions might have on their areas of responsibility. When the MAI burst into the public spotlight in spring 1997, for instance, it took most members of Parliament and even members of Cabinet entirely by surprise.

CORPORATIONS RULE DFAIT

Canadian NGOs are concerned about DFAIT for other reasons as well. For the last two decades, big business has been building an intimate relationship with the trade bureaucrats in the Canadian government. After all, free trade was the brainchild of corporate North America. It is in their interest to get government officials onside.

As early as 1981, Tom d'Aquino, CEO of the Business Council on National Issues (BCNI), the Canadian corporate lobby group, was holding regular meetings with key American corporate leaders and the U.S. Ambassador to Canada, Paul Robinson. (Robinson was a passionate anticommunist and former finance official in the Republican party, a big Ronald Reagan booster and early Brian Mulroney supporter.) The goal of the BCNI rendezvous was to promote a free trade agreement between Canada and the United States. The BCNI, made up of the 150 most powerful banking, manufacturing, resource, insurance, retail, telecommunications, and energy corporations in Canada (many of them branch plants of American transnationals), had been established only a few years earlier. Its goal was to increase the voice and clout of big business in setting the direction of economic and social policy in Canada. Operating as a virtual Shadow Cabinet behind the federal government in Ottawa, the BCNI has had a major impact on every government policy since 1985, including privatization of Crown corporations, competition legislation, government downsizing, energy deregulation, deficit reduction, tax reform favouring the wealthy, and cuts to cultural and social programs.

In an interview for journalist Marci McDonald's 1998 book, *Yankee Doodle Dandy*, d'Aquino said that he had gradually come to see that the transnational corporation was "the train that was leading the world economy," pushing back on the "frontiers" of nation-state policies. He knew he had to bring this "entirely new concept of economic globalization" to Canada. He also realized, however, that neither he nor American politicians nor business interests could be seen as the instigators of any continental initiative. "I knew it had to come from the Canadians." So when Brian Mulroney took office in 1984, the BCNI had a report waiting for him, outlining the rationale and program for a continental trade agreement.

Over the next four years, leading up to the 1988 "free trade" election, in which John Turner opposed Brian Mulroney's infatuation with free trade, an unprecedented collaboration grew up between Simon Reisman and his trade team at the Trade Negotiations Office, the BCNI, and the American Coalition for Trade Expansion with Canada — an industry alliance of six hundred powerful corporations and industry associations, with a combined workforce of sixty million, led by American Express. Many members of this coalition became directly involved, financially and strategically, with the Canadian pro–free trade lobby and the Trade Negotiations Office.

Industry leaders such as Shell, IBM, Weyerhaeuser (who bought out British Columbia forestry giant MacMillan Bloedel in 1999), Allied Signal, AT&T,

Cargill, General Motors, 3M, General Electric, and Dow Chemical not only spent undisclosed millions of dollars promoting the deal in Washington, where it had little political profile, but also gave millions more to the Canadian campaign, siphoning donations to Mulroney's Conservatives through their subsidiaries in the BCNI.

THE FREE TRADE PRICE TAG

Canadian corporations spent, at a conservative estimate, Can$19 million on pro–free trade advertising and in donations to the Conservative party in 1988. For example, Alcan, the Royal Bank, and Noranda each put up Can$400,000. Nineteen foreign-controlled corporations — including Shell, who gave Can$250,000; Texaco, who gave Can$100,000; and Ford, who gave Can$30,000 — contributed directly to the Canadian corporate campaign to promote free trade.

Gordon Ritchie, who served as deputy chief negotiator to Simon Reisman at the Trade Negotiations Office, published a book in 1998, called *Wrestling with the Elephant: The Inside Story of the Canada–U.S. Trade Wars*. In one of its chapters, entitled "Connecting the Levers," he describes the close association that grew up between the captains of Canadian industry and the TNO, a relationship that has grown in intensity since then. Reisman and Ritchie set up a network of sectoral advisory committees to provide them with advice on every aspect of the negotiations, and each group was composed of the chief executives of a particular industry sector. (Like the financing for the Trade Negotiations Office itself, the budget for these industry groups was supplied by External Affairs.)

"In a radical departure from past practice, I assigned two TNO staffers to each of these groups . . . ," wrote Ritchie. "Over the opposition of the traditionalists, I shared our intelligence with these advisors, who were naturally sworn to confidentiality, to a degree never seen before nor, am I told, since. In exchange, they provided us with the very best information and advice they could give. As they came to understand the shape of the deal making, they broke through the traditional business rhetoric to come up with pragmatic and imaginative ways of achieving national objectives. . . . That enabled them to explain to their colleagues in other firms outside the consultations that this or that concession was required to make the agreement possible. . . . Their contribution was absolutely indispensable and changed forever the way the government managed trade policies. . .

"In addition to the sectoral issues, there were a number of overarching questions on which it was essential to solicit the contribution of the business leadership. For this purpose, yet another committee was established, the top-level International Advisory Committee (ITAC), chaired by the chief executive of Northern Telecom, Walter Light. . . . The membership was a Who's Who of the elite of Canadian business, including such icons as David Culver of Alcan, whose company had been hard hit by earlier American protectionism; Alf Powis of Noranda, who may have been the single most important influence on Brian Mulroney; and Philippe de Gaspé Beaubien of Telemedia . . .

"I strongly encouraged successive trade ministers to put in an appearance at these meetings. I also attended every ITAC meeting personally from beginning to end. . . . This arrangement paid substantial dividends. The quality of advice was very high, on such broad issues as the handling of the unfair trade laws. . . . Ultimately perhaps even more important was the ITAC's identification of the pressing need for business to support the agreement once negotiated."

Once established, this relationship between the trade bureaucracy in Ottawa and the country's business elite was never broken. So when the Free Trade Agreement's successor, NAFTA, came up for negotiation, it was not necessary to wage such a high-profile campaign. Besides, the Liberals were now in power, and they were clearly onside by the time they took office in 1993. And they delivered. The North American Free Trade Agreement (NAFTA) came into being in 1994. (So happy was the big business community with the Chrétien Liberals that they rewarded the party with record contributions throughout the 1990s, far surpassing anything they had ever given the Mulroney Tories, even in 1988, the year Mulroney stumped across the country singing the virtues of the FTA.)

So it was not long before the newly formed DFAIT, in partnership with the big business community, launched the Team Canada trade missions to open up new markets in Asia and Latin America. Jean Chrétien and Canada's corporate elite wined and dined with the Chinese leaders who had ordered the student massacre in Tiananmen Square, politicians and business leaders in Latin American countries still openly participating in human rights abuses, and the Suharto regime in Indonesia, shilling while there for Canadian businesses interested in lucrative contracts in war-torn East Timor. In a 1997 trade mission to South Korea with several hundred CEOs, Jean Chrétien was whisked away from a military crackdown on a worker demonstration. When asked to comment on what he had seen, the prime minister had only this to say: "It's a local concern."

The Team Canada trade missions demonstrate the extent to which the Canadian government, through its Department of Foreign Affairs and International Trade, has become a tool of big business to promote their interests. As a result, Canada's international reputation has fundamentally changed. As one senior DFAIT official said, "We used to go with lists of political prisoners we wanted released. Now we go in with lists of companies that want contracts."

Similarly, DFAIT worked intimately with the Canadian corporate community to promote the 1997 meeting of member-nations of the Asia-Pacific Economic Cooperation forum (APEC) in Vancouver. At the 1995 APEC meeting, a permanent business advisory forum — ABAC (the APEC Business Advisory Council) — had been established to work in partnership with APEC political leaders and bureaucrats. And the heads of state of the APEC countries agreed to work closely with these business leaders in order to "examine ways to implement the ABAC recommendations," according to the signed agreement. By the time APEC came to Canada, the relationship was cemented. DFAIT published a list of "Diamond, Platinum, Gold, and Silver Sponsors" — corporations who were given a range of special rewards for their sponsorship, including "exposure to senior government leaders," depending on the level of contribution.

Another DFAIT-corporate collusion became evident in the aftermath of the dispute over the Multilateral Agreement on Investment (MAI). When citizens' groups in Canada heard about the treaty in late 1996, they were told by the office of then Minister for International Trade Roy MacLaren that it didn't exist, and it wasn't until they received a copy surreptitiously in March 1997 that the government confirmed the document's existence. The department hotly denied that it had been secretive in its pursuit of the MAI, insisting that it had consulted widely with the Canadian public over the treaty.

But through access to information provisions, a list of all the groups the government had met with on this issue was obtained, and it shows that DFAIT had misled citizens' groups. Meetings with environmental, culture, and labour groups had not taken place until 1997 — *after* the MAI became a public issue. However, DFAIT had been meeting with the business community throughout 1995 and 1996. In fact, the Canadian Chamber of Commerce and the Canadian Council on International Issues — the international arm of the BCNI — and "member companies" had received private DFAIT briefings on the MAI as early as 1993, four years before the government later admitted it was even involved in such negotiations.

DFAIT's pro-business bias in the MAI talks was evident in a summer 1998 briefing paper it released, closing the door on any possibility of granting citizens the same rights as corporations in the MAI: "It has been suggested that labour unions should equally have access to the investor-state dispute mechanism (giving them equal rights to sue governments for lost power). However, opening up the investor-state mechanism to special interest groups will further complicate the drafting of the MAI."

STRUCTURALLY ADJUSTED CANADA

The ascendancy of trade and finance over all other policy considerations of government, coupled with the undue influence of big business interests over the operations of DFAIT, has serious ramifications for all Canadians. And the scenario has deteriorated even further with the growing influence of foreign-based business interests over the Canadian economy and, therefore, over Canadian trade policy.

In effect, a whole new governing structure has been established to bypass the traditional systems of government and democratic rights of Canadians. This structure vets all government policy — social, environmental, and economic — on behalf of Canadian and foreign-based transnational corporations who are seeking a "level playing field" of deregulation and the privatization of sectors like health care and education, which still remain in the public domain. The Canadian government's new mantra might be "What's good for Seagram's or Nortel Networks or, more likely, Wal-Mart and Coca-Cola, is good for Canada and Canadians." All policy decisions are reviewed by DFAIT on behalf of corporate interests as defined by the BCNI for their impact on trade and profit, and many are proposed and drafted by the global corporate community in the first place. All other concerns, both at home and internationally, including issues of social justice and human rights, on which Canada had traditionally shown leadership, now take a back seat to promoting the bottom line.

NAFTA and the WTO are doing to Canada what the International Monetary Fund and the World Bank did to Third World nations fifteen years ago. Canada is being "structurally adjusted" into the global economy where "winners" — both corporations and individuals — are sorted from losers, and the winners take all.

THE VANISHING BORDER

"So here we are, at the butt end of the twentieth century that was supposed to belong to Canada, only to find that Canada no longer belongs to us," lamented *Maclean's* editorial writer Peter C. Newman in an essay penned on the eve of the new millennium. He was referring to the most recent spate of reports documenting the spectacular rise in American economic domination of Canadian industry and natural resources. As grim as the numbers outlined in Newman's essay are, a May 2000 StatsCan study demonstrated that the situation is steadily worsening. In 1997, the latest year for figures, foreign-controlled companies, mostly American, accounted for 31.5 percent of all corporate revenues in Canada — up from 25 percent in 1988. U.S. direct investment in Canada soared in those same years, climbing to Can$173 billion, from Can$80 billion in 1989. Total direct foreign investment rose to Can$240 billion, from Can$122 billion.

These numbers do not tell the whole story, however. The feeding frenzy has escalated, and there is no doubt that the percentages are now worse than when StatsCan prepared its latest figures. Since 1997, hundreds of healthy Canadian companies have fallen victim to global merger mania — in 1998 alone, two hundred were swallowed. In 1999, the numbers and sizes of takeovers were so great that for the first time, Canadians now control a smaller portion of their own productive wealth than the citizens of any other Industrialized Nation on earth.

Ameritech, a large regional phone company in the United States, has bought 20 percent of Bell Canada; Weyerhaeuser has bought MacMillan Bloedel, an icon of British Columbia's forestry industry; Newcourt Credit

Group, the Canadian financial services up-and-comer, has been purchased by CIT of the U.S.; Nova Chemicals of Alberta has moved to Pittsburgh; and Peoples Jewellers and Shoppers Drug Mart have joined earlier acquisitions of the 1990s, like Tim Horton, the Bauer sporting goods company, Labatt Breweries, and Henry Birks & Sons. Of all these takeovers, only 4 percent were reviewed to ascertain whether any net benefit would accrue to Canada as a result of the merger. And since Brian Mulroney dismantled the Foreign Investment Review Agency (FIRA) in 1985, not one foreign takeover has been denied by the Canadian government.

There is also an untold story behind the StatsCan numbers: many Canadian companies that appear to be Canadian to the core and are counted by StatsCan as such, have, already left the country. Seagram is now run out of Manhattan, and though Nortel Networks maintains offices and some research operations in Canada, its Dallas office has effectively become its world headquarters, and all of its business divisions are run from the United States. Over two hundred Canadian companies — many of the big players, like Four Seasons Hotels, Gulf Canada, Newbridge Networks, and BioChem Pharma — are listed on U.S. stock exchanges, where more than half their stocks are traded.

Analysts in the resource sector warn that the global march to consolidate is moving into high gear in Canada. The planned Can$6 billion merger of Abitibi-Consolidated Inc. and Donohoe Inc. of the U.S. will see the former join a distinguished list of Canadian industry giants like Alcan Aluminium and Norcen Energy Resources that have been absorbed in recent years by mergers with foreign partners. Houston-based Burlington Resources Inc. spent nearly Can$3 billion for Calgary's Poco Petroleum in 1999. And this megacorp joins a wave of American energy giants that are crossing into Canada: Union Pacific Resources Group of Fort Worth, Texas; Houston-based USX-Marathon Group; Pioneer Natural Resources of Irving, Texas; and Dominion Resources of Richmond, Virginia. Their targets, according to industry sources, are Placer Dome, Inco, Renaissance Energy, Fletcher Challenge Canada, Alliance Forest Products, and Domtar.

THE GREAT TAKEOVER RACE

Although it seriously accelerated during 1999, the race to take over Canadian business received its most significant impetus from the Free

Trade Agreement, which came into effect on January 1, 1989. Trade between the two countries has more than doubled since; it now totals a daily $1.3 billion, compared to about $500 million a day in 1988. But in the process, the FTA totally reoriented Canada's economic axis from east-west to north-south. Instead of perpetuating this nation's founding metaphor of a bounteous land stretching from sea to sea, our defining horizon now faces due south. The FTA, later strengthened by the more widely ranging 1994 North American Free Trade Agreement, has placed this country into the jaws of a magnet that has transformed the very essence of being Canadian. We have, willy-nilly, become less the citizens of a country than of a continent.

Peter C. Newman, "The Year of Living Dangerously,"
Maclean's, 20 December 1999

There are many reasons to be concerned about this trend. (Even the Business Council on National Issues and some Canadian corporate leaders are sounding the alarm.) As Canadian author and publisher Mel Hurtig points out, the vast majority of these "investments" are takeovers of existing companies that do not bring new money into Canada or create any new jobs. In addition, decision-making powers and senior jobs have moved south of the border. Fewer research dollars are invested in Canada and fewer charitable donations are available to Canadians, since foreign-based companies spend research dollars in the country where their head office is located and charitable donations are made in their nation of origin.

Most important, however, is the loss of government control over corporate behaviour and the political and economic agenda of foreign-based corporations. Firms that once operated independently are being forced to conduct business according to imported plans and values, and governments have much less authority to insist that some of the economic benefit enjoyed by the private sector be returned to the community — which, of course, fits with the purposes of the transnationals. And if Wal-Mart wants to circumvent provincial labour laws in its treatment of employees — the company calls them "associates" — it does so with impunity, knowing that governments will not risk offending a company with such power. All indicators point to an intensification of this economic model as well as the disappearance of a separate Canadian economy within North America.

ENERGY SELL-OUT

The double bind applies to many sectors — but especially to energy. American energy companies, which already heavily dominated the Canadian oil patch, were major backers of the Canada–U.S. Free Trade Agreement. They worked closely with the industry on both sides of the border and with the Reagan administration to promote a continental energy accord that would lock in deregulation of the Canadian energy sector for all time.

The FTA was negotiated in the mid-1980s against a backdrop of media reports that the United States was running out of power. The American Gas Association reported in 1986 that supplies in the lower forty-eight states were virtually gone, and a 1985 U.S. Congressional report called Canada's regulatory control over its natural gas a "direct restriction of American rights to Canadian gas." It called for the American government to make guaranteed access to Canadian supplies a point of national security. Ann Hughes, the ranking U.S. Commerce Department negotiator, was forthright about her country's wasteful energy habits and admitted that Canada's energy, secured by the free trade deal, would forestall conservation practices in the United States. Edward Ney, then U.S. Ambassador to Canada, said later that access to Canada's energy reserves was the U.S.'s prime motivation for entering into the negotiations.

In his famous 1984 New York "open for business" speech, newly elected Prime Minister Brian Mulroney called the practice of maintaining emergency reserves "odious" and, declaring that Canada had not been built by expropriating "other people's property," promised American business full access to Canada's energy supplies. His government moved quickly to deregulate oil and gas exports and dismantle most restrictions on American foreign investment in the energy industry, further opening up Canada's resources to domination by an ever-smaller, ever-more powerful group of transnational corporations with no interest in Canada.

The National Energy Board was stripped of its powers, and the "vital-supply safeguard" requiring Canada to maintain a twenty-five-year surplus of natural gas was dismantled. No government agency or law now exists to ensure that Canadians will have adequate supplies of their own energy in the future. The United States, however, declared that its twenty-five-year reserve was necessary for national security purposes, and maintained it. Export applicants, Canadian or American, were no longer required to file an export impact assessment and the all-Canadian gas distribution system was abandoned, setting off a frantic round of north-south pipeline construction. Export taxes on our energy supplies were banned, resulting in lost tax revenue for governments and giving American customers, who don't have to pay the GST, a price advantage over Canadian consumers.

Most important, both the FTA, signed in 1989, and NAFTA, signed in 1994, imposed a system of "proportional sharing," whereby Canadian energy supplies to the U.S. are guaranteed in perpetuity. In an astonishing surrender of sovereignty, the government of Canada agreed under the FTA that it no longer has the right to "refuse to issue a licence or revoke or change a licence for the exportation to the United States of energy goods," even for environmental or conservation practices.

This led to a spectacular increase in the sale of natural gas to U.S. markets; since deregulation in 1986, exports have more than quadrupled to over 8.5 billion cubic feet a day. About 55 percent of total Canadian gas production is exported to the U.S., where American distribution companies, supplying a much larger population, have been able to sign long-term contracts at rock-bottom prices. Canadian consumers are left to compete for their own energy resources against an economy ten times as large, with rapidly dwindling reserves and accelerating demand.

The story in oil is the same. Canada now produces 2.3 million barrels a day and ships 1.3 million of those barrels south of the border. This has allowed the U.S. to dip into its reserves without concern. Amid a tripling of crude oil prices, U.S. Energy Secretary Bill Richardson assured Americans in October 2000 that the potential for disruptions along the Eastern Seaboard is minimal, thanks to the fact that Canada is a "secure supplier."

The free trade agreements committed Canada to an energy policy driven by massive, guaranteed exports to the U.S., corporate control of supplies, and an economy more dependent than ever on the exploitation of primary resources. And because the agreements exempted Canadian government subsidies for oil and gas exploration from trade challenge, Canadian tax-payers continue to pay for uncontrolled and environmentally destructive fossil fuel exploration

— a process that has already destroyed habitats in the North and that threatens the sensitive spawning grounds off Cape Breton and Newfoundland. The primary beneficiaries of the destruction and the drain on Canadian pocketbooks are transnational corporations. And Canada has one more excuse to not honour its Kyoto commitments to reduce emissions of fossil fuels.

AUTO PACT OVERTURNED

The auto industry in Canada has been one of the crucial engines of Canada's success in the global economy and accounts for one-quarter of the growth in Canada's exports between 1988 and 1998. For every job created in this sector, five more jobs are created in related industries. It has thrived under a system that is the very opposite of free trade and was established prior to the implementation of the FTA, NAFTA, and the GATT.

The Auto Pact, created in 1965, was a deal worked out between the Canadian and U.S. governments so the Big Three automobile makers — Ford, GM, and Chrysler — could sell their cars in Canada tariff free, in exchange for creating jobs here. The basic principle, anathema to a free trade philosophy, was that, if foreign corporations were going to sell in the Canadian market, they had a duty to produce in that market. The companies agreed to assemble as many vehicles in Canada as they sell here, and they had to meet certain "value-added" requirements to create Canadian jobs in auto parts. The Canadian Auto Workers Union says that without the Auto Pact, there would probably be no auto industry in Canada today.

In a fall 2000 ruling, however, the WTO struck down the Auto Pact, saying that it discriminated against other automakers, particularly manufacturers of cheap imports from Asia. This ruling will eliminate the Big Three's preferential tariff system, imposing additional costs on the very companies that are investing most heavily in Canadian production and jobs. Furthermore, the number of car imports is going to soar, all sides agree — which means trouble for Canadian jobs. As GM spokesperson Tayce Wakefield put it, "Increases in imports are exports in jobs." Once again, the interests of global trade and the transcendent power of DFAIT in the Canadian government have forced the government to abandon an economic policy designed to benefit Canadians.

CULTURAL DIVERSITY TARGETED

The same juggernaut of corporate foreign domination and the imperatives of the free trade agreements have subjected the remains of Canadian culture to further assault. Not satisfied with its already dominant position in Canada, the American entertainment industry is using both NAFTA and the WTO to kill the few measures that still exist to protect Canadian culture. This assault has repeatedly pitted DFAIT against successive ministers of culture, a struggle in which culture invariably loses.

Culture was a contentious issue in both the NAFTA and the WTO negotiations. The Mulroney and Chrétien governments insisted that they had gained full protection for Canadian culture in NAFTA by calling for the inclusion of an exemption for cultural industries and policies. However, this so-called exemption is subject to a "notwithstanding" clause, which gives the U.S. the right to retaliate with measures of "equivalent commercial effect" in *any other* sector, if Canada invokes the exemption clause. In other words, Canada would have to be prepared to pay for the right to maintain a distinct culture. U.S. negotiator Peter Murphy called the exemption a "joke" and said he used it to wring other concessions out of Canada.

The WTO allows no exclusion at all for culture, not even the meaningless one contained in NAFTA. Hence, the U.S. chose the WTO to pursue its case against Canada's modest magazine protections, although it continued to use NAFTA threats of retaliation when Canada attempted to get around the measures at issue. In 1997, the WTO ruled that Canadian magazines are a "good," and that under the National Treatment clause of the GATT, their country of origin is irrelevant. Now, Canadian magazine "goods" cannot be favoured or protected over American magazine "goods" in Canada. The Canadian industry fears a flood of American magazines on the Canadian market and the subsequent loss of dozens, perhaps hundreds, of Canadian magazines. There was never any thought that Canada would ever oppose the ruling. Heritage Minister Sheila Copps was sent out to sell the "compromise" to the Canadian public, backed up when needed by then Minister for International Trade Sergio Marchi. U.S. Trade Representative Charlene Barshefsky was jubilant, stating that the WTO ruling would be precedent-setting for all of Canada's remaining cultural measures.

Christopher Sands of the Centre for Strategic and International Studies in Washington says that the U.S. had two reasons for taking such a hard line against Canada over the magazine issue. The first was that any exemption for Canada would set a negative precedent for other countries, especially in Europe and the Nonindustrialized World, where cultural diversity is emerging as a stumbling block to unfettered international trade.

The other was that the United States was still angry at the role Canadian social and cultural activists had played in rousing opposition to the MAI. "What further startled U.S. policymakers," Sands observes, "was to hear these Canadian arguments echoed in Europe and even Asia. In an increasingly small world, ideas travel fast, and the Canadian concern that the MAI would lead to greater American cultural hegemony touched a chord around the world. The lesson for U.S. trade negotiators: Canada's example matters."

The bureaucrats and politicians at DFAIT couldn't have said it better.

FARMERS ABANDONED

The pattern is repeated in the farm sector. Canada has allowed transnational agrifood corporations to enter the country on their own terms, displacing thousands of family farms and totally dominating many sectors. And the WTO provisions on food security and agriculture have had a further enormous impact on Canadian farmers. Prodded by American agribusiness corporations, the U.S. government has taken repeated action under both North American trade agreements and the WTO to outlaw Canada's food supply management and orderly marketing board systems as unfair trade practices, although it is these very systems that guarantee a fair return at the farm gate.

In another sinister turn of events, under DFAIT's tutelage, farm subsidies have been slashed, along with farm income support. The European Union and, to a lesser extent, the United States, have rightly refused to treat their farmers to such a display of injustice. European wheat farmers receive three times the amount of subsidies that Canadian wheat farmers receive; and Americans receive twice as much. So Canada, in an apparent fit of quixotic self-destruction, has unilaterally disarmed itself — at the expense of one of the lowest-paid and most dangerous occupations in the country.

Meanwhile, the farmer-victims went ahead and did what the government told them to do. They diversified, expanded, invested in new technology, and moved heavily into export and genetically engineered crops — egged on by government policies and representatives. While they increased their exports, all right — by five and a half percent in just over a decade — their net income dropped 25 percent. Nineteen-ninety-nine was the worst year for Canadian farmers since 1926, the year such records began to be kept.

Agriculture, or agribusiness, as it is now called, has undergone more profound changes than almost any other sector. No longer working to produce food for people, farmers are being sent on a mission to gather profits for food corporations. The food on the average North American plate travels over 1,500 miles to get the dinner table; the notion of local producers feeding local communities in exchange for the support of those communities is rapidly fading. The hollowing out of rural Canada is the inevitable and tragic result.

HEALTH CARE AT RISK

Canadian writer and health care expert Colleen Fuller explains that, using the free trade agreements as its overarching legal and financial framework, the Canadian government has switched priorities in health care. Guided by DFAIT and Industry Canada, she says, the overriding political commitment is no longer to provide universal coverage as a public service, but to develop a domestic health industry that can participate effectively in global markets.

In a November 1996 report, Industry Canada declared that it was facing a challenge: how to turn Canada's excellent reputation for high-quality and affordable health services and the world-renowned expertise and skill of Canadian health care workers into a profitable global commodity. Industry Canada officials have concluded that the domestic industry must "consolidate" to create companies big enough to compete on the open market, and that it must attract foreign — that is, American — participation. Without such support, they claim, the whole enterprise will be doomed to failure, as Canadian firms don't have the "requisite outlook and orientation."

While Health Minister Allan Rock is publicly defending universal health care, Fuller observes, DFAIT, as it explains on its website, is gathering intelligence to find investor-partners for "strategic alliances" in priority sectors, such as health care. For this, it enlists the services of Canadian consulates and embassies, which fall under DFAIT's jurisdiction, as "matchmakers" between Canadian and foreign-based private health companies. Forming alliances with U.S. companies, explains DFAIT literature, will help Canadian health care "investors" navigate through unfamiliar territory. Under the "Corporate Advocacy

Program" (CAP), embassy staff are told to promote CAP goals of "investment attraction, retention and expansion of existing U.S. investment in Canada."

A partnership has been established between the International Affairs Directorate (IAD) of Health Canada, DFAIT, and Industry Canada, with the aims of promoting a thriving domestic for-profit health care industry in Canada, seeking foreign investment, and exporting Canadian health care expertise to the world. At an October 1997 press conference, IAD's director general, Ed Aiston, openly acknowledged that Health Canada's role in the project is "a realization that investment in health is beneficial to the Canadian economy and part of the understanding in our Department that Health Canada is not only a regulatory body but also needs to be an ally of the Canadian business community." He added that these initiatives "are carried out in full recognition of the lead of Foreign Affairs and International Trade Canada and Industry Canada."

GOING TO THE BANK FOR A CHECK-UP

In community and home care, large companies such as ComCARE Alliance, Olsten Corp., ParaMed, We Care, Columbia Health Care Inc., MDS, and countless others, both Canadian and U.S.-based, have secured a presence that would have been unthinkable just five years ago. This is happening with the significant involvement of institutions such as the Toronto Dominion Bank, the Canadian Imperial Bank of Commerce, and the investment dealers on both sides of the border.

Colleen Fuller, presentation to the Senate Social Affairs Committee, 6 April 2000

Under NAFTA, once these companies establish a beachhead, it is next to impossible to dislodge them. Corporate rights vested in the agreement would force governments to pay huge amounts of compensation if they ever tried to bring these services back under public control. And the WTO has been weighing into Canada's health system on other fronts. In a fall 2000 ruling, the WTO told the Canadian government to amend its law to give an additional three years of protection on drug patents issued to mostly foreign-based pharmaceutical companies before 1989. If Canada did not do this, it would face the possibility of economic sanctions from the United States. The Canadian Health Coalition has declared that this will likely add another Can$100 million to the cost of drugs in Canada over the next several years as people lose access to the cheaper generic drugs. Canadian consumers will be the losers, since the price hikes will come on top of increases of almost 90 percent in the last decade.

There was not a peep from Health Canada on the ruling. No wonder. As IAD Director General Aiston explains it, Health Canada's goals include efforts to harmonize the regulatory framework governing Canada's health sector with global rules — efforts that will "make us key partners in the Canadian export of medical and pharmaceutical products and in the promotion of foreign investments in Canada."

So it can come as no surprise that Health Canada is also sitting back and allowing the GATS negotiations to go ahead under the direction of DFAIT's Sergio Marchi and Pierre Pettigrew. The stated commitment by all member-countries in these talks is to a continuous, open-ended process of services liberalization, including health care. Already, even under the current GATS agreement, Canada's health (and education and social services) sectors are in jeopardy. Parties have agreed that some rules apply "horizontally" — that is, across the board — whether or not the area has been officially included.

Among the horizontal rules that already apply to health are "Most Favoured Nation" status, which means that once the corporations from one country are operating in your market, you must open your doors to corporations from all countries. In addition, regulations in any given sector must be "least trade restrictive," and all WTO member-countries must be prepared to include market mechanisms wherever possible, even in social programs.

Canada has unfortunately agreed to open discussions on making "National Treatment" a horizontal rule. This would mean that, even if the current exemptions for education and health were maintained (and there appears to be little chance of that), foreign corporations could still be given the right to "establish a commercial presence" in Canada and compete for public funding in these areas.

Perhaps most disturbing, under the current GATS exemption, however, is the fact that a sector must be completely financed by government and have no commercial purpose if it is to be protected from a potential onslaught of transnational competitors. Since very few areas in Canada's health or education sectors are commercial free anymore, health and education as a whole are vulnerable. Alberta's Bill 11, permitting for-profit corporations to compete with public hospitals for public funding to provide health care "services," has already opened the door to U.S. and other for-profit foreign corporations. Now they can use the current GATS agreement to force their way into not just Alberta, but any province in Canada. There is little ambiguity in Alberta's abandonment of the provisions of the Canada Health Act; once Canadian private companies are allowed to provide services in areas covered by the Act, foreign corporations will have unassailable rights under the current WTO to enter Canada. Further, if any future government tries to bring this sector back into the public realm, under NAFTA's "investor-state" rules, it will have to pay huge compensation to any American corporations who have established businesses in Canada. The costs would probably prove to be too onerous for any government. The reality is simple: once privatization is established in any public sector, it will be almost impossible to reverse.

Under the proposed new GATS rules, foreign, for-profit health (and education) corporations will have the right to establish themselves in Canada; they will have the right to compete for public dollars with public institutions like hospitals; standards for health professionals will be subject to WTO rules and reviewed to ensure they are not an impediment to trade; foreign-based telemedicine services will become legal; and no country will be able to stop low-cost health professionals from crossing borders to compete with their higher-paid colleagues. The GATS will kill medicare.

CONSTITUTIONAL CONSTRAINTS

The implications go beyond the individual programs and services involved, like health care, no matter how important they are to Canadians. Fundamentally, because of the ascendancy of a new corporate- and trade-driven regime in the Canadian government, Canada's constitution is being rewritten in front of our very eyes. Because of NAFTA and the WTO, Canada's democratic model of a parliamentary democracy is also being re-routed and drawn into the American constitutional orbit. Alberta constitutional law expert David Schneiderman explains that these trade regimes are grounded in U.S. constitutional principles and law, favouring private property rights law over the more public-oriented system established in Canada.

The most blatant example of this is the "investor-state" provision of NAFTA — Chapter 11 — which allows corporations, for the first time in any international trade agreement, to directly sue the government of a NAFTA member-country for any lost profit, even prospective lost profit, that results from government actions. As trade lawyer Barry Appleton explains, "They could be putting liquid plutonium in children's food; if you ban it and the company making it is an American company, you have to pay compensation."

Chapter 11 has already been used successfully by Virginia-based Ethyl Corp. to force the Canadian government to reverse its legislation banning the cross-border sale of its product, MMT, a gasoline additive that has been outlawed in many countries and which Jean Chrétien once called a "dangerous neurotoxin." S.D. Myers, an American PCB waste-disposal company, also successfully used a Chapter 11 threat to force Canada to reverse its ban on PCB imports, and is now claiming U.S.$50 million in damages. Sun Belt Water Inc. of Santa Barbara, California, likewise, is suing the Canadian government for Can$14 billion because British Columbia banned the export of bulk water in 1993, thereby eliminating any opportunities for the company to get into the water-export business in that province.

The environmental implications of Chapter 11 are far-reaching and self-evident. Any new regulations that are brought to Parliament can be challenged by American corporations with interests in the sector in question. Governments now have to be prepared to pay dearly for the birthrights of their own citizens — in this case, the right to a safe and healthy physical environment. To avoid this scenario, Canadian federal and provincial governments now have to send all their prospective environmental and natural resource protection regulations to DFAIT for examination.

In an October 2000 exchange at a parliamentary Environment Committee meeting, Liberal MP Clifford Lincoln asked senior DFAIT officials Nigel Bankes and Ken Macartney whether Minister of International Trade Pierre Pettigrew was actually fighting against the inclusion of the Precautionary Principle in domestic environmental and health legislation like the proposed new law governing pesticide use — in order to ensure that Canada was complying with the WTO. Nigel Bankes said, "On that specific question, has the department been arguing against simple references to the Precautionary Principle? I think you are correct. I'm aware of at least one instance of that."

Environment ministers now have much less power over their jurisdictions than do their trade counterparts. When the environment ministers of the three NAFTA countries announced in December 1998 that they were going to allow the Commission for Environmental Co-operation (CEC) — the NAFTA side-deal that has become a toothless "environmental watchdog" — to scrutinize these Chapter 11 cases, they stepped far over the line drawn for them by DFAIT and its sister agencies in Washington and Mexico City. Months later, the environment ministers totally retracted the new powers, reining in the agency so far that they nearly dismantled it altogether.

COMMERCIALIZING PUBLIC POLICY

The investor-state suit provisions of NAFTA represent nothing short of a radical departure from both the domestic and international legal norms in at least three fundamental ways. First, by providing corporations with the right to directly enforce an international treaty to which they are neither parties, nor under which they have any obligations. Second, by extending international commercial arbitration to claims that have nothing to do with commercial contracts and everything to do with public policy and law. Third, by creating substantive legal rights concerning expropriation and national treatment that go far beyond those available to Canadian citizens or businesses.

Steven Shrybman, report to Council of Canadians, June 2000

Further, decisions about NAFTA and WTO challenges in one area can have far-reaching implications across the spectrum. U.S. courier giant United Parcel Service of America (UPS) is suing the federal government for over Can$200 million under Chapter 11, alleging that, because Canada Post is a public monopoly, it is able to cross-subsidize its courier services, Xpresspost, Priority Courier, and Purolator. If it is successful, the NAFTA ruling could have enormous implications for other public agencies, such as those providing health care or child care, where there is a mix of public and local private service providers. Arguably, any use of publicly funded infrastructure could be challenged by private American companies who could either claim "national treatment" rights for equal public funding or sue for compensation instead.

These companies and others (including some Canadian companies suing the American government for similar environmental and health regulations) understand that NAFTA and the WTO give them the right to shape government policy. As Jack Lindsay, CEO of Sun Belt, has said, "Because of NAFTA, we are now stakeholders in the national water policy of Canada."

DFAIT and corporate Canada, controlled by U.S. interests, are establishing an adjudicative regime that is effectively supplanting the authority of Canadian courts. The public purpose of the Canadian legal system is being subverted by trade tribunals that are, in essence, private institutions operating in the interests of the private sector. They exist outside the confines of Canadian courts, Canadian tradition, and Canadian law, and they are undermining the very foundations of our judicial system and its democratic heritage.

The result is that instead of addressing economic, social, and environmental policy questions through Parliament, the federal and provincial governments are increasingly creating policy based on U.S. property rights principles. The property and indirectly the political rights of corporations — Canadian and transnational — are enhanced, while the political rights of governments and citizens are, at best, diminished, and, at worst, struck down.

THE NEW CANADA

During fifteen years of life under the new rules of economic globalization, the changes ordinary Canadians have experienced have been nothing short of revolutionary. Canada's economy has been drawn into the American orbit, affecting the judicial system and Canada's economic and cultural structures. But there have been other consequences as well. Socially, Canada now looks more like the U.S. than ever before, with its huge gaps between haves and have-nots. As in the United States, great prosperity abounds in some quarters in Canada, but equally extreme poverty is growing in others.

THE DOWNHILL SLIDE

Since 1989, the year the Canada–U.S. Free Trade Agreement was signed and the year Parliament voted unanimously to eradicate child poverty by the year 2000:

- the number of poor children has grown by 60 percent
- the number of children in families with incomes less than $20,000 has grown by 65 percent
- the number of children in families needing social assistance has grown by 51 percent

- **the number of children living in unaffordable rental housing has grown by 91 percent.**

  1999 Annual Report of Campaign 2000, a coalition of Canadian groups concerned about child poverty, including the Canadian Council for Social Development, the Centre for International Statistics, and the National Council of Welfare

In the last decade, the number of millionaires in Canada has tripled, and corporate salaries have grown at an average rate of about 15 percent per year. In 1999, for instance, compensation for the top one hundred CEOs in Canada grew by 112 percent — regardless of whether their companies' profits rose or fell. In that same decade, Canada experienced the highest rise in child poverty in the industrialized world. During the very years that corporate salaries sky-rocketed, workers' wages rose just 2 percent, less than the rate of inflation. And more and more Canadians are employed in the "precarious" workforce — part-time or self-employed, with no security, pensions, or benefits.

Workers have also been hurt by the dramatic drop in Employment Insurance (EI) benefits. Cuts of about $7 billion a year to the unemployed have left only one-third of unemployed workers now receiving Employment Insurance benefits they have already paid for, compared to almost 80 percent in 1989 (mirroring the trend for similar payments in the U.S.). Because of federal cuts to social programs as a percentage of total federal government spending, social funding is also at its lowest levels since the 1950s.

The cuts to social programs and EI have been so deep that Standard and Poors says the myth of a "kinder Canada" must be put to rest. In 1999, for the first time, says the New York–based ratings institute, Canada spent less on its elderly and unemployed than did the United States.

The cuts to EI and social programs have, not surprisingly, hit the poor far harder than the rest of Canadians. A new study by Statistics Canada researchers John Myles and Garnett Picot shows that low-income families with children were able to stay afloat before these cuts, but that now they are drowning. Study after study has also confirmed that average Canadians are worse off than they were ten years ago, and a new report from the Vanier Institute for the Family indicates that Canadian families are currently facing their worst debt wall since the 1930s.

These fundamental changes to the fabric of life in Canada have affected Canadians and their values. In its annual survey of the country, the polling firm Environics has been mapping the Canadian mood for seventeen years. The 1999 year-end survey revealed some very distressing long-term trends.

Canadians are experiencing a growing sense of insecurity, aimlessness, and personal and social disengagement and a decline in vitality. In fact, the authors warn, for many Canadians, particularly the young, this disengagement is expressed with increasing nihilism. Middle-aged people are pondering the legacy they are leaving their children, which they identify as a growing gap between rich and poor, rapidly increasing child poverty, and environmental degradation.

The respondents are clear about the reasons for this new pessimism: a shredded social security network; technological advances that create inequality of job opportunity; and a system that does not work for ordinary workers, but rather, for a small corporate elite best personified by the power and privilege of banking executives. "These days, we worry less about unlikely threats like random murderers, and more about the very real threat of becoming dinner in a dog-eat-dog society," say the authors. It's hard to get excited by reduced government debts, they add, when people feel that the debt has simply been transferred to them personally.

Many Canadians remember that it was the business press and corporate leaders who demanded that Canada reduce its debt or risk becoming a Third World country. The result, Canadians told Environics, was this: in 2000, it was no longer Canada that was poor — it was Canadians. "Overall," says the study, "Canadians believe that in recent years Canada and its corporations have been doing well, but Canadians have not, and this discrepancy is taking a heavy psychological toll."

As a result, Canadians are becoming less Canadian — less interested in democracy and politics. "At one time," say the authors of the report, "Canadians felt they had power as citizens — one person, one vote. Now they feel that what little power they have is as consumers — one dollar, one vote." Fewer Canadians would now try to put themselves in other people's shoes or to understand where they are coming from. Growing numbers of Canadians say they would participate in the black market to avoid taxes and feel little compunction about ripping off the governments and corporations they see as ripping them off on a daily basis. Canadians are not opposed to paying taxes, they told the pollsters, but feel that the rich don't pay their fair share, so why should they?

A HEMISPHERIC MODEL

Similar attitudes and trends have been identified in the other countries of the Americas as economic globalization has been adopted throughout the hemisphere in anticipation of the "deep integration" of the FTAA. Structural adjustment has caused great suffering in America's Third World Countries, as interest rates on debt payments have soared from 3 percent in 1980 to over 20 percent today. Latin America, as a region, has the highest rate of inequitable income distribution in the world, and after swallowing its free market medicine, poverty is now higher than it was in 1980. The buying power of Latin American workers is also 27 percent lower. Eighty-five percent of all job growth has been in the precarious sector with no benefits or protections.

Mexico, seven years into NAFTA, now has record-high poverty rates of 70 percent, and the average wage lost more than three-quarters of its purchasing power in those years. Ninety million Latin Americans are now indigent and 105 million have no access to any health care whatsoever. Child labour has increased dramatically, and there are now at least 19 million children working in terrible conditions throughout Latin America. Massive environmental degradation has been another side effect of Latin America's desperate rush to exploit its natural resources, and the use of pesticides and fertilizers has tripled since 1996; there are now eighty thousand chemical substances produced and used in South America.

In the face of such suffering, Canadians might expect their government to play its traditional international role and seek ways to alleviate the social and economic injustices of Latin America. But with so much of DFAIT's energy bound up in the Summit of the Americas and the advancement of the FTAA's hemispheric integration agenda, it is business as usual. Canada is exchanging its traditional narrative of "sharing for survival" — under which it created its great universal social programs — for the American social Darwinist narrative of "survival of the fittest." The corporate and political elite in Canada will celebrate their prosperity with the elite of the Americas, while those who can't fit in will be put out of sight and out of mind.

Protecting Essentials

*How people are fighting against the
global corporate assault on subsistence,
economic, and environmental rights*

*T*hey flocked by the tens of thousands to the town of Millau in southern France.
It was the last weekend in June, the first year of the third millennium. Another
mass demonstration against a WTO, IMF, or World Bank meeting? No; it was a
mobilization of popular support for José Bové, a French farmer, who, along with
nine other peasant activists, had been put on trial in the courts for their resistance
to globalization.

José was one of the organizers of the Confédération Paysanne composed of
small farmers in the region who were hit hard by price cuts on their products and
the increasing control of the food industry by big agribusiness corporations. Fed
up, several hundred farmers chose the building site of a new McDonald's franchise
in town as their target. They marched on the construction area, smashing the
emerging fast-food edifice as a symbol of their resistance to the global food and
agricultural industry.

What the Confédération Paysanne called a "festive deconstruction,"

McDonald's condemned as a wrecking party, and José and his nine militant friends were promptly charged with malicious damage and thrown in jail. Mr. Bové refused to post bail and remained in prison, issuing public statements from behind bars. In doing so, he consolidated his own personal integrity at the centre of the resistance and set the stage for what has become known as the trial of the "McDo's 10."

What triggered the protest was the U.S. embargo on the world-famous blue-seamed Roquefort cheese, made in the district of Larzac, where the town of Millau is located. When the European Union refused to abide by the WTO ruling against the E.U. ban on genetically engineered crops and food products, the U.S. retaliated by slapping 100 percent import duties on a wide range of imports, including Roquefort cheese.

One of the main staples of the regional economy, Roquefort cheese is made from the sheep's milk that José and other farmers produce. In a country that takes its food seriously, recognizing that quality food must be slowly prepared and slowly enjoyed, fast foods of all kinds have been labelled "malbouffe" or "bad grub." The very idea that quality food products like Roquefort cheese could be rejected by a global market system that allows McDonald's and other fast-food chains to flourish is anathema to José and his colleagues.

For the multitudes of Europeans who descended on Millau for the trial of the McDo's 10, José Bové and his fellow farmers had become a symbol of resistance to corporate globalization. Political cartoonists throughout Europe had already caricatured Bové's distinctive handlebar moustache, drawing them in the shape of McDonald's golden arches. Underneath one of the cartoons, a caption, in Bové's own defiant words, said it all: "Le Monde n'est pas une marchandise — et moi non plus." (The world is not for sale — and neither am I.)

THE LOCAL IS GLOBAL

As the story of José Bové and the McDo's 10 reveals, there is both a political and a cultural depth to the popular resistance wielded by civil society movements against corporate globalization. In part, what distinguishes Millau from Seattle, as well as Birmingham, Cologne, Washington, and Prague, was the fusion between the local and the global. While the big-city protests involved local people targeting the major institutions of global governance, these cities were, for the most part, immersed in the process of globalization itself. This was not the case with Millau. This town and its region were deeply victimized by corporate globalization. In this French municipality, the local and global dimensions of resistance became one.

Yet, as movement analyst Naomi Klein points out, the deeper roots of popular resistance to corporate globalization are either dismissed or distorted by global corporate moguls and their media allies. Instead, the global civil society movement is portrayed as fractured and diffuse. The pundits argue that, unlike past social movements — the labour, women's, civil rights, and peace movements — there is no overall vision or cohesive ideology behind the opposition to unfettered world trade, finance, and investment. Nor is there a single, charismatic personality leading the movement. And, most infuriating for its opponents, there is no central headquarters to target.

As already noted, the organizing model for Seattle and most of the other big-city mobilizations was neither hierarchical nor centrally controlled. On the contrary, resistance was organized in a highly decentralized and pluralistic way. For the most part, space was provided for groups to plug in, connect, and disconnect at will. This does not mean, of course, that more centralized organizations like labour unions and churches were unable to participate. But they did so within a largely decentralized and nonhierarchical movement-building process. This has proven to be one of the greatest strengths of the emergent civil society movement, making it difficult for the global managing elite and their allies to find a central target to strike down.

Is it possible, however, for a social movement characterized by decentralization and pluralism to be united around a common ideology or vision? The answer appears to be yes. And the most persistent theme underlying the mobilization of popular resistance to corporate globalization is opposition to the systematic assault on democracy and the commons. From Birmingham to Geneva, Cologne to Seattle, and Washington to Prague, the corporate hijacking of democracy and the commons has been the principal target of mass demonstrations. To borrow a phrase from previous resistance movements in Latin America, this is "the logic of the majority."

In this emerging civil society movement, there are at least six battle fronts where people are fighting for their basic rights against corporate globalization. These areas of concern — all integral parts of the defence of democracy and the commons — have to do with protecting the physical essentials of life (subsistence, economic, and ecological rights) and defending the qualities that enhance our shared humanity (social, cultural, and human rights). In a multitude of ways, popular resistance is focused on the corporate hijacking of democracy and the commons all over the world. All of these rights are equally important, but those affecting physical well-being are the most immediate, and their infringement is palpable.

FIGHTING FOR SUBSISTENCE RIGHTS

Of all the universal rights to life that people can claim on this planet, some are essential to human survival. No matter who we are or where we live, for instance, we cannot live without food and water. Subsistence rights are rights to the fundamental, physical conditions that make life possible. While the UN's Universal Declaration of Human Rights recognizes "the right to food," strangely enough, it remains silent on the "right to water" (although reference is made to it in the UN's International Covenant on Economic, Social, and Cultural Rights). Yet, regardless of their international constitutional and legal status, it is obvious that food and water are essential to life, and for this reason, they have deep cultural and spiritual roots in many regions of the world. Based on these foundations, the opposition to the corporate takeover of food and water has been growing, and in many places, women are at the centre of these struggles. People's fundamental rights to food security, fresh water, and food safety are being threatened by the commodification, commercialization, and privatization promoted by transnational corporations.

Food Security

Increasing corporate control of food and the globalization of agriculture is robbing millions of their livelihood and their basic subsistence rights all over the world. With the creation of a global food production and market system, nations and peoples are becoming increasingly dependent on a handful of agribusiness corporations and trading conglomerates for their food supply. Food is being produced, not by farmers for local consumers, but by giant corporations for global markets. Among the food processing conglomerates are names like Nestlé, Unilever, Sara Lee, Nabisco, and Philip Morris, as well as agribusiness giants like Cargill, ConAgra, and Archer Daniels Midland.

From the corporate farm to the supermarket, these food and agribusiness monoliths have concentrated the ownership of production and distribution to the point where they virtually control the global food market system. What's more, they've been highly successful in engineering a set of export-oriented agricultural trade rules through the WTO, designed to take down tariff and non-tariff barriers on agricultural products and cut out government support programs for local farmers and domestic food production. These transformations have begun to set the stage for the elimination of state trading enterprises like the Canadian Wheat Board.

As the National Farmers' Union in Canada told the Citizens' MAI Inquiry in the fall of 1998: "the more international the market becomes, the harder time farmers have exacting a fair return. . . . While the export pie may be getting bigger, the farmers' share — both in relative and absolute terms — is shrinking." Although Canadian farmers have been hard hit by these trends, peasants in Third World countries have been devastated. More and more agricultural land in those nations has been geared for export production, as a means of earning foreign-exchange revenues for debt reduction, at the same time that prices for their agricultural products have been tumbling on world markets. Landless peasants, no longer able to feed their own families, have poured into the cities, swelling the ranks of the urban poor and sowing the seeds of popular resistance.

In Brazil, for example, thousands of peasants — women as well as men — have joined the Landless Workers Movement to protest the country's notoriously uneven distribution of land. Initiated fifteen years ago, the movement sponsors primary schools and food cooperatives in rural areas. But its main goal has been to enable peasants to forcibly occupy farms in efforts to compel the government to speed up its red-tape-heavy redistribution plan. In the spring of 2000, the movement took on its most ambitious campaign yet, as twenty-five thousand rural workers participated in a "blitz operation" that shut down public buildings in fourteen state capitals across Brazil. For days, government operations were paralyzed as landless peasants occupied public buildings or set up camps outside them, blocking officials from entering.

At the same time, an internationally organized movement known as Via Campesina has emerged to fight against the corporate takeover of agriculture and the WTO. Originally composed of peasant leaders and small-scale farmers from fifty countries in both the South and the North, Via Campesina openly challenged government leaders at the 1996 World Food Summit in Rome to make "food security" and "food sovereignty" the centrepieces of their agenda. Less than two years later, they demanded that agriculture be taken out of the WTO negotiations altogether, when world leaders met in Geneva in May 1998 to celebrate the fiftieth anniversary of the creation of the GATT.

In the fall of 2000, the Asian members of Via Campesina organized the Global People's 2000 caravan and mass march across Southeast Asia, promoting local food security and food sovereignty. The caravan started in India and travelled through Thailand, Malaysia, Indonesia, the Philippines, and South Korea, publicizing the Via Campesina's demand that agriculture be removed from WTO talks.

Fresh Water

Although the right to fresh water is taken for granted in many parts of the world, the planet is on the verge of a global water crisis. Currently, more than a billion people lack access to fresh water. By 2025, it is estimated that one-third of the world's population will be facing severe water shortages, and the remaining two-thirds of humanity will be experiencing serious water shortages. Ironically, World Bank officials have predicted that "the wars of the twenty-first century will be fought over water," while at the same time estimating that water will soon become the object of an $800 billion industry.

Suddenly, for-profit corporations are appearing everywhere, providing water-delivery services, bottled water, and bulk water transfers or specializing in river diversions and dam construction. The world's two leading corporations in the delivery and sale of water services, Vivendi and Suez Lyonnaise des Eaux, were ranked sixty-ninth and seventieth in the Fortune Global 500 ratings for 1998. At the same time, the World Bank has facilitated the corporate takeover of water services in Nonindustrialized Countries like Bolivia, Mozambique, and Kenya by making privatization a condition of its loans. At the WTO, meanwhile, the current round of GATS negotiations is preparing an additional set of rules that could give global water corporations all the tools they need to pry open public water services and turn them into profit-making enterprises.

Around the world, popular resistance is just beginning to crystallize, but perhaps nowhere has the opposition been more dramatic than in the community revolt that erupted in Cochabamba, Bolivia, early in 2000. When the World Bank refused to guarantee a U.S.$25 million loan in 1998 to refinance water services in Cochabamba unless the local government sold its public water utility to the private sector and passed on the cost to consumers, the Bolivian government saw to it that the utility was sold to a subsidiary of the construction giant Bechtel. The World Bank then granted monopolies to private water concessionaires, called for full-cost water pricing, pegged the cost of water to the U.S. dollar, and stipulated that the loan monies could not be used to subsidize the poor for water services. As monthly water bills skyrocketed, hundreds of thousands of Bolivian peasants and townspeople took to the streets, demanding that the contract with the Bechtel subsidiary be cancelled. Polls showed that 90 percent of Cochabamba's citizens wanted Bechtel's subsidiary to return the city's water system to public control. After massive protests, the Bolivian government finally conceded in April 1999 and broke the U.S.$200 million contract.

BOLIVIA'S WATER WAR

After water rates were hiked by nearly 35 percent, due to privatization necessitated by a World Bank loan condition, the people of Cocha-bamba shut down their city for four straight days. A series of strikes and blockades took place in January 2000, and nonviolent demonstra-tions resumed after the government broke its promise to secure lower rates in early February. The police blasted protestors with tear gas for two days, leaving 175 people injured and two youths blinded.

In early April, after a week of escalating protests, Bolivian president Hugo Banzer placed the country under martial law and announced that the government would pull out of the privatization process by withdrawing its contract to allow a Bechtel subsidiary to supply Cochabamba's water. But not before a seventeen-year-old boy was shot to death.

"The blood spilled in the streets of Cochabamba," declared protest leader Oscar Olivera, "carries the fingerprints of Bechtel." The next day, Olivera jumped on a plane for Washington, D.C., to confront World Bank president James Wolfensohn.

The fight for water rights is bound to intensify in Canada as well. A recent campaign led by the Council of Canadians calling for a legislated federal ban on water exports gained support from seven out of ten provinces but has so far been rejected by Ottawa. Meanwhile, companies like the Global Water Corporation of Canada are waiting in the wings to exploit any opportunity they might have to export massive quantities of the country's fresh water resources to water bottling enterprises in Asia, using whatever leverage WTO and NAFTA rules provide.

And, as the tragedy of lethal contaminated water in Walkerton, Ontario, has shown, major Ontario provincial government cutbacks on well and water inspection services have made it more difficult for municipalities to supply safe water. At the same time, cash-strapped municipal governments in Halifax and other Canadian cities are entertaining the possibility of inviting big water corporations like Vivendi or Suez to run their water treatment and delivery services.

Food Safety

The fight for foods that are safe also continues to rage at the centre of the battle for subsistence rights around the world. After all, eating safe, and preferably nourishing, food is a fundamental right, essential to personal and physical well-being. But through the science of biotechnological gene splicing, crops and animals have been genetically engineered, leading to the production of what critics call "frankenfoods." This highly dubious diet has been quickly and quietly making its way onto the tables of homes and restaurants, radically altering the quality of what people eat. In North America, close to 75 percent of all prepackaged food is now estimated to contain genetically engineered substances. Yet no long-term scientific testing has been done on the human health impacts of GE foods. Meanwhile, the biotech industry, led by Monsanto (now a wholly owned subsidiary of the Pharmacia Corporation) and including Novartis, Aventis, Astra Zeneca, DuPont, and Dow AgroSciences are expanding the production of these GE crops and foods and using WTO rules and decisions to force their way into new world markets.

Global resistance to GE foods and the biotech industry continues to intensify in many regions of the world, including Europe, where the conflict began. In France, concerned farmers and food safety activists initially formed an alliance and used direct action tactics to prevent Monsanto and Novartis from proceeding with their GE maize crop trials. In the United Kingdom, five young women, clothed in protective suits and carrying heavy-duty plastic bags marked with the biohazard symbol, walked onto a Monsanto field test site and began pulling up GE plant crops. Their actions sparked a movement known as "genetiX snowball," in which hundreds of people formed biosafety affinity groups to remove GE crops from field test sites all over the U.K. Meanwhile, consumers' groups in Germany successfully convinced Europe's largest grain merchants not to purchase GE crops. In several other European countries, consumer boycott campaigns were organized to persuade fast-food chains like Burger King, McDonald's, and Pizza Hut to refuse GE potatoes for their fries. Similar boycotts were aimed at convincing superstores like Sainsbury's to ban GE food products, or at least to segregate them from GE-free foods.

In Asia, the resistance movement took root in India and has since spread across much of the continent. The "Monsanto: Quit India" campaign was launched in one region by an alliance of over one hundred Indian farmer and consumer groups following months of protests. (Close to five hundred farmers in that area had committed suicide in response to failures associated mainly with GE cotton crops.) Responding to a legal petition filed by the Research Foundation for Science, Technology and Ecology, the Supreme Court of India ruled in February 1999 that all field trials of Monsanto's GE cotton be halted.

In other Asian countries, events have been less dramatic but still decisive. In Japan, the Consumers Union obtained two million signatures on a petition, along with the support of 2,300 of 3,300 local government assemblies, calling on Tokyo to require mandatory labelling of GE foods. And in Korea, as a result of public awareness campaigns organized by the Pesticide Action Network in the Asia-Pacific region, the national government announced plans to require labelling of GE products.

Even in the North American heartland of the biotech industry, resistance has been mounting. In November 1998, for example, pressure from citizens' groups in Maine caused Monsanto to withdraw its application to grow genetically engineered corn crops in the state, while on the other side of the country, biotech activists destroyed a test plot of Novartis GE corn on the Berkeley campus of the University of California. Several hundred U.S. restaurants have also joined a nationwide campaign to expose the dangers of GE food products and call for mandatory labelling.

In Canada, a coalition of farm, health, and environmental groups led by the Council of Canadians organized a successful public campaign, which, assisted by Senate hearings and the testimony of government scientists, compelled Ottawa to slap a ban on the use of bovine growth hormone in dairy cattle. More recently, the Council, Greenpeace, and the Sierra Club of Canada shifted their campaign focus to super foodstore chains like Loblaws, demanding that all GE food products on their shelves be labelled. The Council also filed a legal petition against the federal government for failing to protect public health and the environment in its regulation of genetically engineered organisms.

DEFENDING ECONOMIC RIGHTS

Since the Industrial Revolution of the nineteenth century, workers have relentlessly fought for fair wages and working conditions, not only to ensure that their incomes are adequate to meet basic needs, but also to gain a sense of self-worth and human dignity. By organizing in unions to defend their rights and by building a dynamic labour movement in many parts of the world, workers have been able to pose a major ongoing challenge to a system based on unbridled capitalism.

The UN's Universal Declaration of Human Rights recognizes that all people have the "right to work, to free choice of employment, to just and favourable conditions of work, and to protection against unemployment." It also affirms that all workers have "the right to form and to join trade unions." The UN's International Covenant on Economic, Social, and Cultural Rights not only reaffirms these core labour standards, but calls on governments to implement them and to ensure that all people are able to exercise their rights to participate in building up their economies. The International Labour Organization (ILO) has specifically defined worker rights in more than a hundred conventions and has documented worldwide levels of unemployment and exploitive working conditions. The economic rights of women have not always been included in discussions about work and working conditions, but in 1995, the UN World Conference on Women in Beijing further underscored those rights.

Contingent work, sweatshop labour, and debt bondage are three major fronts in the battle for economic rights. In each of these cases, transnational corporations, along with governments and financial institutions, are systematically subverting democratic rights to economic justice.

Contingent Work

A major flashpoint of growing resistance in the new global economy has been the proliferation of contingent work — better known as "McJobs." Precarious, part-time, insecure forms of employment have been on the rise, even in Industrialized Countries, where full-time jobs with benefits, holiday pay, a degree of security, and perhaps union representation were once the norm. Corporations relish their reserves of part-timers, temps, and freelancers because they provide relatively cheap labour. This explosion of contingent work, often involving women, youth, and people of colour, is taking place largely in the service sector, where job growth has soared, especially in the United States.

The brand name corporations that are leading the way in part-time employment in the service sector include McDonald's, Starbucks, The Gap, Wal-Mart, Kmart, Kentucky Fried Chicken, Barnes & Noble, and Borders Books & Music. Due to expanding part-time work, Wal-Mart has become not only the world's biggest retail chain, but also the largest private employer in the United States. While these corporate practices violate a variety of labour rights conventions, the ILO does not have the clout to enforce its own standards. And global governing institutions like the WTO, which do have the muscle, refuse to subject global trade to core labour standards.

Once again, the labour movement has been at the forefront of the battle against contingent work and enforced casual labour — from the campaign waged by the United Parcel Service workers against "part-time America" to the fight by the Canadian Auto Workers against the outsourcing of their jobs at Chrysler and Ford to non-union manufacturers. Yet, since the service sector has been the locus of mushrooming part-time, insecure jobs, resistance has been growing among women, youth, and people of colour, who tend to be the prime victims of these work trends. Although the task of union organizing among part-time and temporary workers has been especially difficult, successful drives have been waged at Starbucks and McDonald's, as well as Wal-Mart and other retail chains. These organizing initiatives have often been led by youth and women workers.

These campaigns against contingent work have embodied new styles of organizing and acting. In the United Kingdom, the infamous McLibel Trial, which pitted McDonald's against two Greenpeace activists who were challenging the company's employment practices, did much to publicly expose the harsh realities of McJobs. Although the activists were found guilty on several counts for libel, the chief justice acknowledged in his ruling that McDonald's contingent work policies were contributing to the depression of workers' wages in the catering industry. On the other side of the Atlantic, American groups like Jobs with Justice have been organizing student, religious, and labour networks and using direct action tactics to make public the contingent work policies of companies like Kentucky Fried Chicken. Janitors for Justice is another movement from the nineties which skillfully used direct action tactics to shut down traffic in downtown Washington, D.C., drawing public attention to the exploitation of janitors and other part-time or contract workers.

Sweatshop Labour

In the 1990s, the exposure of sweatshop labour conditions in the South, involving some of the leading brand name corporations of the North, spearheaded a growing struggle for economic rights. Shifting their production offshore to take advantage of cheap labour conditions, numerous footwear, clothing, and toy manufacturers profited from brutally exploitive and dangerous working conditions for both women and men, particularly in Asia and Central and Latin America. (The brand name players included footwear companies like Nike, Reebok, and Adidas; clothing manufacturers like The Gap, Levi Strauss, Liz Claiborne, and Disney; retail giants like Wal-Mart, Kmart, and JCPenney; and countless toy makers.) For example, the daily wages paid by a Nike supplier to its workers in Vietnam were $1.60, while the price of three square meals alone was $2.10. In many cases, the sweatshop factories employed by these brand name companies were located in free trade or export processing zones, where corporations were allowed to operate outside the labour and environmental laws of the host country. Sealed off from the rest of the economy and society, these cheap labour zones are often surrounded by high fences and patrolled by private security forces.

Although unions have traditionally been at the forefront of the opposition to sweatshop labour, a new style of campaign organizing and resistance emerged in the 1990s to cast the public spotlight on this basic struggle for economic rights. Led by groups like the Campaign for Labor Rights, the National Labor Committee and unions like UNITE! in the U.S., and the Labour Behind the Label Coalition in the U.K., activists have made creative use of "culture jamming" — techniques used to publicly expose the shameful stories of brand name corporations' exploitive labour practices. By tackling the logo, label, or icon that makes these corporations household names, campaign activists create a head-on collision between image and reality. At a 1999 protest rally against Disney, for example, participants parked a giant rubber rat outside a major Disney store. At a New York rally launching "The Holiday Season of Conscience," speakers indicted Nike and Disney for their suppliers' cheap labour practices in front of a giant red swoosh, along with 3-D displays of the Lion King.

MICKEY MOUSE GOES TO HAITI

In producing and promoting a documentary film called *Mickey Mouse Goes to Haiti*, shown in high schools and on campuses all over the U.S., antisweatshop activist Charlie Kernaghan used culture jamming techniques to expose Disney's cheap labour practices. A key part of this kind of culture jamming is the use of creative number crunching. While Disney CEO Michael Eisner earns $9,783 an hour, for example, the average hourly wage of a Haitian worker is 28 cents. It would take a Haitian worker 16.8 years, says Kernaghan, to earn Eisner's salary income at Disney. What's more, the U.S.$181 million in stock options exercised by Eisner at Disney in 1996 is enough to provide for Disney's nineteen thousand Haitian workers and their families for fourteen years.

Based on information from Naomi Klein's *No Logo*

Nike has been the prime target of one of the most effective antisweatshop campaigns. Through the annual International Nike Day of Action, for example, demands for fair wages and independent monitoring are brought home to Nike customers and shoppers at flagship NikeTown stores. In October 1997, demonstrations in eighty-five cities and thirteen countries featured "sweatshop fashion shows" and a game of survival called the "transnational capital auction."

When 1995–96 was designated by campaign activists as the Year of the Sweatshop, stories of exploitive labour practices were exposed in the *New York Times* and on important television programs like *60 Minutes* and *20/20*. During this campaign year, the horrible working conditions at a Gap supplier's factory in El Salvador were exposed when the manager, reacting to a union drive, fired 150 workers and vowed that blood would flow if the organizing continued. During the campaign, talk show host Kathie Lee Gifford's sportswear line at Wal-Mart was publicly revealed as being made by child labour in Honduras and in illegal sweatshops in the United States. In Canada, the Maquila Solidarity Network has played a key role in exposing the cheap labour practices of brand name corporations and in reinforcing the fight for workers' rights in Central America by conducting sweatshop fashion shows across the country.

Debt Bondage

The fight for economic rights includes demands for the cancellation of the international debt loads that are crippling the economies of communities and entire nations in the Third World. Although the UN's Universal Declaration of Human Rights and its accompanying covenants are silent on the issue (since they were drafted before Structural Adjustment Programs — SAPs — were imposed), there can be little doubt that the countries of the South are being systematically denied access to capital and that this prevents people from exercising their economic rights. The lending policies of the IMF and the World Bank, coupled with the SAPs imposed as conditions for the renegotiation of debt payments, have left the majority of Third World nations in a state of debt bondage. Hundreds of millions of people are condemned to live in a state of perpetual poverty as financial resources are allocated for debt payments and economic restructuring instead of the provision of basic needs such as education, nutrition, health, clean water, and sanitation. In addition, the global financial system allows commercial banks, investment dealers, and brokerage houses to freely speculate on currency rates and commodity prices in other countries, thereby intensifying the economic instability of those nations.

In Mexico, a movement called El Barzón emerged in the mid-nineties to take on the country's major bankers over a variety of community debt issues. Composed of campesinos and Indigenous peoples, as well as small businesspeople and landowners, El Barzón — which means a leather strap used to tie the yoke to oxen — grew to be over half a million strong. Initially, the movement took root in rural communities that were fighting the banks' refusal to provide decent loans to small farmers and peasants. In protest, they filled the streets with tractors and blocked the government offices of tax collectors and bank regulators all over the country. Later, the movement spread to Mexico City and other urban centres, where it became known as the "White Army," helping people defend their homes and businesses from debt auctions or property confiscations. When someone was about to lose their house or business, El Barzón would dispatch a white van to the site with a small team of lawyers, equipped with computers and legal documents, to disrupt the proceedings. The slogan on the side of the white van read: *"Debo, no niego / Pago lo justo"* — "I owe, I don't deny / I pay what's fair."

On a more global scale, the Jubilee 2000 Movement has led the way in demanding debt cancellation across the board for all of the world's poorest countries. Organized by the major Christian churches to mark the biblical Year of the Jubilee, which calls for the cancellation of all debts, the movement has managed to mobilize energy in both the North and the South. To push the issue of debt bondage onto the radar screens of policymakers, Jubilee 2000 has rallied by putting people on the street. In May 1998 some seventy thousand people jammed the streets of Birmingham in the U.K., forming a human chain six miles long and chanting "Drop the Debt." The following year, forty thousand joined a human chain in Cologne at the G8 Summit and thirty thousand more formed a similar chain in Seattle at the WTO Ministerial Meeting, demanding action to lift the debt burden. Worldwide, over 17 million signatures have been collected on the Jubilee 2000 Petition, and in October 1999, over a million people took part in a Latin American event — "The Shout of the Excluded" — to call public attention to the burden of debt and injustice.

GUARDING ENVIRONMENTAL RIGHTS

Of all the battlefronts on the globalization landscape, the issue of ecological rights is one of the most pressing. While the fifty-two-year-old Universal Declaration of Human Rights says little about the subject of environmental rights, the 1992 Rio Earth Summit and its Agenda 21 laid the foundation for international environmental action. Since then a series of multilateral agreements have been negotiated, including the Convention on International Trade in Endangered Species, which bans the marketing of endangered species; the Basel Convention on the Control of Transboundary Movements of Hazardous Wastes and Their Disposal, outlawing the export of toxic wastes from rich to poor countries; and the Montreal Protocol, banning trade in ozone-depleting chemicals and products made with those chemicals.

Although these and other tools for ensuring ecological rights exist, they have been consistently trumped by WTO rules, even when those rules supposedly provide protection for environmental laws. Take Article XX of the GATT, for instance. It is meant to allow governments to adopt or retain laws that are "necessary to protect human, animal or plant life and health" (Article XX-b) and laws "related to the conservation of exhaustible natural resources" (Article XX-g). But, as noted in Chapter Four, these articles are subject to another overriding rule — namely, that environmental laws must be the "least trade restrictive," as enforced by the World Trade Organization. Until the recent asbestos case (where the WTO ruled in favour of France's ban on imports of Canadian asbestos), no government has been successful in using Article XX to defend an environmental law from a WTO challenge.

The same holds true for the use of the Precautionary Principle — the provision under which governments are supposed to be able to adopt or retain laws that protect the public against possible environmental or health dangers of particular products, even in the absence of clear scientific evidence that they are not harmful. But WTO rules have managed to twist the application of the Precautionary Principle to the point where the burden of proof regarding product safety lies with governments, not the manufacturers of the product.

Climate Change

The recent discovery of a new lake in the middle of the Canadian Arctic — previously iced over year-round — coupled with a massive hole in the ozone layer the size of the United States, has made climate change through global warming a key controversy in environmental resistance to corporate globalization. Caused by the emission of the main greenhouse gases (carbon dioxide, methane, and nitrous oxide) into the atmosphere, the massive climate changes expected in the first half of the twenty-first century will bring droughts and flooding and increase the spread of infectious diseases. Although the 1997 Kyoto Protocol on Global Climate Change called for a reduction of greenhouse gas emissions to 6 percent below 1990 levels by 2010, the UN's 1995 Intergovernmental Panel on Climate Change insists that 50 to 70 percent reductions over the next two to three decades will be required to stabilize the world's climate. The prime obstacles to achieving these targets have been fossil fuel corporations (oil, gas, and coal), whose industry associations have been vigorously lobbying governments to renege on their commitments to meeting the Kyoto requirements, let alone to making more substantial reductions in greenhouse gas emissions.

Public education and action campaigns have been mounted in most of the northern industrial countries, targeting the major petroleum corporations, as well as governments. In the U.S., for example, Friends of the Earth has made ExxonMobil the prime target of their activity. In mounting its campaign on climate change, Greenpeace International decided to zero in on British Petroleum — a company that promotes itself as being environmentally responsible. The central issue was BP's exploration and production developments in the Arctic. Through a resolution they presented at a BP annual general meeting, Greenpeace representatives were able to convince 13 percent of all BP shareholders to vote in favour of the company pulling out of its Arctic operations. Greenpeace has also been working with insurance companies and banks who are concerned about the impacts of global warming and extreme weather changes, to encourage them to shift investments from fossil fuels to renewable energy sources such as solar energy.

In the United States, the Ozone Action Network mobilized students in an effort to make climate change a major issue in the year 2000 presidential election campaign. In the United Kingdom, Solar Century, a green business, has been actively promoting constructive energy alternatives through retrofitting buildings with solar panels. Meanwhile, in Costa Rica, a coalition of civil society groups issued a common declaration in November 2000, calling their country an oil exploration and exploitation free zone and vowing to wrest it back from the clutches of the big oil corporations. And the David Suzuki Foundation in Canada has been leading the way in ringing alarm bells about the dangers and causes of climate change. Its massive public advertising campaign is aimed at encouraging citizens to put pressure on major government and corporate players who have the power to begin to correct the problem.

Rivers and Dams

The damming and flooding of river systems around the world have long been flashpoints for popular resistance by environmental movements. In recent years, organizations like the International Rivers Network have succeeded in bringing worldwide public attention to the environmental disasters caused by the damming of natural rivers and to the role played by global institutions like the World Bank in building those dams. In India, another citizens' movement focused on the Narmada Valley Development Project, which includes three huge dam systems — the Sardar Sarovar, the Narmada Sagar, and the Maheshwar Dam. During the 1980s, people's organizations were formed in villages throughout the Narmada Valley in response to the projects, and by 1988, they had converged into a single mass organization known as the Narmada Bachao Andolan. The NBA formally called for a halt to all dam construction in the valley, and villagers refused to move or be moved from their homes, declaring that they would stay and drown if it came to that. As resistance mounted throughout the early 1990s, the NBA was eventually able to compel the World Bank to withdraw from the Sardar Sarovar project and to convince the Supreme Court to order suspension of work on the project.

THE NARMADA VALLEY DAM BATTLE

After fifty thousand people gathered to protest the construction of the Sardar Sarovar Dam in India in September 1989, the region was turned into a police state. As news of the villagers' resistance spread, the Japanese arm of Friends of the Earth succeeded in convincing the Japanese government to withdraw its 27 billion yen loan for the project. Then, a sacrificial squad of seven people who had resolved to lay down their lives for the river marched to the site, accompanied by six thousand others, preparing to face off with police battalions. With the glare of the international media spotlight on them, the World Bank announced an independent review of the project. Surprisingly, the review committee reported that the project was environmentally flawed and cast blame on the World Bank, as well as the government.

When the government refused to meet some minimal conditions, the Bank took the unprecedented step of withdrawing from the project. To continue, the government turned to other funding sources. As the monsoon season advanced, hundreds of villagers from Manibeli refused to leave their homes, clinging to wooden posts with their children while the waters rose. After the damage of the monsoon season on the dam site became clear in early 1995, the Supreme Court of India ordered a halt to further construction, but the struggle continues to this day.

Based on information from Arundhati Roy's *The Cost of Living*

Canadians, of course, are no strangers to resistance against the environmental damage of megadam projects. The 1970s campaigns waged by the Cree against the James Bay Project in northern Quebec and against the Manitoba Hydro Project were pioneering examples of megadam struggles that became internationalized, drawing support from movements in other countries. While the Cree were successful in containing some of the environmental damage, the construction of the two projects did cause massive flooding, soil erosion, and displacement of communities.

Today, resistance movements against megadam construction are even better linked and more organized on a global basis. In South Asia, for example, citizens' action groups in India, Pakistan, Nepal, Bangladesh, Sri Lanka, and Bhutan have been working together on a common set of demands, calling on governments and the World Bank to abandon megadam projects in favour of more decentralized, sustainable, and equitable models of water, energy, and land management. When the Sindhi people of Pakistan, following an intense period of constant resistance and creative action, compelled the Pakistani government to cancel the ill-conceived Kalabagh Dam, the NBA (Narmada Bachao Andolan), and other movements in South Asia shared in the victory, and a new people's politics was born in the region.

Fish and Forests

Over the past decade, organizations like the Rainforest Action Network and Greenpeace have played a leading role in fighting for the preservation of old-growth forests in North America, Europe, Asia, and Latin America. In Canada, during the 1990s, groups like Sierra Club Canada and activists from around the world succeeded in blocking some of the attempts of MacMillan Bloedel (now owned by Weyerhaeuser) to clearcut several hundred thousand hectares of old-growth forest in Clayoquot Sound. But victories like this were offset by the fact that the big timber corporations — International Paper, Georgia-Pacific, Kimberly-Clark, Stora Enso, Weyerhaeuser, and Oji Paper — were expanding their operations around the world, creating a massive global industry for wood products. Playing into the timber industry's ambitions, the U.S. called for a "Global Free Logging Agreement" through the World Trade Organization.

When news began to spread that the U.S. would encourage nation-states to sign this agreement at the 1999 Seattle WTO meetings — risking the possible extinction of most of the world's remaining forests — activists immediately launched protest campaigns aimed at Washington and timber industry associations. In June 1999, the International Forum on Globalization and several forestry action groups convened a meeting of activists from all over the world, to map out a common strategy. Briefings were conducted on the WTO, global trade rules, the major timber corporations, and the role of the IMF and the World Bank. Caucuses hammered out follow-up action strategies to be undertaken in jurisdictions ranging from Canada, Japan, and the European Union, to Indonesia, Brazil, and Chile. As a result, considerable opposition was mobilized before the global logging deal died with the collapse of the WTO Millennium Summit in Seattle.

Similar turbulence had hit the fishing industry. Like the cod harvesters off Canada's east coast, giant trawlers were moving into the coastal waters of other countries, dragging weighted nets along the ocean floor, scraping off the fish and destroying almost anything else that came into their path. This insane practice was bringing many species perilously close to extinction. In the lead-up to the Seattle Summit, there were signs that a "Global Free Fishing Agreement" might be concluded there, serving the interests of the big trawling industries and threatening the remainder of the world's fish stocks. Fish workers' protests had already begun, and they continued to escalate, not only against the foreign take of salmon stock on Canada's West Coast, but against foreign intrusions into the ocean fishing grounds of other countries as well. In India, after fish workers in coastal communities waged a prolonged struggle that included harbour blockades, the government rescinded its new Deep Sea Fishing Policy in 1997, terminating the operations of deep sea fishing trawlers in the region. Had the proposal for a "Global Free Fishing Agreement" surfaced at the WTO, it would undoubtedly have been met with a common front of international resistance.

As many corporations tie their long-range plans to the fantasy of infinitely expanding worldwide markets, the already beleaguered physical environment is being subjected to ever-increasing pressures, from which it may never fully recover. In acts of hubris befitting a tragic farce more than a supposedly enlightened society, governments are capitulating to World Trade Organization demands and wiping out the laws and regulations that govern even our food and our water — the basic stuff of life. In such a climate, it is hardly surprising that workers have become the pawns of corporations that move around the globe, seeking out the cheapest labour to create goods for the already-sated consumers of the so-called Developed World.

It is only through the concerted worldwide action of the growing civil society movement that this tidal wave of greed and short-sighted profiteering can be averted.

7

Defending Humanity

How citizens are resisting the
global corporate assault on social,
cultural, and human rights

In 1999, farmer and consumer organizations launched the "Monsanto: Quit India" campaign, following hundreds of farmer suicides due to the failure of genetically engineered cotton crops. It was just the latest manifestation of community-based resistance to the operations of foreign-owned corporations that pose a serious threat to the basic democratic rights and livelihood of the Indian people.

The DuPont Corporation's attempt to relocate a hazardous nylon manufacturing plant from the U.S. to the picturesque state of Goa in India met with sustained resistance by local villagers in the early 1990s. When the federal Environment Ministry in India refused to give clearance to DuPont, based on social, economic, and environmental impact reviews conducted by the Goa state assembly, the U.S. trade representative was dispatched to put pressure on high levels of the Indian government. Not only was the initial decision overturned at the beginning of 1992, but the central government purchased grazing land in

*the village of Tamil Nadu for the DuPont plant and authorized construction to
begin without consulting the local governing body, the Panchayat.*

*The villagers, however, rose up and refused to accept the plant, forming an
Anti-DuPont Committee to lead the resistance. When the villagers organized a
blockade, DuPont representatives and the local police attacked, shooting a youth
at point-blank range. Dozens more were injured in the clashes. Eventually, the
local Panchayat resolved that the DuPont application should be quashed.
Meanwhile, the villagers had begun to repossess the land by herding goats, cows,
and other animals onto the plot. In response to a legal challenge, the High Court
ruling upheld the Panchayat decision to refuse the planning permit.*

*The people of this Indian village demonstrated that it is possible to organize
to resist the global power and pressure of a corporation like DuPont. Even when
the full weight of the U.S. government, reinforced by the actions of their own
national government, was brought down on them, they were able to sustain and
intensify their community-based opposition to the DuPont occupation.*

*And this local uprising is not an isolated case. Ever since the Union Carbide
plant explosion in Bhopal resulted in the deaths of thousands of innocent
people, many Indian citizens have resolved to tell unwanted foreign-based
corporations to leave the country. In recent years, Coca-Cola and Kentucky Fried
Chicken have been just two of the targets of intense popular resistance.*

The defence of democracy and the commons includes more than the
essentials of life — subsistence, economic, and ecological rights. It also includes
other vital and basic elements that contribute to our common humanity —
social, cultural, and human rights. The corporate hijacking of these fundamental rights now poses a growing threat to democracy and the commons
throughout the world. Increasingly, for-profit corporations are taking
over these areas of common life, which in many countries have been the
responsibility of governments and the public sector acting to protect the
common good.

The stories of popular resistance in India may have some important
lessons to offer those engaged in struggles against the corporate infringement
of basic social, cultural, and human rights. Yet the battles now being waged

on these fronts are further complicated by the rules and disciplines of the World Trade Organization, rules which, after all, are designed primarily to facilitate the global expansion of markets for the goods and services produced by transnational corporations. Nevertheless, the struggles for social, cultural, and human rights have become major battlefronts of popular resistance against corporate globalization.

FIGHTING FOR SOCIAL RIGHTS

The recognition of basic social rights such as housing, education, social assistance, and income security has been an ongoing priority for civil society groups in most countries. Throughout much of the last century, labour unions and a variety of other citizens' organizations led the way in the fight for recognition of these rights — a struggle whose historical roots lay in the human suffering and tragedy of the Great Depression of the 1930s. Lack of social safety nets resulted in a decade of massive dislocation, unemployment, hunger, and long-term misery, which governments in most of the industrialized North vowed never to see repeated.

The 1948 Universal Declaration of Human Rights recognized that every person had the right to "a standard of living adequate for . . . health and well-being." It went on to claim that all people had rights to "education, housing and medical care, and necessary social services, and the right to security in the event of unemployment." Given these social benchmarks, many governments began the task of building up the capacity of their public sectors to deliver social programs and public services to protect these citizens' rights.

Over the past fifteen years, however, basic social rights have become the target of a relentless series of assaults through government cutbacks, privatization, and deregulation. For the poor countries of the South, the Structural Adjustment Programs of the IMF and the World Bank have dealt a devastating blow to whatever basic social programs and public services they may once have had. Now, especially in the North, education, health care, and social services have been reduced to consumer items for which transnational corporations see a lucrative, multibillion-dollar market. And the new GATS rules being negotiated at the WTO are designed to open the door for the corporate takeover of public education, health care, and social services on a for-profit basis. Since women play a large role in these caregiving services, they have often been at the forefront of resistance.

Public Education

The corporate takeover of public and postsecondary education has become a hot-button issue in the struggle for social rights. The democratic ideal of universal access to education is evaporating as cash-strapped schools, colleges, and universities throw themselves on the mercy of private corporations to provide funds for everything from cafeterias and computer equipment to textbooks, curriculum development, and research facilities and faculties. The World Bank has already warned governments of Third World countries that they will have to privatize in order to solve their future education funding problems. Meanwhile, in Industrialized Countries like Canada, corporate partnerships with schools are mushrooming. Computer merchants like IBM, Microsoft, and Hewlett-Packard; electronic communications giants like AT&T, Unitel, and Nortel; fast-food enterprises such as McDonald's, Burger King, and Pizza Hut; and soft drink manufacturers like Coca-Cola and Pepsi-Cola have already staked out their turf in schools, colleges, and universities, where a captive market of young people spend up to 40 percent of their time. In the U.S., a whole new for-profit education industry is producing education materials and technical services and making plans to use the new GATS rules being negotiated at the WTO as a means of turning the delivery of public services into global markets.

In response, students, as well as teachers, have begun to organize resistance to the corporate takeover of public education. High school students in France staged a series of walkouts and teach-ins in 1998, primarily because of government cutbacks and privatization. In high schools scattered throughout the United States, students have been organizing protests against the exclusive marketing rights being awarded to brand name companies like Pepsi, Coca-Cola, and McDonald's. At one American high school, a student wore a Pepsi T-shirt on Coca-Cola Day — and was promptly sent home and suspended. In Canada, high school students have been engaging in similar and related battles. When the Youth News Network (YNN) was introduced into Ontario public schools, requiring all students to watch daily broadcasts, students in Meadowvale staged a walkout one May day in 2000, sporting

"Not for Sale" T-shirts and distributing homemade cupcakes with anti-YNN logos on the icing. During that same spring season, Nova Scotia students walked out of their high schools to join teachers and parents in rallies and demonstrations protesting massive government cutbacks to public education.

University and college students have also been blindsided by the corporate takeover of education, and they are resisting. At the National Autonomous University of Mexico, Latin America's largest postsecondary educational institution, with a student enrolment of 260,000, youth activists staged a nine-and-a-half-month strike and occupation in 1999 that effectively shut down classes and other normal operations. Initially, the protest was focused on tuition fees, an issue that was later resolved when the administration more or less conceded to the students' demands. But the occupation was extended by a smaller group of students who maintained that the government's real aim was to eventually privatize the university, in response to the World Bank's proposals that state subsidies for higher education be terminated. The occupation finally ended after an early-morning police raid.

On a smaller scale, similar battles have been waged in Canada since 1995 by the Canadian Federation of Students over sharp hikes in tuition fees, resulting from massive cutbacks in federal funding to the provinces for postsecondary education. Like their counterparts in other areas of the world, Canadian students have been organizing protests against the growing corporate presence on campus and the dominance of corporate figures of the boards of governors of Canadian universities, including Toronto, York, McGill, and Dalhousie.

Health Care

The right to universal health care has become another flashpoint for resistance to corporate globalization. In recent years, the price of prescription drugs has skyrocketed as the world's major pharmaceutical companies, such as Eli Lilly, Merck, Pfizer, and Bristol-Myers Squibb have gained monopoly protection for their drug patents and medical technology through WTO and NAFTA rules governing intellectual property rights. In doing so, they have contributed to the bankruptcy of public health care systems in many countries. Canada has so far been able to withstand these destructive measures, and still remains one of a relatively few countries in the world where all citizens have access to adequate public health care services on the basis of need, rather than ability to pay. But now, even Canadian health care has been targeted as a potential multibillion-dollar market by corporations involved in the for-profit health care industry.

SALVADOREAN PUBLIC HEALTH CARE ON THE LINE

In November 1999, over ten thousand health care workers, doctors, and nurses in El Salvador went on strike, not only to protest the government's failure to live up to collective bargaining agreements, but also to defend the public health care system by calling for modernization without recourse to privatization. The government and hospital administrators responded by firing 221 workers and sending in the national police to occupy work sites and to deal with strikers and protesters. Tens of thousands of maquila workers, campesinos, teachers, students, market vendors, and other public sector workers joined the protest, forming solidarity work stoppages, rallies and marches. U.S. unions and other groups helped form an emergency strike fund. Finally, in March 2000, the Salvadorean government agreed to negotiate with the workers on preserving the public health care system.

Corporate hospital chains like Columbia/HCA, and for-profit HMOs (Health Maintenance Organizations) like Kaiser Permenante and Aetna U.S. Healthcare are planning to make use of the GATS rules being negotiated at the WTO to pry open public health care systems in Canada and other countries, creating new markets for expanded operations. As Canadians know all too well, the battle for the preservation of universal health care is underway. When the province of Alberta introduced legislation permitting hospital services, including services now publicly insured, to be contracted out to private, for-profit companies, a resistance movement soon ignited. It began with a small, ginger group of citizens, calling themselves the Friends of Medicare, holding a vigil outside the Alberta legislature. This action soon mushroomed into a province-wide protest against the government's proposed legislation. While the movement was unable to prevent the passage of the legislation, it succeeded in establishing a solid base of public resistance against a two-tiered health care system, one for the rich and one for the poor.

Meanwhile, in France, health care workers, including the medical mission Médecins sans frontières (Doctors without Borders), have organized campaigns to fight against the GATS threat to public health care. Elsewhere, resistance has also been growing in countries that have already given up on universal health care in favour of a two-tiered system. In the United States, the inadequate treatment provided by HMOs has sparked a wave of protests, not only by patients and nurses, including the California Nurses Association, but also by some physicians. The Center for National Health Program Studies at Harvard Medical School has also produced a slide show and chart book portraying the failures of the U.S. health care system, prompting more Americans to join the struggle to finally establish public health care in the United States. In Britain, where public health care was effectively privatized under Prime Minister Margaret Thatcher, there are signs that the Tony Blair government is now facing resistance to this unfair, two-tiered system.

Since the IMF's Structural Adjustment Programs have effectively wiped out health care services in most Third World nations, the medical services that do remain are now provided primarily on a community level, through cooperatives, unions, churches, and charities. The People's Health Assembly in Bangladesh attempted to improve these services by contacting grassroots organizations engaged in community health delivery throughout the world and inviting them to a pioneering meeting in December 2000. There, the goal was to map out a plan of action to ensure better health care through community-based and -controlled services for the countries of the South. In Africa, community health activists have had to commit enormous amounts of time and energy to combatting exorbitant prices for the drugs used to combat AIDS. They have been engaged with groups like Doctors without Borders in a long-term struggle to convince pharmaceutical giants to curb their patent demands and substantially lower the prices of the drugs needed to stop the killer disease.

In Argentina, Dr. René Favaloro, a world-renowned surgeon who pioneered the heart bypass procedure, committed suicide early in 2000 as a symbolic protest against his own country's failure to develop a just health care system. The clinic he'd established in Buenos Aires to provide equal health care treatment to rich and poor had fallen into bankruptcy after millions of Argentinians, faced with massive government cutbacks, were thrown out of work, losing their health insurance coverage. Private donations to the clinic had also dropped, and government subsidies had been slashed. Three weeks before he put a bullet in his heart, Favaloro told his staff that the prime cause of this social disaster in health care was the free market economics of globalization.

Social Security

Every day, peasants, squatters, and urban slum dwellers in the South are engaged in pitched battles for access to decent housing and water and sewage disposal, to say nothing of jobs and income. In the Industrialized Countries of the North, the homeless, welfare recipients, and the working poor have always been involved in a constant, uphill fight for their rights to social security, which have been steadily eroding as a result of government cutbacks, privatization, and deregulation. But in this age of corporate globalization, resistance movements are encountering new obstacles. Increasingly, governments are abandoning their responsibility to provide basic social security services through the public sector and are allowing corporations to take over the operation of welfare, workfare, and prison programs. The advantage to the corporations, of course, is that they can cash in on the multibillion-dollar pools of public revenues made available through the privatization of government services. In the United States, a new social security industry is emerging, ranging from Andersen Consulting, Electronic Data Systems, and Unisys to defence manufacturer Lockheed Martin. They are all getting into the social security "business," along with a host of smaller companies. As the industry prepares to go global, the new GATS rules will provide them with the tools they need to pry open potential public service "markets" in other countries, as well.

Meanwhile, social rights activists have been recasting their struggles to confront the new realities and forces of global trade in the very services that are essential to the common good. In the United States, the Kensington Welfare Rights Union has organized "Freedom Bus Tours" in cities across the country, emphasizing rights to an adequate standard of living and social services as outlined in Article 25 of the Universal Declaration of Human Rights. Food First, based in San Francisco, has taken a similar approach in mobilizing support for unemployed workers, immigrants, and welfare recipients in their struggles for social rights. In Tennessee, the privatization of prison systems has hit the spotlight as a coalition of public sector unions, religious, student, and inmate family groups, opposed to prisons-for-profit, has mounted a shareholder-action campaign against Corrections Corporation of America, the world's largest marketer of private prison beds.

At the same time, in Europe, urban squatters took a creative approach to publicizing the degradation of social security systems. In May 2000, an organized group of Parisian homeless people occupied the Louvre Museum, where an exhibition on "lost civilizations" was being held: the theme provided the perfect opportunity for squatters to dramatize their plight as displaced people who have lost not only their civilization but all their rights in the high-tech society of the early twenty-first century. And, in Costa Rica, when the government announced the privatization of the country's electrical, transportation, and energy sectors, citizens and workers rebelled with a general strike in March 2000. After two solid weeks of resistance, the government backed off.

In Canada, groups like Low Income Families Together (LIFT) have drawn on the Universal Declaration in mobilizing opposition to the Ontario government's workfare programs. And LIFT has worked to expose the fact that the Canadian and Ontario governments have failed to live up to their obligations under the UN's International Covenant on Economic, Social, and Cultural Rights. In response to Ontario's drastic cuts in welfare payments, other activists stormed the Toronto Stock Exchange in 1997, and during the same period, the Ontario Coalition against Poverty filled shopping carts and jammed the checkout counters of Loblaws stores in Toronto to dramatize the plight of the hungry.

DEFENDING CULTURAL DIVERSITY

It is generally recognized that all peoples have the right to preserve their own languages, values, customs, traditions, and heritage. The Universal Declaration of Human Rights — in its Articles 22 and 27, among others — touches on some of these elements, but a fuller recognition of cultural rights is found in the International Covenant on Economic, Social, and Cultural Rights. In spite of these safeguards, however, cultural rights are violated every day. Around the world, an ersatz culture of Hollywood blockbuster movies and a globalized music, television, and mass market book industry are creating a global monoculture, where one language and one set of customs and traditions predominates. In Latin America, Asia, and Africa, as well as Europe and North America, young people are trapped in a consumer kids' culture that places ultimate value on paraphernalia such as Nike sneakers, Gap clothes, Michael Jordan T-shirts, baseball caps, and all the latest CDs — produced primarily by U.S.-based corporations. This juggernaut is rapidly destroying what remains of individual local traditions, knowledge, skills, artisanship, and values. It was partly this onerous trend that José Bové and the McDo's 10 were resisting in their protest against McDonald's in southern France (see Chapter Six).

Not surprisingly, global trade and investment rules are being used to aid and abet the process of cultural domination. Rules set out in TRIPS (Trade Related Intellectual Property Measures) and GATS (the General Agreement on Trade in Services) are being used to strike down laws, policies, and practices of sovereign nations that have been designed to preserve and protect their individual cultures. Canada experienced a setback when the WTO ruled that this country's cultural policies on split-run magazines contravened GATS rules. The split-run policy required that U.S.-based magazine publishers like *Time* include a special section of Canadian content as a condition for access to the Canadian market, but the WTO claimed that this amounted to a barrier to cross-border trade in services. By the same token, countries attempting to adopt new measures to enhance and/or protect the cultural rights of their citizens can be prevented from doing so under WTO rules. Cultural diversity has been clapped into global handcuffs, and a tide of resistance has begun to emerge.

Theme Parks

One of the prime symbols of the new global monoculture is the entertainment theme park designed to market the so-called American Dream all over the world. The Walt Disney Company, the quintessential representative of the theme park industry, uses virtuoso technology to give hundreds of millions of people the space to pop "in" and "out" of fantasy worlds based largely on a fairy-tale version of American ideals and values. Featuring Mickey Mouse and Snow White, Disney sells its own canned edition of the American Dream and market-tested thrills. After the first Disney theme parks in Anaheim, California, and Orlando, Florida, proved to be roaring successes, the idea was exported to France, Germany, Japan, and several other countries.

Apart from the fact that Mickey Mouse speaks Japanese and Snow White has become fluent in German, Disney theme parks outside the U.S. are not much more than conveyor belts for American-based monoculture. For this reason, Disneyland has become a focus of cultural resistance, especially in France.

When Eurodisney opened in a sugar beet field twenty miles east of Paris in 1992, Parisian intellectuals attacked the project as an assault on French culture. As one theatre director put it, the park, now known as Disneyland Paris, is "a cultural Chernobyl." The French minister of culture refused to attend the opening of the theme park, which he described as a symbol of "the America of clichés and a consumer society." Soon after the official opening, French farmers staged a protest by driving their tractors up to the theme park and blocking its entrance. Their main target was the U.S. government and its demand that French agricultural subsidies be slashed, but the internationally televised act cast the global spotlight on issues of cultural domination, as well.

Media Empires

Today, the main engines of global monoculture are the media entertainment empires that have been created through megamergers and are now dominating the planet's air waves. As if Time Warner was not big enough, its merger with America Online (the world's largest Internet company) has produced the most powerful media entertainment empire on earth. Now Time Warner/AOL joins Disney/ABC, Rupert Murdoch's News Corporation, and Viacom in controlling the world's information and communications industry.

Not long ago, communications were considered to be of such strategic importance in distributing news and information and in shaping citizens' attitudes that governments worked hard to maintain a degree of public ownership and control over radio, television, and other mass media. Politicians saw the importance of ensuring that news and information were not commercially driven and that cultural diversity was safeguarded. In Canada, the Canadian Broadcasting Corporation was established with a mandate to preserve and protect the nation's cultural identity and diversity, both within the country and in relation to the United States. Now, all of this has radically changed. The recent mergers between CanWest Global and the *National Post*, and between BCE, CTV, and the *Globe and Mail* have created giant, for-profit media corporations that control the airwaves, linking newspaper, television, and the Internet. News is now presented as monocultural entertainment,

defined largely in the image of big business. At the same time, current negotiations taking place at the WTO could establish a set of global rules designed
to expand the corporate domination of telecommunications, including the
Internet and digital systems. And the hands of governments will be tied even
more as WTO rules prevent them from providing subsidies or support mechanisms for public broadcasting.

Resistance to the trend has been scarce. Global media giants are a formidable force to counter, and the changes taking place in the communication
and information industries have been occurring at such a torrid pace that
members of the cultural community — artists, actors, writers, entertainers,
filmmakers, and publishers — have found themselves on the defensive.
Nevertheless, the cultural community has been finding ways to forge
international links in the fight for cultural rights and diversity. In September
2000, representatives from 160 civil society organizations concerned about
cultural rights issues in thirty different countries met in Santorini, Greece, to
form the International Network for Cultural Diversity. Although the delegates
to the Santorini conference tackled a wide range of issues, including what
to do about the power of the media entertainment empires and threats to
public broadcasting, energies were focused on developing an international
charter as a new legal instrument for protecting cultural diversity. These and
related proposals were presented to cultural ministers from twenty countries
who were simultaneously holding a meeting in Santorini, chaired by
Canadian Heritage Minister Sheila Copps.

FRENCH CULTURAL COMMUNITY BLASTS MAI

At the height of MAI negotiations concerning a global investment
treaty in 1998, French artists, entertainers, and filmmakers decided to
take to the national airwaves themselves to express their resistance.
The occasion was the annual César Awards, which in France, are syn-
onymous with the Academy Awards, or "Oscars," in America. At a key
moment in the nationally televised event, the emcee openly
denounced the proposed MAI as a threat to cultural rights and diversity. The MAI would give Hollywood direct access to French markets
and culture. While the incident provoked a major uproar in official
Paris circles where the MAI was being negotiated at the OECD, it

> galvanized popular opposition throughout the country. Later, France pulled the plug on the MAI negotiations by walking away from the table.

Indigenous Knowledge

Indigenous knowledge and cultural heritage are now being used to boost the profit margins of worldwide corporations — with the help of the WTO's TRIPS agreement. Agrochemical and pharmaceutical corporations have been using property rights and patent laws to claim ownership over seed varieties and medicinal plants, especially in the richly biodiverse regions of the Nonindustrialized World. In one instance, acting on behalf of these two industries, the U.S. government used the TRIPS agreement to charge the government of Thailand with passing laws to protect the cultural rights and heritage of the country's traditional healers. For Indigenous peoples, whose long-standing knowledge of nature has evolved collectively through many generations, actions like these appear ludicrous. At the International Conference of Indigenous Peoples, held in the Philippines in July 1999, the delegates declared that "Western property rights regimes pose a direct threat to Indigenous cosmologies and values. . . . No corporation or individual can claim invention or discovery of medicinal plants, seeds, or other living things."

The case of the neem tree in India is a classic illustration. Revered by Indigenous communities for centuries for its medicinal value and its usefulness as a biopesticide, the neem has been nicknamed the "village pharmacy." Products that derive from the marvellous tree are used for purposes ranging from cleaning teeth to treating acne and ulcers. Since the early 1970s, a number of American and Japanese corporations, including W.R. Grace & Company, have taken out patents on numerous products extracted from the tree, even though neem-based medicines and biopesticides have been produced by Indigenous communities for centuries. In May 2000, however, an alliance of Indian and European groups, led by physicist and author Vandana Shiva of the Research Institute for Science, Technology and Ecology, won a major legal victory that protected one of the neem tree's products. After facing considerable pressure, the European Patent Office decided to withdraw the patent it had previously granted to W.R. Grace for a chemical formulation derived from the tree — setting a major precedent in favour of Indigenous people's defence of their cultural rights.

SAFEGUARDING HUMAN RIGHTS

Human rights violations have been roundly condemned in the UN's Universal Declaration of Human Rights, the accompanying covenants, International Labour Organization (ILO) conventions, and resolutions resulting from the Beijing Conference on women's rights. From time to time, the UN Commis-sion on Human Rights has also played a role in mobilizing nation-states to eliminate the practices that inherently promote violations of these rights — offences like physical torture, bodily harm, sexual abuse, racial discrimination, exploitive work, and any form of slavery.

Yet, the dominant institutions of the global economy are largely immune to this body of human rights law. WTO, IMF, and World Bank rules are not subordinate to the Universal Declaration of Human Rights or its accompanying covenants, and the WTO's refusal to incorporate human rights and labour standards into its operations render them null and void anyway in the context of the global economy. Action on human rights violations is left to institutions like the United Nations Commission on Human Rights (UNCHR) and the ILO, which, unlike the WTO, have no power to enforce their laws.

Besides exploited workers, the main victims of human rights violations around the world are women, children, migrants, and Indigenous peoples. Intensified by the pressures and forces that characterize the new global economy, their struggles are especially fierce in areas where the flesh trade is active or where military repression and exploitive labour practices reign.

The Flesh Trade

In the new global economy, participants in the flesh trade have even more opportunity for profit than they had in the past. Taking advantage of the increasing numbers of women who have lost jobs and livelihoods because of the capricious nature of unfettered transnational trade, pimps operating on behalf of businesses, unrestrained by governments, rake in large profits from the sale and use of women's bodies. In many countries, "sex tourism" has become a growth industry, based on offering women and children as prostitutes to foreign visitors. Through the Internet, women can be instantly recruited into the flesh trade and marketed on a global basis. So, too, can children, who have become an increasingly popular "commodity" for flesh traders because they are less likely to transmit AIDS to the clients of this highly exploitative commerce.

For the women's movement around the world, the global flesh trade has become an important human rights issue. In country after country, women's groups have been focusing their education and action campaigns on this new variation of a degrading and life-threatening business. Take, for example, the Women's International League for Peace and Freedom (WILPF). Under the auspices of their program "Women Define Globalization," they have launched an education and action campaign that links flesh trade issues to a wide range of other economic and social forces affecting women in the new global economy. Through workshops and conferences, the WILPF enables women to see how global corporations are exerting power over their daily lives and hijacking their democratic rights. Similarly, the National Action Committee on the Status of Women (NAC) in Canada has been giving priority to building solidarity with women's struggles against economic and sexual exploitation in other countries, especially in Southeast Asia and Latin America. They successfully lobbied Ottawa to amend the Criminal Code so that Canadians engaging in sex tourism with children in other countries can be charged with rape back home.

Military Repression

In recent years, Nigeria and Burma have become key targets of action against military oppression. In Nigeria, solidarity campaigns have been organized in support of the Ogoni people. They claimed their lands were being devastated by oil spills and toxic waste dumps resulting from the operations of international petroleum giants working nearby, but when they launched objections, they became the objects of ongoing repression at the hands of military and state police. The prime targets for resistance have been the Nigerian military regime and Royal Dutch/Shell. It was well known that as the largest petroleum producer in the country, Shell worked hand in glove with the Nigerian military to ensure protection against social unrest related to the company's oil operations.

In Burma, campaigns have been organized in support of the country's pro-democracy movement led by Nobel Peace Prize holder Aung San Suu Kyi.

Since 1988, Burma has been ruled by a brutal military junta. In a scathing report of human rights violations, the ILO has officially documented and denounced forced labour practices used by the junta to construct an oil pipeline across the country, violating Indigenous land claims as they went. In providing military security for the pipeline's construction, for instance, the army went into villages and forced people to carry their munitions for them. In order to financially suffocate the junta, the Burmese pro-democracy movement has called for the kind of foreign disinvestment strategies that helped bring about the dismantling of apartheid in South Africa.

BARRING INVESTMENT IN BURMA

In February 1995, the city council of Berkeley, California, passed a resolution barring the city from purchasing goods and services from companies with investments or operations in Burma, where human rights are flagrantly violated under the country's oppressive military regime. The Berkeley action had a domino effect across the U.S. According to the latest count, some twenty-two cities and two states had adopted "selective purchasing agreements" pertaining to companies operating in Burma, and another half dozen cities were passing similar resolutions affecting investments in Nigeria. Both Massachusetts and Vermont passed selective purchasing laws regarding Burma and similar legislation is pending in New York, Texas, and Washington state. Since the passage of the Massachusetts law, several big name corporations have divested their operations in Burma, including Apple Computer, Eastman Kodak, Texaco, Hewlett-Packard, and Philips Electronics.

Based on information from Naomi Klein's *No Logo*

Resistance groups have also called for foreign disinvestment in Nigeria and in other countries suffering under oppressive regimes. However, WTO rules are being cited by opponents to thwart these efforts. When citizens' groups in the United States lobbied their state and local governments to adopt policies of not doing business with any company operating in Burma or Nigeria, the state of Massachusetts took the cue and actually did enact a law to terminate government purchasing contracts with companies doing business in Burma. This courageous action was, of course, met with little joy on the part of the companies who were shut out, but instead of taking their business elsewhere, European and Japanese corporations affected by the new legislation because of their extensive Burmese operations took steps to have the law challenged under WTO rules. At the same time, a corporate lobby group called USA*ENGAGE formally challenged the Massachusetts law in state court, claiming that it violated the American Constitution by interfering with the exclusive authority of the executive branch of the U.S. government to conduct foreign policy. The membership of USA*ENGAGE includes AT&T, Boeing, BP America, the Chase Manhattan Bank, Coca-Cola, Dow Chemical, IBM, Intel, and Siemens, as well as Monsanto and Union Carbide. The state court ruled in favour of USA*ENGAGE, but the resistance has continued through court appeals and a heightened public education campaign.

LABOUR STANDARDS

The only way to prevent corporations from exploiting cheap labour pools in Third World countries, union leaders insist, is to urge all countries to adopt the core labour standards established by the International Labour Organization. The 120 conventions adopted by the ILO include the right of workers to unionize, to engage in collective bargaining, to receive fair wages for their labour, and to have adequate health and safety standards in the workplace. Yet many countries do not enforce such standards, and the human rights of unionists working in those jurisdictions are often in jeopardy. In 1999 alone, 140 trade unionists either disappeared or committed suicide or were assassinated after being threatened because of their defence of workers' rights. Nearly 3,000 more were arrested, and 1,500 were either injured, beaten, or tortured.

Throughout Southeast Asia, where many regimes have failed to enact or enforce appropriate labour standards, workers are beginning to take measures to improve their conditions. In Cambodia, twenty thousand workers in two hundred garment factories walked off the job in June 2000, demanding an increase in their forty-dollar monthly wage. And since the fall of the Suharto regime in Indonesia, labour disputes have become a daily affair. In Vietnam, sixty-three strikes took place in 1999, primarily at foreign-owned factories. However, when the International Confederation of Free Trade Unions and its affiliates in the labour movement around the world mounted a relentless campaign to have core ILO labour standards adopted by the WTO and its member-countries, many Third World governments rejected this as a move by the North to undercut the South's comparative advantage in low wage costs. Given this North-South disconnect, the Canadian Labour Congress, for one, has begun to understand that simply inserting a labour clause in the WTO may not be sufficient and that more dialogue with unions and civil society groups in Third World countries is essential.

The exploitation of child labour by transnational corporations operating in Third World countries is another result of nations of the South attempting to gain greater international market share. A longstanding problem, exploitation of child workers became a live issue within and outside the labour movement in 1995. That was when thirteen-year-old Canadian teenager Craig Kielburger disrupted Prime Minister Jean Chrétien's 1995 trade mission to India in order to cast the public spotlight on children who were working there and throughout Southeast Asia in bonded slavery. Through his Toronto-based organization, Free the Children — heavily funded by the labour movement — young Kielburger has taken his crusade against the exploitation of child labour into high schools and grade schools all over the world. The issue has also proven to be an effective lever in the trade union struggle to mobilize public support for core labour standards that would eliminate the sweatshops and related forms of cheap labour used by many transnational corporations.

• • •

Child labour and other human rights, the protection of social rights and cultural diversity — these are some of the major battlefields in the conflict between the proponents of corporate globalization and the defenders of common humanity. There are, to be sure, other areas of flagrant violations (to animal rights, for example, or peoples' rights to peace). And every issue can be crosscut on the basis of gender, race, and class realities. But to use the Internet analogy again, these battlefields are the "hubs," and the diverse campaigns being waged are the "spokes." Each activist element is autonomous, but all are interconnected.

The unifying theme that permeates the various battlefields is the mission to defend democracy and to guard the commons. This vision binds them together in a coherent struggle for societal transformation and planetary survival. There can be no democracy in the global economy as long as there are no public spaces and institutions to ensure that the rights of people as citizens and the well-being of the earth are maintained and secured. By the same token, there can be no commons in the global economy unless civil society movements are able to effectively participate in defining, shaping, and implementing the public spaces and institutions required to ensure universal access to the basic needs of life.

The battle to save democracy and the commons is not an idealistic fantasy. It is grounded in international agreements like the Universal Declaration of Human Rights, its accompanying covenants, and the charters emerging from numerous UN summits. More important, the fight to preserve these rights is firmly rooted in the political cultures of particular peoples and nations. Transnational corporate monoculture and the governments and corporations that promote it are militating against justice and the right that all human beings have guaranteed access to the basics of life and to human, social, and cultural rights. Civil society groups are working to completely reverse the trend before it's too late.

8

Citizens' Agenda

*How citizens' movements are laying
the foundations for rebuilding democracy
and transforming the global economy*

"*A*ll *great social movements have been fired by a fierce imagination," declared
a Winnipeg participant. It was 1998, and a Citizens' Inquiry was being
conducted all across Canada after the collapse of negotiations surrounding the
Multilateral Agreement on Investment.*

*The MAI defeat had come to symbolize massive resistance to corporate
globalization and its failures, but the Chrétien government wasn't noticing. So
the Council of Canadians seized the moment and organized a series of hearings
in eight cities in the fall of 1998. The Council and forty other national organizations set up sessions in Vancouver, Edmonton, Saskatoon, Winnipeg, Toronto,
Montreal, Halifax, and St. John's and called the series "The MAI Inquiry: A
Citizens' Search for Alternatives."*

*The commissioners on the Inquiry panel were well known in Canada and
knowledgeable about globalization. Before they began their tour, a Citizens'
Handbook had been distributed throughout the country, highlighting the need to*

reorganize the global economy. This reconfiguration would be built on the Three Rs of democracy: Rights, Rules, and Responsibilities. And the handbook included a Citizens' Report Card for evaluating the performance of institutions like the WTO, the IMF, and the World Bank.

Hundreds of civil society groups made submissions to the commissioners as they made their way across the country, and thousands of individual citizens filled out and handed in their report cards. The result was a harvest of creative plans for transforming economic and social structures in Canada and around the world. Proposals included a six-point plan for achieving food security and food safety; a set of proposals for "remaking the economy through women's eyes"; and a strategy for the creation of "community parliaments" as a means of increasing local democratic control over the economy.

Other visions included a "genuine progress index" for evaluating the hidden and long-term costs and benefits of economic policy making; a new international treaty, in which citizens' rights would take precedence over investor rights and corporations would be held accountable for violating the Universal Declaration of Human Rights; an international charter for protecting cultural rights and diversity; and a variety of policy tools and strategies for controlling financial speculation, curbing capital flight, and making transnational corporations environmentally and socially accountable to communities.

As the final report of the Citizens' Inquiry demonstrated, there is certainly no shortage of creative imagination when it comes to proposing ways of reorganizing the global economy to serve the democratic rights of people and to ensure the survival of the planet. Yet citizens all over the world are seldom, if ever, given the chance to collectively define and shape their economic, social, and ecological futures. Through the Citizens' Inquiry, the groundwork was laid for reclaiming democracy and the commons in the new global economy.

For Canadians, there is nothing especially new about citizens organizing themselves democratically to develop alternative economic policies and strategies. Every year a vast group of civil society organizations (labour unions, community associations, environmental groups, women's networks, religious organizations, international associations, and other public interest groups) participate in a process to develop alternative federal, provincial, and city budgets. Originally designed by CHO!CES, a Winnipeg-based social action network, the process involves representatives of civil society groups and policy specialists working together to design and promote alternative budgets based on priorities different from those of the governments in power.

Under the auspices of the Canadian Centre for Policy Alternatives and CHO!CES, an Alternative Federal Budget has been designed and promoted every year since 1995. Each year, participating civil society organizations make choices about priorities for expenditures while the policy analysts work on calculations about revenue generation and fiscal strategies. Participating groups embark on negotiations over whether spending priorities should include, for example, a new pharmacare program on prescription drugs for families and seniors or a national, universally accessible childcare program. Macroeconomic, fiscal, and taxation policies are put on the table, along with measures to stimulate environmental investment, green jobs, and the rebuilding of public infrastructure. The benefits are many, but foremost among them perhaps is the fact that these alternative budget-making processes offer citizens concrete opportunities to develop and exercise their skills in making public policy, based on different economic, social, and environmental priorities.

Elsewhere, similar kinds of citizens' agendas are being developed by civil society movements to reclaim democracy and the commons. A prime example is the Sustainable Chile program, in which a national coalition of civil society groups has been developing specific proposals for social transformation of the economy, based on models of sustainability. In six regions of Chile, civil society groups have developed a participatory process in which grassroots movements work with technical experts in designing alternative policies and programs for a sustainable Chile. Since 1998, the Sustainable Chile program has developed alternative plans for twenty-two sectors of the economy, including forestry, mining, agriculture, fishing, energy, water, urban development, and biodiversity, along with health, education, and social and environmental services. In April 1999, a national citizens' agenda for a Sustainable Chile was launched publicly during the country's presidential campaign.

To cultivate widespread public awareness and support of the Sustainable Chile platform, civil society groups chose Sara Larrain, a well-known social and environmental activist in Chile, to be their presidential candidate. During the three-month campaign, the citizens' agenda for a sustainable Chile was promoted in cities, towns, and rural communities throughout the country, and it received five minutes' play on national television every day for a thirty-day period. Following the election campaign, civil society groups began developing strategies for promoting and implementing their own citizens' agendas for sustainability at the provincial and regional levels. And this agenda and process are now beginning to spread throughout Latin America as national coalitions of citizens' movements form around similar people's agendas for sustainability in Brazil, Uruguay, Argentina, and Paraguay.

Three other notable international initiatives have appeared in the past two years as antidotes to the new poisons of unfettered global markets and their social and environmental implications. The International Forum on Globalization (IFG), based in San Francisco, has just published a set of proposals — "Alternatives to Economic Globalization," co-edited by John Cavanagh and Jerry Mander. This document is expected to be used as a basis for stimulating public discussion and debate in civil society movements through a new round of teach-ins on alternatives to the global economy, to be held in both Third World and Industrialized Nations. The Third World Network, which works with governments as well as civil society organizations in the South, has also formulated a platform of policy changes in global trade, finance, and investment. And the Hemispheric Social Alliance, composed of civil society groups in North and Latin America, has outlined a platform of "Alternatives for the Americas" covering a wide range of areas, including investment, finance, trade, sustainable energy, agriculture, the environment, immigration, labour, and human rights.

These initiatives demonstrate that people in many countries are hungry for a new politics — citizens' politics — in an age when rampant corporate globalization has alienated the majority of those who will be affected by multinationals. People are increasingly losing confidence in the will and ability — let alone the authority — of governments to serve their needs and the needs of the earth itself. In corrupt and dictatorial regimes, this attitude toward government has been the norm, but the same reactions have now become more prevalent in liberal democracies like Canada, where laws, policies, and programs are now more obviously the products of collusion between governments and corporations than they were in the past.

Profound changes in the nature and role of the state are essential. What's more, people now understand themselves differently as citizens, their self-perception having been radically twisted and distorted by living in a global market economy. According to new "market maketh" philosophies, people are relegated to being consumers first and foremost, not citizens. "I shop; therefore, I am" has become the motto of our times. As today's youth know all too well, the dominant message is not to exercise one's role as a citizen in the political community but to be a consumer in the global marketplace. By becoming global shoppers, people lose their identity as members of a political community and instead become integers on the marketing grids of transnational corporations in the global market.

Those who are not satisfied with an identity contingent on the whims of a corporate modelling of the world are among the participants in the search for a new citizens' politics. In the mass mobilizations that took place on the streets of Seattle and elsewhere, people were not only saying "No" to the old order; they were also saying "'Yes" to a new order. The old order, rooted in the paradigm symbolized by the Washington Consensus, has been slowly but steadily disintegrating since its acceleration following the end of the Cold War, so global managers and their institutions — namely, the WTO, the IMF, and the World Bank — are currently experiencing a crisis of legitimacy. The "Battle of Seattle" and related mobilizations have demonstrated that neither the global management elite nor their government allies can safely say any longer that they enjoy the confidence and support of civil society around the world. Arising from the ashes of the old order are the embers of a new and fundamentally different way of governing and doing business.

The MAI Citizens' Inquiry held in Canada, coupled with initiatives like the Sustainable Chile project and the international work being done on alternatives to economic globalization are signs that people are determined to build a citizens' agenda for transforming the global economy based on a new paradigm. The exact nature of that new paradigm remains to be seen, but imperatives for societal transformation and planetary survival will be central features, and currently, demands for reclaiming democracy and protecting the commons are taking centre stage.

Based on the diverse proposals presented at the Citizens' Inquiry, a common platform emerged as a base from which to forge a citizens' agenda for transforming the global economy. This platform contains six components:

- reclaiming core principles,
- re-democratizing our governments,
- reconstructing trade regimes,
- revamping global finance,
- re-regulating foreign investment, and
- re-chartering transnational corporations.

Although some diversity exists among civil society organizations, in regards to both emphasis and position, it is also fair to say that an emerging consensus is forming around these six components as a common platform for transforming the global economy. The first two will be taken up in this chapter, and the remaining four will be addressed in Chapter Nine.

RECLAIMING CORE PRINCIPLES

To develop an effective citizens' agenda for transforming the global economy, operating principles need to be clarified. But the task is not as straightforward as it might first appear, since many of the core principles in which healthy societies are rooted, and by which they are nourished, have themselves been co-opted, twisted, and distorted. Take, for example, "democracy" as an operating principle. Now often equated with the free market and unbridled capitalism, the very meaning of democracy itself has become mangled. So, too, has our understanding of what it means to be a "citizen." It is not sufficient, therefore, to simply express and affirm core principles for transforming the global economy. In many cases, it is essential to reclaim, retrieve, and redefine these core principles.

During the Citizens' Inquiry, for example, one witness pointed out that the term "democracy" was originally derived from two Greek words: "demos," meaning "people," and "kratos," meaning "power." This understanding of democracy as "people power" has been all but lost in our political culture. Yet democracy, by definition, implies that people have the authority to govern themselves and that sovereignty, first and foremost, resides in the people. In turn, people collectively decide to pool their sovereignty by creating and recreating governments with the authority to act for the common good. While the traditions and processes for electing leaders, developing policies, and making and reinforcing laws differs from country to country and culture to culture, all peoples have in common the right to shape their own lives, communities, and nations through self-government.

GANDHI REVISITED

In India, civil society movements have been reviving Mahatma Gandhi's principles of Swaraj and Swadeshi as inspiration for exercising democratic control and building sustainable communities. "The people's democratically driven agenda," says Indian physicist and feminist Vandana Shiva, "is for greater localization, both political and economic. Political localization implies more decisions being transferred to local space. This is Gandhi's concept of Swaraj. Economic localization implies that whatever can be produced locally with local resources should be protected to build a vibrant local economy, so that livelihoods and the environment are both protected. This was Gandhi's concept of Swadeshi."

Movements in India are consciously retrieving these and other Gandhian principles, to forge a new citizens' politics in opposition to the corporate-led globalization and governance of the WTO, the IMF, and the World Bank.

In effect, the authority for developing a citizens' agenda is itself rooted in this essential definition of democracy and the notion of popular sovereignty. But for most citizens' movements today, the meaning of democracy goes beyond this to include the following basic operating principles, which form the cornerstones of a common platform for transforming the global economy.

Democratic Rights

Civil society movements insist on the full recognition and implementation of people's basic democratic rights, as enshrined in the Universal Declaration of Human Rights. Among them are the rights to food, clothing, and shelter; to employment, education, and health care; to a clean environment, cultural integrity, and high-quality public services; to fair wages; to collective bargaining and the formation of unions; and to participation in decisions affecting these rights.

These individual rights are reinforced, in turn, by the collective rights encoded in other UN declarations, such as the International Covenant on Economic, Social, and Cultural Rights and the International Covenant on Civil and Political Rights. A citizens' agenda would insist that these basic democratic rights and freedoms become the cornerstones for managing the global economy. And in developing global rules for trade, finance, and investment, the rights and needs of citizens would take precedence over the interests of investors and transnational corporations.

The Common Good

In order to recognize and implement these basic democratic rights, however, governments need to preserve and protect certain areas of the economy and society for the sake of the common good — areas known as the commons. The commons, also defined as any aspects of life that are of universal importance, may include, but are not limited to: *food security* (that is, adequate supplies of safe, quality foods); *environmental safeguards* (including regulations to prevent pollution; to prohibit toxic waste disposal, habitat loss, and ozone depletion; and to limit greenhouse gas emissions); *strategic resources* (such as finance, energy, and communications, which are of critical importance to nations and people's livelihoods); *vital resources* (seeds, genes, water, air, and other elements of biodiversity); *public services*, including essential services like health care, education, and social security; *cultural integrity* (such as Indigenous cultural expression through the works of local artists, writers, and entertainers); *labour standards* (trade unions, fair wages, and collective bargaining, as well as restrictions on child and other forced labour); and *human rights* (protected in order to prevent discrimination, torture, sexual abuse, and other bodily harm). To preserve and defend the commons, governments have the right, as well as the responsibility, to intervene in the market when necessary and to institute regulatory measures, including the establishment of public enterprises.

Sustainable Communities

Democratic rights and the common good can be protected best through the creation of local sustainable communities, in which local resources are used by local people to produce goods and services for distribution close to home, within ecological limits. This core principle runs counter to the dictates of corporate globalization on several levels. Rather than promoting export-oriented economies, which, in turn, require the construction of more and more transportation corridors, fossil fuel use, refrigeration, and packaging, many citizens' groups encourage greater economic self-reliance and the restoration of local and regional sources of products and commodities. And as a countervailing force to the concentration of economic and political power promoted by transnational corporations and the World Trade Organization, civil society groups recommend reliance on the principle of subsidiarity. In other words, political decisions affecting local communities should be made at the local level as much as possible. Governments should have the right and responsibility to favour the creation of local sustainable communities through policies like "site here to sell here" and they need to enact laws requiring capital to be more firmly grounded in local communities.

Political Sovereignty

In certain strategic areas of global economic governance — notably trade, finance, and investment — too much political sovereignty has already been transferred from nation-states to transnational corporations and global management institutions like the WTO. Surprisingly, in nominally democratic societies, this transfer has been made to global institutions that have no democratic accountability to citizens of any country in the world. And the surrender of political sovereignty by nation-states has occurred largely without the consent of their citizens, in whom sovereignty is supposed to reside in the first place. If the core principles of democratic rights, the common good, and sustainable communities are to be brought to life, then democratically elected governments must have the powers required to establish and implement clear economic, social, and ecological objectives for national development. To do so, political sovereignty must be reclaimed and revitalized. However, this cannot be achieved authentically without more active and effective participation of citizens in governing processes.

Effective Participation

For active citizen participation to come about, new mechanisms are essential. Simply restoring political sovereignty to national governments will not be sufficient, because virtually all countries are currently operating on a democratic deficit. Decisions bearing on trade, finance, and investment are made by senior government bureaucrats in collusion with corporate managers from key sectors of the economy. If public consultations are undertaken (see Chapter Five), the record shows that they are conducted primarily as public relations exercises. If the rules of the global economy are going to reflect the principles of democratic rights, the common good, and sustainable communities, citizens must be able to speak up and participate in national government decision making about trade, finance, and investment priorities. For their voices to be encouraged and heard, however, new mechanisms for democratic participation and control must be developed in all countries.

International Solidarity

Civil society movements reject the corporate-driven model of globalization that is being exported all over the world today. This does not mean, however, that these movements embrace the return of economic nationalism or the re-bordering of the world. On the contrary, they recognize that there is much to be gained by living and acting in a spirit of international solidarity. According to the International Forum on Globalization (IFG), internationalism embraces the global flow of ideas, information, culture, money, and goods, not in order to concentrate wealth and power in the hands of a few, but to help realize people's basic democratic rights, protect the common good, and build local sustainable communities. In a word, internationalism implies global solidarity among civil society movements — a development that has been greatly facilitated by Internet communication.

These tenets should be strategically applied not only to the global economy, but also to all other levels of the economy simultaneously — local, regional, and national. Unless efforts to change the rules and institutions governing the global economy are matched by struggles to transform local and national economies, there can be little hope of authentic change.

RE-DEMOCRATIZING OUR GOVERNMENTS

Re-democratizing our governments may sound like an "oxymoron." On the one hand, some people will say we already live in a democracy, because we elect our governments and members of Parliament on a regular basis and then have the opportunity to "throw the bums out" a few years later if we don't like what they're doing. On the other hand, some will argue that we don't live in a democracy, nor have we ever, since governments don't really represent or respond to the basic needs of people, leaving citizens with little choice but to take matters normally left to governments into their own hands. In a similar vein, civil society groups in countries with a tradition of authoritarian and dictatorial regimes see the state as the enemy of progressive social change, while those from countries with a tradition of social democracy sometimes have a more positive view of the role that governments can play. In either case, why re-democratize governments?

For one thing, in countries like Canada, where citizens live with a delusion of democracy, it would be refreshing to introduce the real thing. As author and broadcaster Judy Rebick has pointed out, we need to make a distinction between two models of democracy: "representative democracy" and "participatory democracy." The Canadian parliamentary system is based on the representative form of democracy, where citizens virtually delegate their democratic voice to a group of government representatives for up to five years, but do not hold them accountable from day to day and week to week. While this has been the predominant view of democracy in our political culture, we have precious little experience with direct or participatory forms of democracy, in which citizens exercise their rights to be self-governing people by shaping and making decisions about laws, policies, and programs. For these reasons, says Rebick, Canadians must learn to "imagine democracy."

By probing concrete examples of what she calls "active citizenship," not only in Canada but also internationally, people begin to get a glimpse of participatory democracy, which embodies an ongoing "interaction between active citizens, elected politicians, and career officials" in governmental planning and decision making. As a Canadian example of this form of democracy, Rebick cites the cross-country public forums that took place before the referendum on the proposed Charlottetown Accord in 1992, in which citizens from all walks of life discussed, debated, and formulated a position on asymmetrical federalism as a way of resolving the Quebec-Canada issue — something politicians had not been able to do on their own. Internationally, she refers to the Brazilian city of Pôrto Alegre, where citizens are elected each year to serve alongside city councillors as they make decisions about municipal spending priorities. The elected citizens offer their advice following extensive discussion and debate in community assemblies, through what's called a participatory budget process.

Democracy is still a long way off, however, since the state itself and the right to democratic self-governance has been largely hijacked by transnational corporations. Beginning in the late nineteenth century, the legal status of corporations as "natural persons" with powers of free speech and assembly was entrenched by a series of court rulings, first in the United States and then in other countries around the world. Corporate profits, contracts, and the rate of return on investment were redefined as "property" and were legally protected from meddling either by citizens or by their elected representatives. As a result, corporations acquired more political rights than individual persons had as citizens. Then, over a quarter-century ago, the Trilateral Commission was formed by American powerbrokers, bringing the CEOs of the world's largest corporations together with presidents, prime ministers, and senior government officials. Concerted efforts began to be made to reinvent the role of the state. In its 1974 report, entitled *The Crisis of Democracy*, the Trilateral Commission declared that there was "an excess of democracy" in the world that has led to "a deficit in governability."

The solution, said the trilateralists, lay in having stronger governments in a weaker democratic framework. Building on the trilateralist vision, big business coalitions were established in the capitals of the major Industrialized Nations — the U.S. Business Roundtable, the European Round Table of Industrialists, the Japanese Keidanren, and the Business Council on National Issues in Canada. They had the lobbying and political machinery necessary to advance laws, policies, and programs based on the corporate agenda. Eventually, the trileralists mapped out proposals for global governance through the IMF, the World Bank, and later the World Trade Organization. So by the 1990s, the role of the state had effectively been remade in the image of the transnational corporation, with big business lobby machinery firmly entrenched in the halls of political power, playing a highly influential and even decisive role in determining laws, policies, and programs.

The central threat to democracy today is therefore the "corporate security state." For the most part, the state has been redesigned primarily to defend and protect the "sovereign" interests of transnational corporations, rather than the democratic rights of its citizens. In this age of corporate globalization, the prime role of the state is to provide a favourable climate for profitable transnational investment, production, and competition. Priority is placed on providing "security for investors," not "security for citizens" — at all levels of government, national, regional, and local. The "corporate security state" has, for all intents and purposes, become constitutionalized through the new body of rules administered by the WTO and the IMF for global trade, finance, and investment.

A NEW MODEL OF GOVERNANCE

The corporate security state obviously needs to exit the world stage if local economies, public services, and social programs are going to survive. Otherwise, these and other benefits will founder in the storms of market turbulence. All antiglobalization citizens' groups need to prepare action plans for dismantling the corporate security state and for replacing it with a model of democratic governance. Such a plan of action would be a multifaceted one, and the first steps in implementation would be something like this:

- define the new model of democratic governance,
- dismantle the mechanisms of the corporate security state,
- overhaul the functions of the state to make them more democratic,
- strengthen the capacity to build sustainable communities, and
- democratize the major institutions of global economic governance.

This new model would be based on a combination of representative and participatory democracy. In Canada, our model of representative democracy should be made "proportional" to ensure that the number of seats more closely represents how people actually vote. Under a model of proportional representation, a party receiving 42 percent of the vote, for example, would get 42 percent of the seats, while those parties obtaining 22 and 15 percent of the popular vote would be assured of a proportional number of seats. Experience in several European countries shows that political instabilities that might arise in a multi-party system can be offset through adjustments in the application of the proportional representation model.

This would be only part of the solution, however, since even representatives who are fairly elected are still more than capable of acting against the common good. So institutional mechanisms must also be designed to maximize citizen participation in public policy making. Using these instruments for participatory democracy, members of civil society could become effectively involved in policy making on all issues, including trade, finance, and investment, and this would set the stage for Canada to help bring democratic governance to the operations of the global economy.

Even a system like this could be overwhelmed by corporate influence, just like the system that exists today, unless other measures were taken to level the playing field. Each country suffers from particular mechanisms of collusion between corporations and governments, so strategies for dismantling that machinery will vary. In some countries, for example, it makes sense to target all forms of bribery and corruption as the principal tool used by corporations to manipulate public policy making. In the United States and Canada, this would involve restricting, if not removing, all types of corporate financing for election campaigns and political parties as forms of legalized bribery and cronyism. Tight rules also need to be put in place to substantially reduce the power of the big business lobby machinery in national capitals, including the Business Council on National Issues in Ottawa, where policy think tanks and batteries of lawyers are deployed to draft policies and laws for governments on behalf of their corporate clients. Similar action is required to eliminate the use of political advertising by corporations and big business coalitions to whip up public support for their own policy demands through newspapers, radio, television, and now the Internet.

The roles and functions of the state also need to be redesigned and over-hauled for the exercise of democratic governance. In Ottawa, for example, public servants in the Department of Foreign Affairs and International Trade (DFAIT), the Department of Finance, and Industry Canada would have to be retrained in order to serve the public more effectively by re-regulating international trade, finance, and investment policies that realize citizens' democratic rights, defend the commons, and build local, sustainable communities. Other government departments such as Health, Human Resources, Heritage, Environment, and CIDA (Canadian International Development Agency) would also have to be re-tooled to play a more effective role on this front. To help counterbalance corporate influence in the meeting rooms and hallways of government offices, new institutional mechanisms must be developed to maximize citizen participation in decisions relating to the global economy. One option would be to establish a constituent assembly, composed of elected representatives from a wide range of civil society groups, which would have the mandate and resources to formulate and promote policy positions on global trade, finance, and investment, based on the core principles of democracy.

DEMOCRACY IN LONDON TOWN

An innovative experiment in local democratic governance occurred in the early 1980s through the Greater London Council (GLC) in the United Kingdom. To counter the corporate globalizing agenda of Margaret Thatcher's national government, a newly elected Greater London Council under the leadership of Ken Livingstone called for more active citizen participation in local government. Instead of funding community groups only for the provision of services, the GLC also provided funds to citizens' groups involved in economic and social change. And these citizens' groups elected representatives to sit on council committees, where they were active in making policy, program, and strategy proposals. While the GLC experiment was imperfect and short-lived, it provides creative insights into new structures for blending participatory and representative forms of governance.

Protect the Local Globally

Concrete measures also need to be taken to strengthen the capacity of local citizens and governments to build sustainable communities. Local governments, for example, could be equipped with the kinds of industrial and tax policy measures required both to enforce "site here to sell here" policies and to increase community- or worker-owned industries, cooperative enterprises, and credit unions. Adapting the school board model of citizen participation, community boards composed of elected representatives could be established with the mandate and tools to oversee the investment plans of domestic and foreign-based corporations and to examine bank loan and financing practices for community reinvestment. This would guard against capital flight and ensure that corporations act in the interests of local citizens.

In order to protect the local environment, community land trusts, designed to enhance public stewardship over agricultural and forest lands and governed by boards of elected citizens, should be set up in all regions of the country. Similarly, sustainable urban community boards, consisting of elected citizens, should be put in place, with the mandate and tools required to effectively improve urban design and implement better community housing, mass transportation, and pollution control.

Even with all these changes, democracy will still be eroded unless the major institutions of global economic governance are democratized. Of the two prevailing systems of global governance in the world — the United Nations and its multiple agencies and the Bretton Woods Institutions (the WTO, the IMF, and the World Bank) — the UN system is still the better option for exercising international democratic governance in accordance with the core principles of democracy. The United Nations' Charter, the Universal Declaration of Human Rights, and the international covenants governing economic, social, cultural, civil, and political rights provide the UN with a broad mandate to revive citizens' democratic rights in concert with national and local governments. In keeping with the UN's original mandate, the essential functions of global economic governance should be transferred from the Bretton Woods Institutions to the United Nations.

However, structural changes will also be required at the United Nations. Not only is the UN cash strapped, but it, too, is in the process of being hijacked by transnational corporations, as evidenced by Kofi Annan's recent Global Compact initiative. If the UN is to fulfill its obligations for global governance, bold measures must be taken to restore funding commitments (beginning with the U.S.) and to purge the institution of corporate influence.

By reclaiming the core principles of democracy, dissolving the mechanisms of the corporate security state, and initiating a process for redemocratizing our governments at national, regional, and local levels, the stage would be set to breathe new life into transforming the governing institutions of the global economy. To do so, strategic initiatives need to be undertaken to prune the powers of the WTO, the IMF, and the World Bank, with a view to eventually dismantling them as they now stand.

9

Democratic Control

How citizens' movements are
developing a plan of action for
transforming the global economy

*C*ommenting on the UN's Global Compact and several related initiatives,
William Greider of The Nation had this to say: "The purpose obviously is
public relations — improving the tarnished images of global corporations and
portraying weak-willed international institutions as attentive and relevant to
the turmoil of worldwide controversy. But even empty gestures can prove to be
meaningful, sometimes far beyond what their authors had in mind.

"An enduring truth, a wise friend once explained to me, is that important
social change nearly always begins in hypocrisy. First, the powerful are persuaded
to say the appropriate words, that is, to sign a commitment to higher values and
decent behavior. The social activists must spend the next ten years pounding on
them, trying to make them live up to their promises or persuading governments to
enact laws that will compel them to do so. In the long struggle for global rules
and accountability, this new phase may be understood as essential foreplay."

The period following the Battle of Seattle may well be characterized as a time *for "essential foreplay." But the civil society organizations that have been at the forefront of waging relentless campaigns against the unholy trinity of the WTO, the IMF, and the World Bank have been deadly serious about moving from resistance to transformation. After laying down the cornerstones for democratic governance, civil society groups have been busy developing their own agenda for changing the rules and institutions that govern global trade, finance, and investment. At the same time, they have been determined to tackle the dominant institution of our times — namely, the transnational corporation.*

For the global managing elite, such "dialogue" is used as a pretext for modest reforms. But the antiglobalization movement is not interested in simply reforming the global economy. Nothing short of overhauling the major institutions of global economic governance and bringing them under democratic control will be sufficient.

After Seattle, an important debate erupted in civil society circles, based on the question "Should we fix or nix the WTO?" (These were the words of Lori Wallach, Director of Public Citizen's Global Trade Watch in Washington, D.C.) The issue was similar to one that set off the strategic debate among civil society groups after the passage of NAFTA in 1994 — about whether people should campaign for the renegotiation or the abrogation of the deal. But there are notable differences between the WTO and NAFTA. While both are composed of a body of trade rules, the WTO is a more wide-ranging global institution with 134 member-countries. So when representatives of civil society groups from around the world met in Boston to hammer out a common strategy on the WTO in March 2000, they realized that to dismantle it, they would need to do much more than convince a couple of governments to withdraw from the club.

The collapse of the WTO Summit talks in Seattle and the consequent failure to launch the Millennium Round of global trade negotiations had provided civil society movements with some important strategic space, but four months later in Boston, it became clear that more time was required to develop a more sophisticated strategy. While most participants may have wanted to nix the WTO, it was agreed that an interim strategy would be needed to continue building momentum. As Walden Bello of Focus South in Thailand proposed, the strategic focus for the time being needed to be put on "curbing the powers of the WTO." In practice, this would mean pruning back its powers in key areas of the global economy, escalating demands to protect the commons in other vital areas, and strengthening institutions that could act as countervailing powers to the WTO.

RECONSTRUCTING TRADE REGIMES

The Boston meeting resulted in a "Shrink or Sink" declaration and an interim strategy: "We need to replace this old, unfair, and oppressive trade system," the declaration said, "with a new, socially just, and sustainable trading framework for the twenty-first century. We need to protect cultural, biological, economic, and social diversity; introduce progressive policies to prioritize local economies and trade; secure internationally recognized economic, cultural, social, and labor rights; and reclaim the sovereignty of peoples and national and subnational democratic decision-making processes. In order to do this, we need new rules based on the principles of democratic control of resources, ecological sustainability, equity, cooperation, and precaution."

The "Shrink or Sink" declaration went on to target several major bodies of trade rules that need to be carved out of the WTO, along with corresponding powers, which must be contained or redirected. These were the key goals identified at the Boston meeting:

- remove health, education, water, energy, and other basic human services from international trade, along with a rollback of the GATS' powers to enforce "progressive liberalization" and foreign investment in the service sector,
- remove the Trade Related Intellectual Property Rights (TRIPS) regime from the WTO, restore national patent protection systems, and ban the patenting of life forms in all national and international regimes,
- exempt all forms of sustainable agriculture from WTO trade rules, and prohibit government subsidies in Industrialized Countries to expand agricultural exports, in order to prevent dumping of agricultural products in Third World countries,
- eliminate the WTO's Trade Related Investment Measures (TRIMS), thereby allowing all countries, especially in the Third World, to increase the capacity of their own productive sectors, and

- eliminate the WTO disputes settlement mechanism, which not only "enforces an illegitimate system of unfair rules and operates with undemocratic procedures," but "also usurps the rule making and legislative role of sovereign nations and local governments."

In short, the declaration maintains that either the WTO can be made to "shrink" by adopting these measures or it will have to be made to "sink" under its own weight.

TRICKS OF COMMUNITY TRADE

A grassroots movement in India has found a way of using the trade rules of the WTO agreement to assert community ownership and control over the biodiversity of their regions. To offset agrochemical and pharmaceutical corporations moving in to claim ownership over local seed varieties, food crops, and medicinal plants, community groups have been registering their biological resources and taking out community patents themselves. The movement, known as Jaiv Panchayat, or "living democracy," maintains that these are common resources, which belong to the community and should never be privatized or brought under corporate control. According to India's constitution, local governments have jurisdiction over local biological resources, and in eight out of India's twenty-seven states, the community patenting process has been spreading like wildfire from village to village, creating new obstacles for corporations that might be intending to make use of the TRIPS to expand their ownership and control of biological resources.

Drawing a Line Around the Commons

Putting the WTO on a power-restricted diet would do much to restore democratic processes in many countries, but civil society groups need to go beyond these measures by calling for the protection of the global and local commons. There are certain goods and services that should not be traded, commodified, patented, or privatized in the global economy. In particular, there are four categories of goods and services that should be traded only on restricted terms or not at all: *pernicious goods* such as toxic waste, nuclear arms and waste, and genetically engineered organisms, which should not be traded because of their detrimental effects on the environment or public health, safety, and welfare; *life building blocks* such as air, genes, the human genome, and bulk water, which should not be commodified or traded for commercial profit because they are essential to human and ecological survival; and *common inheritance goods* such as seeds, plants, and animals, which may be traded but not patented for ongoing profits. Finally, *democratic rights*, including food security, health care, education, culture, and social security — which some governments have declared as common entitlements of citizens in their respective countries — should not be subject to global trade rules enforced by the WTO.

The time has come to draw a line around the commons, demarcating how far the international trade system should be allowed to go in marketing goods and services. Few if any of the original post–World War II architects of the Bretton Woods global trade system would have endorsed a process by which fundamental democratic rights and the common building blocks of life itself on this planet would be commodified, privatized, and sold to the highest bidder on the global market. But this scenario has begun to emerge, making it vital to oppose any moves to subject the global and local commons to world trade rules. By the same token, governments, in collaboration with civil society, need to assert public and democratic control over that which is sacred and essential to life on this planet. At the very least, as the "Shrink or Sink" declaration insists, global trade regimes like the WTO must not be allowed to exercise supremacy over the numerous multilateral agreements that have been negotiated under the auspices of the UN on the environment, health, human rights, Indigenous peoples, animal welfare, food security, and women's and workers' rights.

As the powers of the WTO are effectively curbed, steps can also be taken to strengthen the countervailing powers of other international organizations. Instead of allowing trade-related health, labour, environment, and human rights standards to be brought under the WTO regime, these vital contributors to a healthy common life should come under the jurisdiction of the UN agencies that have primary responsibility and expertise in these fields. As the International Forum on Globalization advocates, this would mean promoting measures designed to strengthen components of the World Health Organization, the International Labour Organization, the United Nations

Environmental Programme, and the United Nations Commission on Human Rights that would help protect the commons. The upgrading of these international agencies, however, must be carried out in collaboration with, not as a substitute for, effective and responsive democratic governance at the national and local levels. (See Chapter Eight.)

According to the International Forum on Globalization, a renewed and revitalized United Nations Conference on Trade and Development (UNCTAD) could play an important countervailing role in relation to the WTO. UNCTAD has significant support and legitimacy among Third World countries, since, over the past three decades, it was the main vehicle used to work toward restructuring the global economy in support of their national development priorities. And in the aftermath of Seattle, UNCTAD is in a pivotal position to play a critical role as the ultimate arbiter on trade and development issues. To do so, however, UNCTAD would need to undergo internal changes of its own. Many of the practices that have marked its approach in the past need to be discarded in favour of a new paradigm that nurtures ecological economics and local sustainable communities. UNCTAD's prime decision-making constituency also needs to be broadened to include not only Third World governments and their officials but also civil society groups.

Creating New Trade Regimes

The ultimate goal of these strategies is the dismantling of the WTO. But what, if anything, should replace the WTO? Most civil society movements favour some sort of rules-based global trade system, but they are calling for new rules and a new system. Some argue that a return to the less onerous General Agreement on Trade and Tariffs (GATT) that existed prior to the WTO is the way to go, as long as its processes are reformed to become more open and democratic. Others contend that the strengthening of regional trade bodies would be preferable to maintaining a global trade system.

The best option, however, may lie in restoring and renewing the original vision of a more comprehensive International Trade Organization (ITO), which, as noted in Chapter Three, was proposed as a "leg" of the United Nations, alongside the IMF and World Bank, before the emergence of the GATT. Following a vigorous debate after World War II, the 1948 Havana Charter proposed the creation of the ITO with a mandate to promote trade and investment as a means to certain ends — in this case, to generate full employment, protect workers' rights, and defend against "global cartels" of corporate power. It also included provisions for ongoing civil society partici-pation. Although the U.S. Senate effectively killed the original ITO, the model it proposed for the role of trade and investment in an emerging global econ-omy could be revived within the new framework of promoting democratic rights, the commons, and sustainable communities.

Of course, even the most complete revamping of the global trade regime would be futile unless national governments also reconstruct their domestic trade policies. In Canada, for instance, the mandate and structure of the Department of Foreign Affairs and International Trade (DFAIT) needs to be overhauled to promote a trading model that enhances basic democratic rights, preserves the commons, and builds sustainable communities. Similar to the WTO, the powers of DFAIT need to be pruned to allow for other government policy departments — environment, culture, health care, human resources, labour, and international assistance — to play a more effective role in determining Canada's trade policies and providing a corresponding set of checks and balances.

The same goes for participation of the provinces, which would, of course, depend on a shared commitment to Canada's renewed international trade objectives. To be sure, the current juggernaut of corporate-government collu-sion that lies at the core of trade policy making at DFAIT must be completely removed and replaced. Instead, a creative and effective mechanism for civil society participation needs to be developed, with built-in procedures for dem-ocratic accountability, through an elected citizens' constituent assembly or other, similar body.

REVAMPING GLOBAL FINANCE

The crisis of legitimacy that has engulfed the global financial system since the 1994 collapse of the Mexican peso continues to fester. IMF-sanctioned policies have lured foreign speculators into setting the stage for a series of financial meltdowns that have since swept through four Asian countries, Brazil, and Russia since 1997. Meanwhile, the IMF slapped together a multi-billion-dollar bailout package that benefited Wall Street speculators more than anyone else, whereby uncollectible private debts were effectively converted into public debts and millions of people were thrown into perpetual poverty.

Take the case of Korea during the last Asian financial meltdown. After high-level consultations with the world's largest commercial and merchant banks, the U.S. Treasury insisted that the IMF bailout agreement lift the ceiling on foreign ownership of Korean industrial assets to 55 percent and allow 100 percent ownership of Korean banks. Foreign corporate predators moved in for the kill, buying up Korean industrial assets at bargain basement prices. Although there was massive financial flight from South Korea by speculators, some creditors decided to take advantage of the crisis by rolling over their loans. Instead of lending money at 0.25 percentage points above the London Inter Bank Offered Rate (LIBOR), they charged a full 6 percentage points above that rate, thereby reaping huge windfall profits. In effect, the bailout filled the pockets of the global financial managers but failed to rescue Korean firms, as two hundred companies were shut down and four thousand workers were driven into the ranks of the unemployed every day during the height of the crisis.

Similarly, two decades' worth of Structural Adjustment Programs (SAPs) designed by the IMF and the World Bank, purportedly to help Third World Nations repay debts to the North, have trapped most of these countries in a vicious cycle of increasing social cutbacks and poverty, coupled with economic stagnation and decline. As referred to earlier, even the World Bank's own study shows that 54 percent of the people in twenty-eight borrowing countries experienced stagnating per capita income, rising poverty, and declining life expectancy. When a debate over debt relief for the world's poorest countries took place in the U.S. Congress in the spring of 2000, serious questions were raised as to whether the IMF should be involved at all. "As we have painfully discovered," declared one Congresswoman, "the way the IMF works causes children to starve."

As civil society campaigns like "Fifty Years Is Enough" in Washington, D.C., and the Canada-based "Halifax Initiative" accelerated their resistance to the IMF and the World Bank, the publicly discredited Bretton Woods Institutions responded with some minor cosmetic surgery. Attempting to distance the World Bank from its hardline Structural Adjustment Programs, Bank president James Wolfensohn called for a review of the SAP program and announced that "reducing poverty" would be the Bank's new priority. Long on rhetoric about poverty reduction through linking the "macroeconomic" and "social aspects" of development, the Bank was nevertheless short on developing a concrete strategy to achieve these goals.

Meanwhile, the IMF's "solution" turned out to consist merely of allowing the rich Industrialized Countries more time to peddle their free market "adjustments" (the Structural Adjustment Programs) by funding them for a longer period through its newly named "Extended Structural Adjustment Facility." At an IMF–World Bank meeting in September 1999, however, IMF economists admitted to civil society representatives that they really did not have a plan for reducing poverty and were looking to the World Bank for leadership. As one much-consulted labour leader from the Philippines remarked later: "It's the same old approach of deregulation, privatization, and liberalization, but with safety nets."

Tearing Down and Building Up

In the midst of this legitimacy crisis and institutional disarray, civil society movements have been developing their own agenda for transforming the global financial system. In December 1998, representatives of civil society groups from around the world came together for a working conference in Washington, D.C., called "Toward a Progressive International Economy" and developed a plan of action. Cosponsored by the International Forum on Globalization (IFG), the Third World Network, the Institute for Policy Studies, and Friends of the Earth (USA), the event generated a series of policy proposals and action strategies that could be implemented in international, national, regional, and local arenas. Many of the policy proposals were later expanded upon in the IFG's "Alternatives to Economic Globalization" and publications produced by the Third World Network.

Appropriating a strategy used to dismantle nuclear power plants, the IFG proposed that an international commission be established to oversee the process of decommissioning the IMF and its assets. Half the commission members would be from civil society organizations that had played a pivotal role in casting the public spotlight on the wreckage caused by the IMF. Among the immediate steps to be undertaken by the commission would be the dismantling of all Structural Adjustment Programs in the Third World and the former socialist countries, a reduction in IMF professional staff from one thousand to two hundred, and a corresponding reduction in capital expenditures and operational expenses. The commission would also be responsible for working out a plan for the disposition of outstanding debts owed to the IMF. A similar decommissioning strategy could be deployed at the same time for the World Bank.

Once the decommissioning processes for the IMF and the Bank were underway, immediate steps would be taken to create an International Insolvency Court (ICC), as initially proposed by UNCTAD, the global church coalition Jubilee 2000, and the Canadian government, led by Paul Martin. The IIC's mandate would be to work out negotiated settlements for debt relief for low-income countries. It would be a completely independent body, composed of a balanced representation from both creditor and debtor nations. To carry out its mandate, the IIC would contain both a Conciliation Panel and an Arbitration Panel. The Conciliation Panel would be responsible for facilitating negotiated settlements between creditor and debtor governments. In cases where parties failed to reach a settlement, the Arbitration Panel would be responsible for making a final and legally binding decision. UN agencies like UNCTAD would be called upon to provide debtor counties with assistance in preparing and presenting their case to the court. The court would also be mandated to ensure that all privately incurred debts remained private (unless guaranteed by governments through a democratic process consistent with established law).

To replace the IMF, an International Finance Organization (IFO) should be established under the auspices of the United Nations. As proposed by the International Forum on Globalization, the IFO would "work with UN member-countries to achieve and maintain balance and stability in international financial relationships, free national and global finance from the distortions of international debt and debt-based money, promote productive domestic investment and domestic ownership of productive resources, and take such actions as necessary at the international level to support nations and localities in creating equitable, productive, and sustainable livelihoods for all."

Unlike the IMF, the IFO would have neither lending capacity nor enforcement powers. Its primary functions would be to "maintain a central data base on international accounts, flag problem situations and facilitate negotiations between countries to correct imbalances." On the basis of policy studies, for example, the IFO would facilitate the negotiation and implementation of international agreements to dampen speculative financial movements and to prevent the use of offshore banks and tax havens for money laundering and tax evasion. Similarly, the IFO could facilitate negotiations for the introduction of a Tobin tax on financial transactions (named after its proponent, Nobel prize–winning economist James Tobin), as a means of curbing speculation and the destabilizing effects of fly-by-night portfolio investments.

In order to provide countries with access to short-term emergency loans, Regional Monetary Funds would be created. This proposal was based on the premise that finance, as the renowned British economist John Meynard Keynes consistently advocated, should be kept under national and local control as much as possible. Regional monetary institutions like this would be in a much better position than an international one to deal with financial crises quickly and effectively. Their member-countries would have a strong shared interest in avoiding any contagion effects. In the event of unanticipated shortfalls in foreign exchange, these Regional Monetary Funds would be designed and equipped to provide "quick response, short-term emergency loans" to countries on a need basis. Each regional fund would be accountable to the member-countries in its region and sensitive to local national concerns and interests. Countries outside the region would be free to participate as observers in a particular RMF meeting, but no country could become a voting member of more than one regional fund.

Creating Speed Bumps

These initiatives would provide more space for all countries to regulate capital movements. In order to ensure financial stability in what has become a volatile global casino economy, Ottawa should, for example, re-regulate capital flows through "speed bump" measures, setting down requirements like these: a percentage of all foreign direct investment must be deposited in Canadian banks; all portfolio investments must remain in the country for at least one year; all foreign currency accounts and foreign exchange transactions for purely speculative purposes must be prohibited.

The capacity of the Bank of Canada to play a more active role in global money markets should also be restored by requiring that all commercial chartered banks (e.g., the Royal, CIBC, Toronto Dominion, and Scotiabank) deposit a percentage of their reserves with the country's central bank. (This would restore the ability of the Bank of Canada to intervene in global money markets in order to control inflows and outflows of capital, among other things.) To curb excessive speculation on money markets, Ottawa should also place a ban on loans to hedge funds and institute a ban on offshore banking in tax havens. A financial transactions tax, similar to the Tobin tax, could also be applied not only to trading in stocks, bonds, and currencies but also to dealings in options, futures, and derivative contracts. Moreover, the safety net that the Canada Deposit Insurance Corporation provides for Canadian speculators against bankruptcies should be eliminated because it simply encourages investors to risk more and more speculation.

PARTICIPATORY FINANCIAL PLANNING IN BRAZIL

In Pôrto Alegre, a city of over one million people in Brazil, where the Workers' party has been elected to government, citizens effectively participate in financial planning by setting the city's budget priorities every year. In sixteen geographic and socially distinct sectors of the city, citizen delegates are elected annually to serve along with city councillors. In March and April, citizens' forums involving five hundred to seven hundred people (including participation by poor neighbourhood associations) are organized in each of the sixteen districts. Financial reports from the previous year are discussed and a process is developed for setting spending priorities for the coming year. In May, the elected citizens fine-tune proposals for budget priorities, and the submissions from all sixteen districts are integrated into a draft budget. The draft budget is then sent to the mayor and municipal councillors for final approval.

By the same token, Ottawa and the provinces could introduce legislation that would enable civil society groups and local communities to exercise more control over capital flows through mutual and pension funds. Tax incentives, for example, could be used to direct mutual and pension fund investments toward more productive local activity. And changes in pension fund legislation should be introduced to allow workers more direct control over the investments that are made daily with their own pension contributions, often in corporations or financial speculations that are diametrically opposed to their own interests. By exercising more control over their investments, workers can ensure that a high proportion of their money is invested in local productive enterprises that create jobs and contribute to the creation and enhancement of sustainable communities. To encourage more capital to remain in the country for investment in local community development, Ottawa should reduce the foreign content provisions of Registered Retirement Savings Plans (RRSPs), which are currently pegged at 20 percent.

RE-REGULATING FOREIGN INVESTMENT

The ill-fated Multilateral Agreement on Investment (MAI) was to have been a crowning achievement as a global investment treaty. From the standpoint of the twenty-nine member-countries of the OECD, the so-called "rich nations' club" that negotiated the treaty in Paris, the MAI was to have provided a set of global rules designed to open the doors of nation-states all over the world to foreign investment. But to the civil society movements that joined together and mobilized to oppose it, the MAI symbolized the dawn of a new age of global corporate rule. It was a bill of rights for transnational corporations. After all, here was an international treaty that would, in effect, constitution-alize the sovereignty of transnational corporations over nation-states and democratically elected governments, provide rules allowing corporations to regulate governments rather than the other way around, and donate a set of power tools to corporations to help them force those rules on governments through a set of legally binding mechanisms.

The collapse of the MAI negotiations at the OECD in the fall of 1998, of course, became a watershed for the movement against corporate globaliza-tion. But it may have come as a surprise to the well-heeled backers of the MAI that many of the deal's civil society critics were not opposed to the idea of a set of global rules for investment. The problem was that the MAI embodied the wrong rules, negotiated by the wrong people, in the wrong international venue. Many anti-MAI campaigners were calling for a totally different kind of investment treaty — one that would bring transnational corporations and their operations under the rule of law, rather than providing them with their own special bill of rights and freedoms. Right in the midst of the anti-MAI campaign itself, there were no fewer than five international projects working on alternative global investment rules. Among them was an Internet dialogue between movement activists and academics from a variety of countries, called "Towards a Citizens' MAI," coordinated by the Polaris Institute in Canada.

During this period, the search for alternatives to the MAI by civil society groups from OECD countries was carried out mostly in dialogue with movements in the Nonindustrialized Nations. "The major issue," insisted Martin Khor of the Third World Network, "is not whether or not foreign investment is good or bad or whether it should be welcomed," but "whether or not national governments should retain the right and powers to regulate [foreign direct investment]." Most Nonindustrialized Countries, he said, want foreign investment and are trying their best to attract it. The challenge for governments is "to maximize the positive aspects while minimizing the negative aspects" of foreign direct investment (FDI). To do so, they must be able to: subject their FDI policies to a broader set of national objectives and development needs; encourage the entry of the type of FDI considered desirable for these objectives and disallow the kinds that would be inappropriate; and impose certain conditions on FDI and its operations in the country.

Indeed, it was the 1974 UN Charter on the Economic Rights and Duties of States that recognized the responsibilities of national governments to regulate foreign investment in order to serve the economic, social, and environmental priorities of development. At the core of this Charter is the principle that capital itself has social obligations. After all, capital formation is a social process built on present and past generations of human labour and on extractions of aeons-old resources from the earth. Just think of the economic and social infrastructure that corporations use — roads and bridges; services like sanitation and public education; and natural resources like forests, minerals, clean water, and petroleum — to produce the products that generate revenue and profit for the corporation and its shareholders alone. For these reasons, there is both a social and an ecological mortgage on all capital: corporations owe a debt to society and nature. In turn, this "stored value of capital" provides legitimate grounds for putting obligations on investors and corporations.

Any global rules must therefore be designed to allow national governments to exercise regulatory powers requiring transnational corporations to meet their social obligations. Part of this design must include flexible policy tools that governments can use to ensure that foreign investment plans are harmonious with the development of true democratic rights, with the protection of the commons, and with the establishment of local, sustainable communities. Unlike the case with the MAI, governments should be given the freedom to make distinctions between rules for foreign and domestic corporations by requiring that foreign investors meet certain performance standards.

New global investment rules should also recognize that governments have a responsibility to secure control over strategic sectors of their economies (such as finance, energy, and communications) through public enterprises and to take whatever measures may be necessary to protect the commons — the environment, health care, education, and culture. And while various incentives will be used to attract foreign investors, governments must also be free to use the same incentives to ensure that transnational corporations fulfill their social obligations through those investments.

The 1974 UN Charter did specify that foreign-based corporations should be compensated for any losses incurred when the state expropriates its property. This seems reasonable enough, but the MAI proposals twisted the term "expropriation" to make it apply to *indirect* takings, including loss of profits that might result from legislation (such as environmental or health protection laws). If there were to be a global investment treaty, compensation by the state for expropriation would, at the very least, need to be strictly limited to *direct* takings of real estate or other property.

Investor-state mechanisms allowing corporations to sue governments directly (which already exist under NAFTA and most bilateral investment agreements) should also be eliminated. If there is to be a dispute resolution process, citizens must be given the legal standing before the courts that governments and corporations have, and disputes should be settled through the national courts of the host country. In addition, any negotiations relating to a global investment treaty must *not* take place at the WTO, but under the auspices of the United Nations, with effective civil society participation.

Yet it makes little sense to press for the development of global investment rules along these lines unless there is a corresponding commitment by national governments to re-regulate foreign investment. Despite the views of naysayers, Canada continues to be one of the world's best long-term investment locations, given its abundant supply of natural resources, skilled labour, and consumer markets, along with a comparatively safe and stable economic climate. So, if foreign-based corporations want to invest here, citizens should demand that Ottawa require that certain social obligations and performance standards be met. At the outset, Investment Canada, the toothless agency designed to promote foreign investment in Canada with few or no strings attached, should be scrapped. In its place, a Canada Development Agency needs to be established with a mandate to implement a national development plan based on principles of a civil society. This new agency should, as the MAI Citizens' Inquiry recommended, do a "social audit" on major foreign investment plans, assessing their impacts on jobs, the environment, community, health, safety, and related issues. Based on the results of the social audit, specific social obligations and/or performance requirements would then be pegged and included in an "investment covenant" between the corporation and the community.

Given the global realities of capital mobility today, Ottawa's attempts to re-regulate foreign investment along these lines would no doubt be countered by transnational corporations threatening to shift their production operations elsewhere. While such threats are sometimes overstated, the fact remains that a strategy to curb capital flight would have to go hand-in-hand with a plan to re-regulate foreign investment. As the Citizens' Inquiry proposed, diversifying Canada's investment options with a view to reducing dependence on foreign direct investment should become a strategic priority for reducing capital flight. For example, publicly owned enterprises, unlike their private counterparts, are not likely to pack up their operations and move or go on an investment strike because they are, by their very nature, contained within political boundaries. By investing in new public enterprises, Ottawa could reduce dependence on foreign investment and diminish the risk of capital flight. However, given the fact that Crown corporations tend to operate like private corporations in today's economy, this strategy would work only if serious measures were simultaneously taken to revitalize public enterprises and make them democratically accountable in their operations.

NATIONAL INVESTMENT FUND

To reduce dependence on foreign investment, labour and community groups in Canada have proposed the creation of a National Investment Fund, combined with Community Development Boards. As developed by the Alternative Federal Budget, the National Investment Fund would pool money generated through a levy on the assets of all financial organizations, including banks, mutual funds, and pension funds. This pool of capital would then be disbursed

through Community Development Boards for job creation and local
or regional development needs and priorities. And instead of investing exclusively in mutual funds, citizens would be encouraged to buy
National Investment Bonds, which could also be used for retirement
savings. At the national level, the Fund's board would be composed
of elected representatives from the Community Development Boards,
as well as representatives from financial organizations and the
federal government. The Community Development Boards would all
be composed of elected citizens.

Based on information from the Alternative Federal Budget
compiled by CHO!CES and the Canadian Centre for Policy Alternatives

The Alternative Federal Budget also calls for concrete annual proposals regarding how public investments could be made in transit systems, co-op housing, waste reduction and recycling, retrofits for public buildings, and not-for-profit child and elder care centres. In order to redirect the billions of Canadian dollars that flee the country every year for investment in foreign business ventures, the AFB has proposed that Ottawa establish an Enterprise Development Bank to provide low-cost debt or equity capital for domestic companies willing to undertake new job-creating investments that coincide with national development objectives and criteria. Similar measures could also be taken to redirect other pools of capital, such as a portion of the more than $450 billion in worker pension funds, toward a program of creative public and social investment in Canada, with the consent and participation of the labour movement in this country.

To be effective, citizens would also need to take action at the local level to ensure that both foreign and domestic investment contributes to the creation and maintenance of sustainable communities. Across Canada, the movement for community economic development has focused on promoting strategies that employ local people and resources to produce goods and services for local community needs. These initiatives, however, could be supplemented by local investment policies designed to stimulate the build-up of sustainable communities. The planks of such a community investment policy could include job quotas for local residents; "site here to sell here" provisions; procurement of goods and services from local businesses; pollution controls and rules on toxic waste disposal; community permission for the extraction of local natural resources; basic labour and worker rights standards; requirements for community reinvestment; and conditions that must be met if a plant is shut down and moved elsewhere. For cities and municipalities to enact community investment polices along these lines, provincial enabling legislation may be necessary.

While this investment agenda would move Canada far ahead on the road to becoming a more civil and democratic nation, most of its initiatives would be ruled out of order under the investment chapter of NAFTA (Chapter 11). This poses a strategic problem. If Canadians are to move forward with this agenda, then NAFTA, or at least Chapter 11, needs to be abrogated. But it is highly unlikely, given the current political climate, that Ottawa would be prepared to invoke the NAFTA abrogation clause. A more feasible strategy may consist of civil society organizations calling on Ottawa to reopen negotiations on NAFTA based on a range of hot-button issues: culture, energy, water, lack of protection of the environment, the NAFTA investor-state mechanism (which allows corporations to sue governments directly for violation of investment rules) and the national treatment clause (whereby foreign-based corporations are guaranteed equal, and often more favourable, treatment than domestic and local companies.) If, by chance, satisfactory changes resulted, then NAFTA would effectively be declawed. If, on the other hand, Washington, D.C., and Mexico City refused to negotiate on these terms, Ottawa would be in a position to serve the six months' notice of intent to withdraw, as required under the NAFTA abrogation clause.

RE-CHARTERING TRANSNATIONAL CORPORATIONS

At the dawn of the twenty-first century, the transnational corporation stands as the dominant institutional force at the centre of human history and the planet itself. Corporatization has become both the prime objective and the driving motivation behind the new models of global governance, and the international trade, finance, and investment regimes that now rule people and life on earth. Above all, this is why corporations have been the main symbols and targets of the resistance movements against globalization sweeping across the world.

For many society activists, it is no longer sufficient to single out individual corporations that cause harm to people and the environment, in efforts to make them become more socially responsible and accountable. Instead, the movement has begun to target the corporation itself, particularly the transnational corporation, as the ruling institution of our times. Historically, the corporation is really a creature of the state. The first trans-national corporations in Western Europe were the great exploration enterprises like the East India Company and the Hudson's Bay Company, which were given royal charters to search for new land and riches in the name of their nations and empires.

In Canada, corporations like the Hudson's Bay Company and the Bank of Montreal were originally granted royal charters by the King of England through Parliament, to open up British North America. While the practice of granting royal charters continued after Confederation, Ottawa and the provinces eventually assumed the responsibility of legally chartering corporations. But it was the state that ultimately sanctioned the existence of corporations by giving them the licence and the authority to operate.

Without a charter, no corporation has the legal right to own property, borrow money, sign contracts, hire or fire, or accumulate assets or debts. And in the United States, corporations initially existed at the pleasure of the state legislature to serve the common good. State charters, dating back two centuries or more, often specified what social obligations a corporation needed to perform in exchange for the right to operate.

If a particular corporation failed to live up to its obligations, the state legislature had the authority to revoke its charter. In some American states, citizens were active in writing the rules and operating conditions for corporations, not just in the charters, but also in state constitutions and laws. Through their legislators, members of the public were able to keep a short leash on corporations, spelling out the rules they had to follow and holding their owners liable for harms or injuries caused. However, an 1886 Supreme Court ruling recognizing corporations as "natural persons" under the U.S. Constitution struck down hundreds of these state laws, and new legislation was passed, granting corporations protection for property and investment rights and limited liability for harm or injury.

Citizens' movements have now begun to reclaim their sovereign rights to ensure corporate responsibility, insisting that state-sanctioned charters granting corporations the licence, mandate, and authority to operate, be reviewed, renewed, and if necessary, revoked. In Pennsylvania, for example, citizens' groups have initiated an amendment to the state's corporation code, calling for corporate charters to be limited to thirty years and requesting the establishment of a corresponding review process, in which the corporation must prove that it is operating in the public interest before its charter can be renewed. In California, a coalition of citizens' organizations (including the National Organization for Women, the Rainforest Action Network, and the National Lawyers Guild) have petitioned the Attorney General to revoke the charter for the Union Oil Company of California (Unocal), citing California's own corporation code authorizing revocation procedures. The coalition has fortified their petition with a battery of evidence they say documents Unocal's responsibility for environmental devastation, exploitation of workers, and gross violation of human rights.

Elsewhere, U.S. authorities have begun to respond. "When a corporation has been convicted of repeated felonies that harm or endanger the lives of human beings or destroy the environment," declared New York State Attorney General Eliot Spitzer in 1998, "the corporation should be put to death, its corporate existence ended, and its assets taken and sold at a public auction." Although Spitzer has yet to use his authority to revoke a charter, he has taken up battle with several corporate giants, including General Electric. In Alabama, Judge William Wynn filed a legal petition in 1998 to dissolve six tobacco companies on the grounds that they had broken state laws prohibiting the sale of tobacco to children. Wynn referred to his actions as a "citizen's arrest," but the ruling judge, after meeting with the tobacco companies' legal team, dismissed the case.

In Canada, citizens' groups have also begun to mount campaigns to both preserve and alter laws affecting the chartering of corporations. In British Columbia, the Citizens' Council on Corporate Issues, in alliance with other organizations (including the Council of Canadians), mobilized public pressure on the B.C. government to prevent the removal of charter revocation procedures from the province's corporations code. The provincial bar association had been called upon by big business interests to "modernize" and bring "corporate laws up to . . . twenty-first-century" standards. But defensive moves by citizens' groups in 1999 were successful in blocking the proposed changes, thereby keeping the law intact. And with the Canadian Business Corporations Act currently under review in Ottawa, a network of twenty-five citizens' groups called the Corporate Responsibility Coalition is lobbying for significant changes in the corporations code. These include making it legal for corporations to be held liable for crimes committed through company operations and for initiatives to be taken by shareholders and/or concerned citizens' groups to dissolve a corporation if it repeatedly breaks the law.

IT'S THE CORPORATION, STUPID!

In a feature article following the Battle of Seattle and succeeding demonstrations in Washington, D.C., London, and Davos, *Adbusters* magazine had this to say about "the corporate crackdown":

"The corporation won't come out of this intact. The new activists — and this is what Bill Clinton, Paul Martin, Mike Moore, and all the keepers of the old order don't get — are no longer protesting against the harms that corporations do, they are protesting against the corporation itself. These new activists want to go back to the beginning, back to the laws and legal precedents that gave birth to the corporate 'I'. They want to tinker with the corporate genetic code, to change the laws under which charters are granted and revoked, the laws that protect investors from even the foulest taint of their investments, and the rules and regulations under which corporations operate from the local to the international level."

Kalle Lasn and Tom Liacas, "The Crackdown,"

Adbusters, August-September 2000

Communities and municipalities outside Canada have also begun to take steps to hold corporations liable for their actions. In Point Arena, a small town on California's north coast, the municipal council passed a resolution in April 2000 stating that corporations will not be recognized as "persons" in their community. Now, the U.S.-based citizens' rights group Alliance for Democracy is taking this model resolution against corporate personhood and spreading it from town to town. After a referendum in November 1998, the university town of Arcata, California, was given a clear mandate to "ensure democratic control of all corporations conducting business within the city."

Recognizing that local enterprises are all too often the victims of corporate globalization, an alliance of 140 small businesses in Boulder, Colorado, has proposed the adoption of a "community vitality act" designed to put a limit on the number of chain corporations allowed to operate in the city. And applying the "three strikes and you're out" remedy for criminal practice, Pennsylvania's Wayne Township passed a law stating that any corporation with three or more regulatory violations over seven years would be forbidden from establishing operations in their jurisdiction.

In order to assist national governments in curbing the powers of transnational corporations in the new global economy, the International Forum on Globalization has proposed that a United Nations Organization for Corporate Accountability (OCA) be established. The OCA's primary function would be to support the initiatives of national governments and citizens in making transnationals more accountable. It would provide information and advisory services and facilitate the negotiation of bilateral and multilateral agreements related to the operations of global corporations. According to this proposal, the authority to regulate and enforce rules governing the operations of transnational corporations in certain jurisdictions would be in the hands of national and local governments. The OCA would provide both governments and the public at large with comprehensive and authoritative information on corporate practices, which could then be used as a basis for legislative, legal, or boycott actions.

According to the IFG, the proposed OCA would: maintain comprehensive and readily accessible public records for the thousand largest global corporations; focus international attention on the implications of corporate concentration in such key sectors of the global economy as banking, media, resource, high-tech, and agribusiness industries; document unfair competitive practices such as predatory pricing designed to drive smaller competitors from the market; publish an international watch list of corporations that engage in persistent patterns of regulatory infractions and illegal activity; document and publish the public costs incurred by corporations that pay substandard wages, sell harmful products, or discharge harmful wastes; and coordinate the negotiation of agreements allowing those harmed by the reckless practices of a corporate subsidiary in one country to sue and recover damages from the parent corporation in another country.

One of the major targets of the movement to change the nature and structure of corporations today is the existence of "limited liability" laws. For the most part, the chief executive officers of transnational corporations and their shareholders enjoy virtual immunity from legal responsibility for harms committed by the corporation against the environment, workers, or communities. So, for example, when Union Carbide was found responsible for the deaths of thousands of people in Bhopal because of a plant explosion, and when Exxon destroyed a coastline because of the *Exxon Valdez* oil leak, the shareholders who invested in these corporate giants were not held liable for their companies' actions halfway around the world. If these investors had been held partially responsible, the nature of the stock market itself would have undergone a dramatic transformation. And in future investment decisions, instead of going for the fast buck, investors would be highly motivated to evaluate the environmental, labour, and human rights track record of a corporation before becoming a shareholder. Just as important, CEOs and other executives would have to put priority on these social obligations instead of focusing blindly on increasing shareholder profits alone.

New legal measures are also being developed whereby transnational corporations could be held accountable in their home base country for harms and injuries that their companies or subsidiaries cause in other countries. In the United Kingdom, for example, cases have been brought, on behalf of workers, before the British courts against Rio Tinto for uranium dust exposure and against Thor Chemicals for mercury exposure affecting workers in other countries. (The Thor case was settled in favour of the workers; the Rio Tinto case is still pending.) As the World Development Movement in the U.K. sees it, these cases could set a precedent by establishing that: the head offices of transnationals are responsible for the decisions they make which affect the actions of their subsidiaries; low standards for overseas operations are not considered acceptable when it is known such practices would be considered dangerous at home; cases regarding overseas injuries will be heard by the British courts if this is the only way that justice can be achieved.

Similarly, the U.S. Congress is debating the McKinney Bill (introduced by Representative Cynthia McKinney), which would establish a standard for the overseas operations of U.S.-based corporations, along with enforcement mechanisms. The standards include: the payment of a living wage to workers; a ban on mandatory overtime for workers under eighteen, pregnancy testing, and retaliation against whistle blowers; respect for basic International Labour Organization standards such as the right to unionize and to health and safety protections; and adherence to both international and U.S. federal environmental laws and regulations. The code would be enforced, first, by giving preference to compliant corporations in the process of granting U.S. government contracts and export assistance and, secondly, by empowering the victims, including non-U.S. citizens, to sue American corporations in American courts.

In effect, all these initiatives are part of the movement for re-chartering transnational corporations in the new global economy — one which goes far beyond the United Nations' Global Compact as a means of bringing trans-national corporations under democratic control and into compliance with the rule of law. After all, the Global Compact is a voluntary and toothless exercise in which corporations essentially monitor their own practices. For many of the participating corporations, like Nike or Rio Tinto, which have already been the targets of campaigns waged by civil society groups, the Global Compact is merely a PR exercise which provides an opportunity for a much needed facelift. But, as William Greider reminds us in his article in *The Nation* cited at the beginning of this chapter, "social change almost always begins in hypocrisy."

10

Global Mobilization

*How civil society is building a
global movement for action as
a political counterweight to
corporate globalization*

"*What civil society movements need is our own international forum, where we
can develop and promote our own agenda and strategies for transforming the
global economy," said one of the organizers of the World Social Forum at Pôrto
Alegre, Brazil, in January 2001.*

*The World Social Forum (WSF) was designed as a symbolic and political
counterweight to the World Economic Forum, where, every year, the CEOs of the
world's thousand largest global corporations meet with presidents, prime ministers, and senior government officials in Davos, Switzerland, during the last week
of January. While the Davos event provides an annual occasion for corporate
and government elites to formulate strategies for the global economy, the World
Social Forum is to be a yearly event, where representatives of hundreds of civil
society organizations around the world can meet to develop alternative strategies
for transforming the global economy.*

The site of the World Social Forum has its own symbolic value for civil society movements organizing against corporate globalization. In Pôrto Alegre, direct citizen participation in planning and decision making is alive and well. Every year, the government of that city works with an elected citizens' forum to review program expenditures of the city and region. (See Chapter Nine.) It's a living example of a new democracy in action. As the elected government of Pôrto Alegre, the Brazilian Workers' party has also been active in helping urban and rural grassroots organizations build community-based resistance and alternatives to economic globalization. And the Pôrto Alegre government has provided the WSF with a state-of-the-art venue that holds 2,500 people.

The prime targets for strategic discussion and debate at the WSF in Pôrto Alegre were transnational corporations and the unholy trinity of global economic governance — namely, the WTO, the IMF, and the World Bank. Through five days of plenaries and workshops, the WSF provided opportunities for civil society representatives to exchange experiences in mobilizing resistance, proposals for developing alternative economic agendas, and plans for strengthening North-South alliances around the world. As the daily activities unfolded, it became more and more evident that the World Social Forum had become a dynamic and living counterweight to the World Economic Forum in Davos.

What's more, principles of participatory democracy were embodied in the initial planning and organizing of the WSF. In preparation, mobilizing committees of civil society groups were put together in as many countries as possible. Each country-based committee was encouraged to develop proposals for thematic workshops; submit topics for sessions on strategy, tactics, and organizing methods; and convene events to prepare delegates for the WSF and/or simultaneous with the WSF for the many civil society groups who were not able to attend. The proceedings of the World Social Forum were also broadcast around the world on the Internet.

THE MOBILIZATON OF CIVIL SOCIETY

As the World Social Forum signified, the mobilization of civil society is now taking organizational shape at global, national, and local levels. At the dawn of the twenty-first century, this movement may be the most important political development, nationally and internationally, to arise in decades. As noted in the Introduction, not only is civil society the fastest-growing sector of society, says Johns Hopkins University political scientist Lester Salamon, it is expanding at four times the rate of the economy. According to Salamon, more than one million nonprofit organizations are registered in India, and Brazil has three hundred thousand. Since the fall of communism in the Soviet Union, the new Russia has seen an average of one hundred thousand newly registered civil society groups each year for the past seven. France, which once banned charitable organizations, now has sixty thousand new registrations a year. And in Canada, there are eighty thousand registered charities and another hundred thousand nonprofit organizations.

All told, says Salamon, civil society sector represents the eighth-largest sector of the global economy. Some civil society groups have the indispensable task of delivering social services and in that role often have no choice but to make compromises with the economic and political elites. However, a growing number of nongovernmental organizations are concerned with public policy and are engaged in struggles for social change. In the past, this segment of civil society — embodied in labour unions, co-operative enterprises, women's networks, farmers' associations, environmental groups, religious organizations, civil rights associations, and peace networks — has been critical to generating democratic social change, both in Canada and elsewhere in the world. Today, it is the resurgence of this segment of civil society that offers the best hope for transforming the global economy and building a democratic future for planetary survival.

The strength of this bourgeoning civil society movement lies in its combined mixture of old and new elements. Labour unions continue to be an indispensable component of any social movement for transforming the global economy simply because they are the prime vehicles not only for defending workers' rights but also for providing an effective counterweight to the means of production. The women's, ecological, and peasant movements of our times also play a key role in the new civil society movement against corporate globalization. They represent vital constituencies and bring essential visions and values to the struggle for democratic social change. Civil rights, progressive religious, and end-the-arms-race movements offer different, and equally important, strengths. All these groups are alive and active and working to redefine their roles in the emerging, broader-based, civil society movement against corporate globalization.

At the same time, youth-led networks have brought with them a whole new set of visions, energies, and organizing styles. As a type of urban environmental protest, Reclaim the Streets, originating in Britain, has shown what can be done to mobilize thousands of people to take back the commons for collective use — represented by the communal space of city streets — by organizing parties with dance, music, and art to express a combination of rave and rage, often in support of workers', environmental, and human rights campaigns. The Direct Action Network and the Ruckus Society in the U.S. have revived the use of nonviolent civil disobedience in the struggle for democratic social change by training cadres of youth activists for direct action and dramatic stunts, making use of affinity groups and network organizing methods. Moreover, new forms of movement building and resistance have also emerged in the South. The Landless Workers Movement in Brazil, for example, combines social service and social change tactics by, on the one hand, sponsoring primary schools, food cooperatives, and makeshift home construction for peasant families, while on the other hand launching land reforms through the direct occupation of estate farms and public buildings. In India, the Jaiv Panchayat movement has not only turned the tables on the world's major agrochemical and pharmaceutical corporations by securing communal control over local plant life and biodiversity, but they have done so by using a creative organizing style of working with children, parents, and municipal councillors on a village-by-village basis.

The new movement has also gained momentum as a result of network organizing across sectors in international settings and within countries. The international People's Global Action (PGA), for instance, mobilizes a worldwide network of activists around the major meetings of the IMF, the World Bank, and the WTO. When the G7 leaders met in Cologne in June 1999, the PGA, Reclaim the Streets, and other groups cosponsored a "global carnival against capital." It also facilitated an intercontinental caravan of five hundred Indian farmers, which travelled across Western Europe, making protest stops at each country's headquarters of Cargill, Monsanto, and other agribusiness giants. ATTAC!, initially organized in France, has become the base for a series of European campaigns on a range of globalization issues such as the elimination of tax havens, the restructuring of the WTO, the promotion of the Tobin tax to curb speculative financial transactions, and the dismantling of free trade negotiations like the Transatlantic Economic Partnership. And Jubilee 2000, founded on the Biblical law of restoring lands and forgiving debts every fifty years, has encouraged faith communities around the world to press for the cancellation of the Third World's onerous debts.

TRANSFORMING CAPITALISM AND DEMOCRACY

So what is to be made of this dynamic social movement? How should it be publicly identified? To simply call it a "civil society movement" is not quite enough. Although civil society makes up that vitally important independent public space between the state and corporations, it is still, as the Italian social movement strategist Antonio Gramsci put it, a maze of "conflicting attitudes, values, and interests." The movement needs a name so that it can be distinguished from other social movements. Yet the name "antiglobalization movement" does not completely fill the bill. Most of the youth activists associated with the movement are not necessarily against globalization, but rather against the corporate-led model of globalization. For those who are committed to building alternatives and transforming the global economy, the "anticorporate globalization" label does not fully capture what this movement is all about either. Perhaps, as some activists contend, the new movement is so diffuse and decentralized that it can't be adequately named.

One possibility exists, however. Most civil society groups currently on stage or working behind the scenes have one set of goals in common. They are all fighting for fundamental democratic rights along one or more of the six tracks mentioned in Chapter Six: subsistence rights, economic rights, environmental rights, social rights, cultural rights, and human rights. So "new democracy movement" may be the most fitting way to describe what is happening. On many of these battlefronts for democratic rights, demands are being made by civil society groups to defend and protect key areas of our common life — food, water, health, education, the environment, seeds, genes, culture (to name a few) — from being sucked into the vortex of a global market controlled by transnational corporations. Activists are also fighting for sustainable communities, where citizens will be able to exercise democratic control over local economic development and environmental concerns within the global economy. Weaving its way through all of these demands is the call for a fundamental redistribution of wealth and power.

Developing a new democracy along these lines at local, national, and international levels is the only possible antidote to corporate globalization.

> **EXERCISING LOCAL DEMOCRATIC CONTROL**
>
> The rule of the World Bank and the WTO has implied rule by super-state institutions serving the one-sided interest of commerce and beyond the democratic control of people. As the state withdraws from environmental and social regulation in the "free trade" era, local communities are getting organized to regulate commercial activity by asserting their environmental rights to natural resources, land, water and biodiversity and their democratic rights to decide how these resources should be used. . . . Now, in each sector, the biggest multi-national corporation has been forced to recognize that it is the clearance from citizens, not just from the government, that is necessary for democratic functioning.
>
> Vandana Shiva, Afsar H. Jafri, and Gitanjali Bedi,
> *Ecological Costs of Economic Globalization: The Indian Experience*

At its core, it appears that this new movement is really about the task of transforming both capitalism and democracy. After all, "corporate globalization" — the latest rendition of the capitalist theme — has distorted notions of democracy to the point that fundamental rights are at risk. For generations, people were told that the greatest threat to democracy was the existence of communism. The collapse of the Berlin Wall and the triumph of capitalism was supposed to usher in an era in which democracy would flourish, but increasingly, this promise has become "the big lie" for both younger and older generations. If anything, the globalization of unbridled capitalism through the worldwide operations of transnational corporations, largely facilitated by the WTO, the IMF, and the World Bank, has exposed some of the deeper structural problems of democracy itself. Instead of experiencing the fruits of democracy — greater equality, sustainability, and participation — people are faced with growing economic and social inequities, further destruction of the environment, and loss of control over their economic, social, and ecological future.

Although the Bretton Woods Institutions were originally established to eliminate or at least mitigate these inequities, the new democracy movement must continue to expose how the WTO, the IMF, and the World Bank have now become the predators themselves. After increasing the human misery and suffering of the poor majority in the South through their Structural Adjustment Programs over the past two decades, the IMF is now providing massive bailout packages for Wall Street investors speculating on Third World currencies and commodities. Meanwhile, the World Bank continues to finance megadam projects that cause massive flooding of communities and environmental damage. Intensified collusion between governments and transnational corporations — all carried out under the protective arm of the World Trade Organization — means that world commercial interests can set rules that trump the economic, social, environmental, cultural, and consumer protection legislation of sovereign nations. In every area — agricultural products, natural resources, manufactured goods, intellectual property, and public services — WTO rules are designed, first and foremost, to serve the global market interests of transnational corporations by providing a set of power tools for binding enforcement.

Now that the prime role of governments is to provide safeguards for investors, not citizens — a turn of events worthy of a Dickensian satire — the corporate security state has become a major challenge for the new democracy movement. Under the centralized nation-state, says Vandana Shiva, the real threat to democracy lies not in state protectionism but in corporate protectionism. In Canada, the three-part powerhouse of DFAIT, together with the Departments of Finance and Industry, largely establishes the rules and controls the framework for public policy making in Ottawa, in collusion with corporate lobby machines like the Business Council on National Issues. All other departments — including agriculture, environment, health, human resource development, heritage, and fisheries — have been subordinated to the rules and disciplines laid down by DFAIT, Finance, and Industry. The controlling powers of this junta and its distortion of democracy must become a central target of resistance and change in Canadian politics.

The role of the state or government is also crucial to achieving the aims of the new democracy movement. Of course, many of the anarchist elements associated with the movement reject this position. One can certainly understand and appreciate the negative attitudes that people have toward the corporate-driven model of government that burdens countries of both the North and the South. Yet many civil society movement activists in the South, while recognizing all too well the weaknesses and vulnerabilities of their own governments, insist that the state remains an indispensable mechanism for achieving social justice and planetary survival. What the movement must do is to put priority on democratizing and transforming government and its institutions. The time has come, says Shiva, for civil society to redefine democracy "in terms of people's decisions in their every day lives" and to redefine the nation "in terms of people, not in terms of the centralized state." This requires a dispersal of both economic and political decision-making powers throughout society and a multiplicity of institutions.

What's more, democratic governance is essential for the task of transforming the global economy. How else can one expect to carry out the main goals of the citizens' agenda outlined in Chapters Eight and Nine: reconstructing trade regimes, revamping global finance, re-regulating foreign investment, and re-chartering transnational corporations. All of these strategic objectives require intervention by the federal government. DFAIT itself would have to be dismantled and reorganized. But none of this can happen unless the role of the Canadian state is redefined for the purpose of defending democratic rights of citizens, promoting the commons, and building sustainable communities. Although the national government in Ottawa needs to retain and even strengthen certain powers in order to deal with transnational capital in the new global economy, there must be greater democratic participation and control by citizens in the exercise of these powers. Mechanisms for participatory democracy and citizen participation in policy making and action must be put in place.

The new democracy movement needs to be vigilant on this front. The creation and re-creation of democracy must become the *raison d'être* of this movement. Democratizing the state at all levels — local, national, and global — should be a top strategic priority. The movement, of course, is not a political party, nor should it become one. As the French farm movement leader José Bové put it: "We are a counter-power, not a substitute for politics. We have no fixed answer for everything . . . [Our role is to make] people think." Even so, political action will be necessary to enact the kind of citizens' agenda being proposed for transforming the global economy. It is not enough, however, for a political party to adopt this agenda as part of its platform. As long as the institutions of governance function as a corporate security state in this country and elsewhere, it does not make a great deal of difference which political party is in power. That's why the new democracy movement must be geared to play a vigorous role in democratizing government. Nor should the movement disband once a "good government" is elected. The power of big business and the forces of greed will always be knocking on the door.

A GLOBAL COUNTERWEIGHT

In taking on these political challenges, the new democracy movement is not powerless. A crisis of legitimacy still hovers over the unholy trinity of the WTO, the IMF, and the World Bank. The defeat of the MAI, the shutdown of the Millennium Round of the WTO in Seattle, and the adoption of the Biosafety Protocol by environment ministers in Montreal in January 2000 have given the movement a dose of public confidence. And the victories have continued: Australia and New Zealand's joint bid to enter a free trade regime with the Association of Southeast Asian Nations was recently rejected; worker rights and environmental standards were included in a bilateral free trade agreement between the U.S. and Jordan; and the Middle Eastern country of Qatar decided to reverse its decision to host the next WTO Summit, scheduled for November 2001. Despite the booming economy in North America, the authority of transnational corporations is being questioned now more than at any other time since the early 1970s, when the big oil giants were suspected to have provoked the energy crisis in order to jack up gas prices. A number of the movement's successes have resulted from citing principles and requirements of the UN's Universal Declaration of Human Rights; the International Covenants on Economic, Social, and Cultural Rights and Civil and Political Rights; charters from the United Nations' Social Summits; and Multilateral Environment Agreements. This international legal foundation has so far proven to be useful ammunition in the fight against corporate globalization.

> ### BEING COHERENT ABOUT A SWARM OF MOSQUITOES
> So how do you extract coherence from a movement . . . whose greatest tactical strength so far has been its similarity with a swarm of

> mosquitoes? Maybe, as with the Internet itself, you don't do it by
> imposing a preset structure but rather by skillfully surfing the struc-
> tures that are already in place. . . . There are so many groups involved
> in anticorporate campaigns that nothing but the hubs and spokes
> model could possibly accommodate all their different styles, tactics
> and goals. . . . The charge that the anticorporate movement lacks
> "vision" falls apart when looked at in the context of these campaigns.
> It's true that the mass protests in Seattle and DC were a hodgepodge
> of slogans and causes. . . . Trying to find coherence in these large-
> scale shows of strength, the critics are confusing the movement with
> the thing itself — missing the forest for the people dressed up as
> trees. This movement is its spokes and in the spokes there is no short-
> age of vision.
>
> Naomi Klein, "The Vision Thing," *The Nation*

Since the Battle of Seattle, momentum has been on the side of the new democracy movement. But one year later, there are fears that the movement could subside from burnout. Nevertheless, now is certainly not the time to slow down. If anything, now is the time to turn up the heat, from the mobilization against the FTAA Ministerial Meetings through to the next Ministerial Meeting of the WTO. Yet this is also the time to dig in and prepare for the long haul. If this new democracy movement is going to be strong enough to win future battles, let alone the war itself, concerted steps must be taken to strengthen the capacities of the movement on national and international fronts. The following is a six-step plan of action designed to help the movement meet that goal.

1. BUILD A COMMON FRONT OF CIVIL SOCIETY ORGANIZATIONS

In most countries, the civil society groups actively working on the multiple issues related to corporate globalization are often scattered and disconnected. The same is true at the international level. Although the Internet has been a dynamic force in connecting individual activists, and though groups do come together from time to time to form tactical alliances around particular issues or campaigns, there is seldom a place where groups can converge and forge solidarity on an ongoing basis. Using the six battlefields of democratic rights discussed in Chapters Six and Seven, steps can be taken to identify the variety of front-line groups and organized constituencies that could be brought together to form a common front. The vision of a new democracy movement would help bring key civil society groups together to discuss purposes of forming a common front and how to work around shared goals and strategies for transforming the global economy. Keeping in mind the need to respect pluralism and decentralization, the hub and spokes structure mentioned in Chapter One should be considered as the organizational model for forming a common front. Elected representatives from each of the participating groups would form the hub, with the spokes being the various campaigns focused on the many different issues of corporate globalization.

Given the wide diversity of organizational styles and philosophies, it would be no easy undertaking to develop a common front along these lines at the international level. Yet the best hope for doing so may be the World Social Forum launched in Pôrto Alegre as civil society's counterweight to the World Economic Forum, in January 2001. Through the WSF, the major global campaigns waged against the WTO, the IMF, and the World Bank by groups like the Third World Network, Fifty Years Is Enough, and the Shrink or Sink campaign can be brought together under one roof, along with numerous other anticorporate campaigns. The annual WSF will not only provide an opportunity for developing more effective coordination and interaction between these global campaigns, but it will also give more civil society organizations in the South a chance to play a more active role in shaping those campaigns. Eventually, the WSF could become the place for an annual summit meeting between civil society leaders from countries all over the world.

Labour unions could play a key role in organizing the common front of new democracy organizations. They represent a significant portion of workers in most countries, and they are the only sector of civil society that has an effective degree of leverage in negotiations with those who control the means of production. However, the International Confederation of Free Trade Unions (ICFTU), which plays a major role in developing policy positions for the labour movement on issues of globalization, has frequently become a stumbling block for many civil society organizations who want to forge alliances. It operates in isolation from the larger NGO community and often offers compromise, such as accepting trade agreements as long as they include a "social clause" — a position that is unacceptable to the movement as a whole. Concerted efforts must be made by other civil society organizations to call on labour unions to commit themselves as full and active players in building a common front, within each country and internationally as well.

In Canada, for instance, the Canadian Labour Congress and its affiliates have joined forces with the Council of Canadians and over fifty other national civil society groups to form the Common Front on the WTO (CF-WTO). Many of the organizations in the CF-WTO are also participating members of Common Frontiers, which is currently focused on the negotiation of the Free Trade Area of the Americas, and the Halifax Initiative, which works on issues of debt relief and IMF/World Bank Structural Adjustment Programs. All three of these working alliances have valuable contributions to make to a common plan of action for transforming the global economy. So one of the movement-building challenges in Canada is to bring these three working alliances together to form a broad-based common front to tackle the corporate-government policy-making juggernaut in Ottawa and to fight for a new model of democratic governance. At the very least, a summit meeting of these civil society organizations and alliances could be organized each year to clarify common principles, issues, and strategies. Eventually, the hub and spokes metaphor could be applied to facilitate communication flows and maximize network organizing among the participating civil society organizations and their constituencies.

2. STRENGTHEN THE PARTICIPATION OF MARGINALIZED GROUPS

The mass demonstrations on the streets of Seattle, Washington, Birmingham, Melbourne, and Prague revealed that the resistance movement against corporate globalization has so far been largely composed of white, middle-class people. Even on the youth blockades and in their direct-action training camps, the absence of people of colour along with the poor and marginalized is noticeable. Since the prime victims of the global economy are poor and nonwhite, the new democracy movement needs to reach out to a wider diversity of races and classes. This will be a long-term task, however. The community-base-building organizations of the North with the greatest numbers of poor people and people of colour are preoccupied with their own local battles, thereby making it difficult to develop links with the issues and struggles of globalization. As one U.S. youth activist who works among the urban poor observed: "For people of color, our bread and butter issue is not globalization, it's how are we going to feed our kids." The same has been true of many grassroots women's groups. It was not until the Battle of Seattle erupted that many of these community-based networks in the North took notice of the movement against corporate globalization.

In the long run, however, the credibility of the new democracy movement depends on mobilizing the participation and leadership of the poor, the marginalized, and people of colour. What has been missing in part is an approach that emphasizes "globalization from below" as a counterweight to "globalization from above." A survey of U.S.-based organizations following the Battle of Seattle revealed that a significant portion of grassroots or community-base-building groups working on issues ranging from contingent work to toxic wastes in their communities felt that they were disenfranchised by having little or no participation in the "antiglobalization movement." The survey showed that many of the otherwise excellent education materials and tools on issues of globalization were produced by public interest and policy research groups in Washington, D.C., and that there was little or no input from grassroots or base-building groups. Not only was the language used in these materials often technical and legalistic, but little effort had been made to communicate in terms of race, class, or gender. New educational tools need to be developed in the North that start from a "globalization from below" perspective.

PASSION FOR JUSTICE

Yes to partnership and solidarity — based on passion, which is to say of people that feel and touch each other. Governments and institutions are, by nature, incapable of feeling the passion for justice which is a source of strength and power. Individuals as human beings, not as officials or NGO professionals, can bring back life in this world. Relational power, first and foremost, with the dispossessed, will be the basis of the New Diplomacy [Democracy]. Or it will not be new at all.

Alejandro Bendaña, Centro de Estudios Internacionales, Managua, Nicaragua

In developing campaign strategies, priority must be put on outreach to antipoverty organizations, grassroots women's groups, immigrant communities, Indigenous people's organizations, associations of people of colour, and homeless networks. Allied movements from various countries in the South could also provide some useful guidance, tools and tips. At the same time, other civil society groups also appear to be missing in action. Applying the grid of the six battlefronts, a significant number of environmental, cultural, education, women's, international development, human rights, and church/religious organizations could be encouraged to engage in the movement's campaigns. Concerted efforts should also be taken to reach out to the people in these constituencies whose lives and concerns are clearly affected by what these agents of global corporate governance are doing.

In Canada, new challenges and opportunities are emerging. Solidarity links, for example, need to be forged between several key labour union, student, and public interest organizations in the emerging new democracy movement, and militant antipoverty organizations like the Ontario Coalition against Poverty, Aboriginal groups like the Assembly of First Nations, and grassroots community-based groups through the Solidarity Network based in Ottawa. Connections must be made between the daily struggles of the urban poor and Aboriginal peoples and the new GATS rules affecting health, education, and social services, which are currently being negotiated at the WTO. New tools for popular education and outreach also need to be developed that are consciously designed to reflect race, class, and gender perspectives. A solidarity exchange conference could also be planned and organized to bring together base-building organizations of poor and marginalized peoples and to explore ways of forging links between local community struggles and resistance to corporate globalization.

3. Organize Local Community-Based Advocacy Networks

To be authentic, however, a movement must also put priority on organizing local communities for action. The struggle cannot be left to national and international organizations alone. After all, there is no point in repeating the oppressive rule of globalized powers that take no notice of the damage they do to local communities, economies, and natural environments. In some ways, this goes hand in hand with attempts to revive the politics of localization based on Gandhi's principles of Swaraj (relocating political decisions in local communities closest to where people live and work) and Swadeshi (relocating economic decisions in local communities where local resources can be used to produce goods and services).

One way to proceed is to organize community-based advocacy networks composed of activists from a variety of local civil society organizations such as unions, environmental groups, women's associations, farmers' organizations, and neighbourhood groups. The purpose of these networks would be to organize local campaigns of resistance and alternatives. Emphasis would be put on highlighting the links between local community issues and NAFTA, the FTAA, and the operations of corporate global governance institutions like the WTO, the IMF, and the World Bank. As a form of political organizing, advocacy networks differ from both conventional civil society organizations and formal coalitions. They require a high level of personal commitment and responsibility and depend on substantial cross-sectoral teamwork. Campaigns may be initiated by one organization, but the basic planning and organizing is carried out by a team of committed activists from several different groups and sectors. Effective use could also be made of the affinity group process developed by youth activists.

The Vancouver-based group Trading Strategies is a good example. Cochaired by the local bodies of the Council of Canadians and the Canadian Auto Workers, Trading Strategies brings together activists from organizations ranging from the West Coast Environmental Law Association, the B.C. Teachers Federation, the Vancouver District Labour Council, and a host of health care, women's, cultural, student, research, public interest, youth, and community organizations. Organized along lines similar to the hub and spokes model, Trading Strategies acts as a common platform base for a variety of campaigns, each consisting of a small team of activists working on issues like the GATS negotiations at the WTO, GE foods and biotechnology, or the impacts of NAFTA decisions on local concerns about forestry and water. Proposals for campaigns are brought to the table either by individual activists or by member-organizations, and once there is a general consensus, a team of committed persons goes to work on the planning and organizing. Through this process, Trading Strategies has played a key role for local organizing drives against the MAI and in preparation for the Battle of Seattle.

Across Canada, community-based advocacy networks like Trading Strategies could be organized in key urban and rural communities. As local counterparts to the Common Front, they could provide a solid community base for the new democracy movement. By organizing around local issues that relate to national and international campaigns, these community networks would give concrete expression to "globalization from below." More importantly, they would provide a vehicle through which local grassroots groups could actively and meaningfully participate in the emerging new democracy movement.

4. DESIGN CAMPAIGN STRATEGIES TO BUILD THE MOVEMENT

There is an overwhelming tendency on the part of civil society organizations in the North to put greater emphasis on organizing short-term campaigns than on building a movement for transforming the global economy in the long run. Single-issue campaigns are important for influencing public opinion and policy debates in democratic societies and they do lead to positive policy changes. However, they too often tend to ignore the root causes of the issues they are organized to address. Campaigns that are primarily designed to gain media attention and not to mobilize citizens contribute little to authentic social movement building. As a vehicle for reaching out to the broader public and forging debates on issues of corporate globalization, campaigns could have a more vital role to play in developing a new democracy movement if they are organized to achieve these objectives as well.

Choosing the right targets is an important task in organizing campaigns for resistance and alternatives. Take, for example, action organized in opposition to the WTO negotiations on a new round of GATS rules affecting public health, education, environmental regulations, and social and cultural services in Canada. Unless the campaign is designed to unmask and expose the operations of DFAIT and its collusion with big business, and follows the money to determine which corporate players are calling the shots on Canada's trade agenda, it will be limited in its impact. Similarly, campaigns on debt relief aimed at changing the policies of the IMF and the World Bank should also target and expose the role played by the Finance Department and the commercial banks in Canada and the U.S. Wall Street–Treasury complex in perpetuating the spiralling debt crisis that plagues Third World and former Eastern Bloc countries. In other words, campaigns must be designed to target and expose the root causes. And getting at the root causes often requires a deeper understanding of the nature and role of capitalism and democracy.

Campaigns can also serve movement-building priorities by providing opportunities for citizens to develop leadership capacity and to learn new skills. They can actually serve as "schools" for activists in the movement. Instead of simply using people as troops to be mobilized, organizers could put a priority on developing people's capacity for team leadership. One effective approach to campaign development is to create teams of people with different skills and to integrate their talents around the work to be done. Through campaign teams, people can develop and hone their skills as researchers, workshop leaders, community organizers, strategists, and media and political spokespersons. While team leadership development can become a focus of national and international campaigns, it is community-based campaigns for resistance and alternatives that provide the best opportunities. But nationally organized campaigns should be designed to facilitate the development of community-based team leadership. To be effective, greater attention must be given to making local or community links with the issues in designing the campaign.

5. DEVELOP THE CAPACITY TO MOBILIZE COLLECTIVE POWER

In democratic societies, one of the most effective ways for citizens to bring about social change is to withdraw their consent and cooperation from established authorities. By working, buying products, paying taxes, and obeying laws, people give their consent and cooperation to those who govern. By collectively withdrawing their consent, they can provoke a "crisis of legitimacy," undercut the strength of their opponents, and shift the balance of power. Even by threatening to withdraw, citizens can collectively exercise power in such a way as to publicly question the legitimacy of established authorities. In response to such threats, the ruling elites will often prefer to make concessions than to have their power completely undermined. Once the balance of power has been shifted, civil society organizations will discover opportunities for strategic moves.

> ## REVERSING ACQUIESCENCE
> The power of existing social relations is based on the active coopera-
> tion of some people and the consent and/or acquiescence of others.
> It is the activity of people — going to work, paying taxes, buying
> products, obeying government officials, staying off private property
> — that continually recreates the power of the powerful. . . . This
> dependence gives people a potential power over society — but one
> that can be realized only if they are prepared to reverse their acqui-
> escence.
>
> Jeremy Brecher, Tim Costello, and Brendon Smith, *Globalization from Below*

In building a new democracy movement, it is crucial that civil society organizations strategically develop and strengthen their capacity to exercise this
form of collective power. Although civil society movements have used more
than two hundred identifiable methods of nonviolent action to express with-
drawal of consent or organized dissent, the most frequent ones are strikes,
boycotts, and civil disobedience. Many civil society organizations involved in
campaigns to transform the global economy have not yet begun to make
effective use of these tactics. Yet even when tactics of nonviolent direct action
are deployed, full strategic consideration is not always given to the forces at
play and how best to take advantage of opportunities to shift the balance of
power. In mobilizing resistance to the MAI, for example, or the Millennium
Round of the WTO or the World Bank funding of the Narmada Dam in India,
strategic opportunities for shifting the balance of power emerged because
a "crisis of legitimacy" around these institutions was provoked, in part, by
the collective use of various direct action tactics. While victories were scored
in these battles, certain strategic opportunities were missed that could have
been seized had there been a more complete picture of the corporate and
government players involved, including their own interlocking relationships
and manoeuvres.

At the same time, the power of civil society organizations to undermine
the authority and legitimacy of corporations and the governments who
serve them is largely contingent on the exercise of direct action based on a
commitment to nonviolence. It is one thing for governments themselves to

react with violence against protest demonstrations by unleashing police or military forces, but when certain factions of the anarchist movement have gone on rampages to destroy buildings and other property in the streets of Geneva, Seattle, and Prague, they have run the risk of creating a "crisis of legitimacy" for the rest of the civil society movement in the minds of the public at large. One can well understand the feelings of anger, despair, and even bitterness toward governments and corporations for what they are doing to humanity and the planet. Many young people who resort to property damage come from poverty and communities without power. For them, all conventional means of protest have failed, and they see these actions as a form of survival. But social movements generally lose their own power and authority when violence becomes the means for social change. Morally and politically, this is also the wrong foundation on which to build a new democracy. Consolidating the commitment and support of civil society organizations for the use of nonviolent forms of direct action must therefore be a priority in building a new democracy movement.

Civil society organizations also need to be better equipped to counter the co-optation tactics being used by the agents of corporate globalization to restore their lost authority and legitimacy. Following the lead of the World Bank's well-honed campaign to co-opt civil society groups, WTO officials, government trade bureaucrats, and some corporate executives have been tripping over each other since Seattle to "dialogue with civil society." In Canada, similar moves have been made by Finance Minister Paul Martin and DFAIT. While not all "dialogue" initiatives are necessarily meant to derail civil society groups, the strategic aim is clearly to facilitate a relegitimization of these dominant institutions. Worse still, when the efforts to co-opt do succeed, leaders are separated from their rank and file and groups are neutralized. Closely related are divide-and-conquer strategies designed to create splits in the movement. Blatant attempts have been made to label civil society organizations as "good" or "bad," depending on whether they accept or reject the basic corporate state agenda for the global economy and on whether or not they engage in direct action tactics. Anticipating that these kinds of divide-and-conquer moves will be made, civil society organizations must learn to take preventive measures.

6. CREATE SPACE FOR ONGOING
REFLECTION ON MOVEMENT PRINCIPLES

At the core of any social movement, there must be a unifying vision and set of principles, if it is to be sustained for the long haul. There is a very real danger of activists hopping from one set of issues, campaigns, and mobilizations to another without taking the time to reflect on the underlying structural causes and the fundamental purposes for action. If citizen activists don't reflect on their actions and strategies of resistance in the light of the deeper structures of capitalism and democracy itself, there is the risk of losing energy and spinning wheels. The same holds true for building economic alternatives through a citizens' agenda. Unless the limits and possibilities of pursuing a set of economic alternatives in the context of the present structures of capitalism and democracy are critically examined, activists' hopes and expectations can quickly dissipate. The goal of building a movement for transforming the global economy will suffer if citizen activists get caught up in the treadmill of reacting to one issue and campaign after another without taking the time to make sense of it all. It's a sure recipe for making activists burn out and causing social movements to peter out.

RUSHING FROM ISSUE TO ISSUE WITHOUT A COMPASS
The problem obviously isn't the importance of such fights, but the absence of a larger context. Since the latest mobilization is a matter of do or die, there is no space or patience for consideration of a long-term strategy that goes beyond specific grievances or threats. Hopes are raised without clarifying, or even asking, whether these hopes can be met within a capitalist society. A powerful enemy is identified — the corporate sector — without exposing the basis of that power as residing not in capital's latest initiative or trend, but in the overall nature of the capitalist system. . . . The energy consequently mobilized suffers from a collective inability to sustain itself and make itself cumulative. Impressive battles are fought without addressing what needs to be done to win the war.

Sam Gindin, *Canadian Dimension*

To build and sustain a new democracy movement, therefore, steps must be taken to provide citizen activists with the time and space they need to reflect on their struggles for resistance and alternatives. The unifying vision of the movement provides the basis for reflection. Since transforming democracy is one aspect of this vision, it is important for citizens to reflect on their actions in the light of the nature and role of democracy. By the same token, if changing the global economy is another aspect of the movement's unifying purpose, rethinking the nature and role of capitalism should also be part of the process. While this can be done at any time, the best moment for doing so is often at the end of a campaign. Reflection should be rooted in the living struggles of citizen activists themselves, with full respect for a plurality of views. At times, a creative dialogue between activists and academics could be useful for deepening the reflection. By going through this kind of process at least once or twice a year, citizen activists will be able to internalize the unifying vision of the movement, clarify strategic goals and priorities, and better guard themselves against burnout.

At the same time, space needs to be provided for the formation and training of movement leaders, organizers, and activists. In the United States, citizen movement activists have made use of the Highlander Institute in Tennessee to train community organizers for almost half a century. A similar institute is needed in Canada to enable citizens to build skills in corporate research, popular education, strategic planning, campaign development, direct action tactics, community organizing, and media work. Through such an institute, activists could root their work in the history of social movements and deepen their understanding of the dynamics of capitalism and democracy. Moreover, a set of common indicators should also be developed for evaluating the effectiveness of the movement's strategies and campaigns. What effect has the movement had, for example, on shaking up the corporate globalization paradigm? What changes, if any, has the movement been able to generate? What strategic opportunities have been opened up? What blows have been dealt to the legitimacy and authority of institutions like the WTO, the IMF, and DFAIT or specific transnational corporations? What shifts have taken place in the balance of power? And, above all, what real impacts has the movement had on the lives of people, their communities, and the earth itself?

In addition, civil society organizations must give serious attention to overcoming their own internal democratic deficits. In their counterattacks, the corporate elite has attempted to delegitimize certain civil society organizations on grounds that they are not themselves democratically representative or accountable. In building a new democracy movement, steps need to be taken by membership-based civil society organizations to renew and revitalize their own internal processes for effective participation in policy development and actions.

• • •

This six-step plan of action for building and strengthening the new democracy movement calls for new ways of visioning, thinking, energizing, and acting in the present for the sake of the future. In this spirit, the Council of Canadians has launched a task force with a mandate to develop a plan of action for building a citizens' agenda for social transformation in this country. The plan of action is to be focused on three dimensions: a vision for social transformation, the formation and training of citizen activists, and corresponding changes in the Council's own campaigns and program of action. In carrying out its mandate, the task force intends to engage people from other civil society organizations, as well as the membership of the Council, before submitting its proposals to the Council's annual general meeting in the Fall of 2001. Through this undertaking, further insights into building a new democracy movement are bound to emerge.

As citizens of the world, we find ourselves on the brink of what may well turn out to be a critical moment in history. In an age of increasing global corporate rule, there is no choice but for civil society organizations to take some bold initiatives of their own for the sake of social transformation and planetary survival. Since the Battle of Seattle, the global junta has been busy repairing and fortifying the power structures of the WTO, the IMF, and the World Bank. But the cracks in this unholy trinity of global corporate governance are still apparent — the cracks that were opened up by the defeat of the MAI, the Asian financial meltdown, and the shutdown of the WTO Millennium Summit. While this moment will pass, the challenge is to seize the strategic opportunities at hand to build a new democracy movement that will be strong enough to shift the balance of power. This will be the only way to bring about a fundamental transformation of the global economic order.

Above all, it is important to recall that the real strength and power of civil society, as distinct from governments and corporations, lies in the passion of people — the capacity to feel, touch, and relate to one another and thereby bring life back into this world. This is the passion for justice, for creation, for participation. It is the power to hear, feel, and respond to the cries of the poor and the dispossessed and the groaning of the earth itself. It is the capacity to energize people to fight for their fundamental democratic rights as citizens through a new politics of resistance and transformation. At the heart of this new politics lies a vision of hope as a moral imperative. This is not the kind of "cheap hope" that stems from Western optimism and the belief that progress makes life better for all. This is a "costly hope," which comes through struggle with the powers and principalities of the world. That's why the politics of transformation must go hand-in-hand with the politics of resistance.

The challenges looming on the horizon appear to be both awesome and formidable. It may well take the rest of our lives to lay the foundations for the building of a new democracy. But, hey! What else have we got to do?

Suggested Reading

Anderson, Sarah, and John Cavanagh, with Thea Lee. *Field Guide to the Global Economy*. New York: Institute for Policy Studies and The New Press, 2000.

Balanya, Belen, Ann Doherty, Olivier Hoedeman, Adam Ma'anit and Erik Wesselius. *Europe Inc.: Regional and Global Restructuring and the Rise of Corporate Power*. London: Corporate Europe Observatory and Pluto Press, 2000.

Barker, Debi, and Jerry Mander. *Invisible Government, the World Trade Organization: Global Government for the New Millennium?* San Francisco: International Forum on Globalization, 2000.

Brecher, Jeremy, Tim Costello, and Brendan Smith. *Globalization from Below: The Power of Solidarity*. Cambridge, MA: South End Press, 2000.

Bruno, Kenny, and Joshua Karliner. *Tangled Up in Blue: Corporate Partnerships at the United Nations*. San Francisco: Transnational Resource and Action Center, 2000.

Cavanagh, John, and Jerry Mander (eds.). *Alternatives to Economic Globalization*. San Francisco: International Forum on Globalization, January 2001.

Council of Canadians. *Confronting Globalization and Reclaiming Democracy*. Ottawa: 1999.

Friends of the Earth International. *The World Trade System: How It Works and What's Wrong with It*. Amsterdam: 2000.

Hines, Colin. *Localization: A Global Manifesto*. London and Sterling: Earthscan Publications Ltd., 2000.

Khor, Martin, Walden Bello, Vandana Shiva, Dot Keet, Sara Larrain, and Oronto Douglas. *Views from the South: The Effects of Globalization and the WTO on Third World Countries*. San Francisco: International Forum on Globalization, 2000.

Klein, Naomi. *No Logo: Taking Aim at the Brand Bullies*. Toronto: Alfred A. Knopf Canada, 2000.

Korten, David C. *The Post Corporate World: Life After Capitalism*. San Francisco: Kumarian Press and Berrett-Koehler Publishers, Inc., 1999.

Shiva, Vandana. *Stolen Harvest: The Hijacking of the Global Food Supply*. Cambridge, MA: South End Press, 2000.

Shrybman, Steven. *The World Trade Organization, A Citizens' Guide*. Ottawa and Halifax: The Canadian Centre for Policy Alternatives and James Lorimer and Co. Ltd., 1999.

Sinclair, Scott. *GATS: How the World Trade Organization's New "Services" Negotiations Threaten Democracy*. Ottawa: The Canadian Centre for Policy Alternatives, 2000.

Rebick, Judy. *Imagine Democracy*. Toronto: Stoddart Publishing Co. Limited, 2000.

Roy, Arundhati. *The Cost of Living*. Toronto: Vintage Canada, 1999.

Wallach, Lori, and Michelle Sforza. *Whose Trade Organization? Corporate Globalization and the Erosion of Democracy*. Washington, DC: Public Citizen, 1999.

Index

Culver, David, 102
currency speculation, 64–66, 185–86, 189–90

Daley, William, 76
dams, 140–41, 209
d'Aquino, Tom, 99–100
David Suzuki Foundation, 139
Davos (Switz.). *See* World Economic Forum (WEF)
debt, 57, 121, 136–37, 188. *See also* Jubilee 2000; Structural Adjustment Programs (SAPs)
Delta Force, 12, 48
democracy, 4, 27, 168–78, 180, 204, 210–11
Democratic party convention, 32, 39
democratic rights, 169–70
"dialogue," 3, 27–28, 41, 45, 91–93, 180, 221
Dingwall, Dave, 99
Direct Action Network, 11, 32, 206
Disney. *See* Walt Disney Company
Dominion Resources, 106
Domtar, 106
Donohoe Inc., 106
Dow Chemical/Dow AgroSciences, 101, 130, 160
Dresdner Bank, 78
drug patents, 98–99, 114–15
DuPont Corporation, 77, 130, 144–45

Eagleburger, Lawrence, 46
Earth Summit (Rio), 53, 81, 137–38
East India Company, 197
Eastman Kodak, 74, 159
East Timor, 103
economic rights, 132–39
education, 18, 147–48
Eggleton, Art, 98
Eisner, Michael, 135
El Barzón, 136–37
Electronic Data Systems, 151
Eli Lilly, 148
El Salvador, 136, 149
Elwell, Christine, 92
End of Oil Action Coalition, 37
energy, 59–60, 108–10
Engering, Franz, 24
Enterprise Development Bank, 195
Environics, 120
environment, 53, 78–81, 117–18, 137–43

Ethyl Corp., 117
Europe, 27, 82
European-American Business Council (EABC), 75–76
European Commission, 84, 94
European Patent Office, 156–57
European Round Table of Industrialists (ERT), 75, 174
European Union, 14, 24, 75, 78, 93, 124, 142
ExxonMobil, 139, 201

Favaloro, René, Dr., 150–51
FBI, 12, 39, 48
Federal Reserve Bank, 45
Fifty Years Is Enough, 18, 186, 213
Financial Leaders Group, 77–78
Financial Services Agreement (FSA), 70
Fischer, Stanley, 33
fisheries, 79, 142–43
flesh trade, 157–58
Fletcher Challenge Canada, 106
FMC Corp., 76
Focus South, 180
food, 82–84, 126–28. *See also* agriculture
genetically engineered, 83–84, 130–32
Food First, 151
Ford Financial Services Group, 78
Ford Motor, 19, 101, 110, 133
foreign investment, 77–78, 105–8, 191–94
Foreign Investment Review Agency (FIRA), 106
forestry, 141–42
Four Seasons Hotels, 106
France, 24, 130, 138, 147, 150, 153–54, 155–56
Free the Children, 19, 161
Free Trade Area of the Americas (FTAA), 16, 32, 35–36, 76, 96, 122, 212, 214, 217
Friedman, Thomas L., 9
Friends of Medicare, 149
Friends of the Earth, 11, 33, 47, 52, 139, 140, 187
Fuller, Colleen, 113, 114

Gaidar, Yegor, 67
Gandhi, Mahatma, 169, 217
The Gap, 13, 19, 133, 134, 136, 153
Gates, Bill, 1, 9